THE PROSE OF WILLIAM CARLOS WILLIAMS

The Prose of
William Carlos Williams

By

LINDA WELSHIMER WAGNER

WESLEYAN UNIVERSITY PRESS

Middletown, Connecticut

For my parents,
Esther and Sam Welshimer

"You read too much, Willie, that's what's the matter with
    you . . ."
"I don't read at all."
"Then what the hell do you do?"
"I'm an agent."
"For what?"
"The word . . . the eternal word."
                    —William Carlos Williams, in a work sheet,
                    in Yale Collection

Sometime we will have to resign ourselves to the fact that
art is what the artists make it, and that the spectator has damn
well to take what he gets.
                    —Pound to Joyce

Contents

Acknowledgments

MY thanks to Frederick Eckman, with whose help I began this project; to Mrs. Florence H. Williams, for her kindnesses; to Emily Wallace, for her excellent bibliography of Williams' writings; and to Norman Holmes Pearson and John C. Thirlwall for their suggestions.

Materials from the Lockwood Memorial Poetry Collection, State University of New York at Buffalo, and the Collection of American Literature, Yale University Library, are used by permission of those libraries and of Mrs. Williams. A letter to Williams from David Lyle, in the Yale Collection of American Literature, is quoted by Mr. Lyle's permission. Permission to quote from Dr. Williams' prose and poetry, both published and unpublished, has been given by Mrs. Williams, by James Laughlin of New Directions, by Beacon Press, and by City Lights Books, as specified on the copyright page of this volume.

Parts of this book have appeared in various forms in *Criticism, The Journal of Modern Literature, The Kenyon Review, The Novel, Papers of the Midwest Modern Language Association, South Dakota Review, Studies in Short Fiction,* and *Tennessee Studies in Language and Literature.* I thank the editors who have allowed me to reprint this material.

I am grateful to the College of Arts and Letters, Michigan State University, for a research grant which enabled me to finish this book.

L. W. W.

East Lansing, Michigan
May, 1970

THE PROSE OF WILLIAM CARLOS WILLIAMS

Introduction

IN 1964 Wesleyan University Press published my study of Dr. Williams' poems. The approach then was chronological and technical, with little reference to Williams' many books of prose. Now that my work is complete, I have tried to make *The Prose of William Carlos Williams* more than just a "second half," the full meaning of which would depend on the first book. (The chapters on *Paterson* and the late writing, however, will probably be more meaningful if used in conjunction with the earlier study.) Because Williams' work sheets and his statements about his writing are so plentiful, it has been possible here to use materials other than those included in the first book. The unity of Williams' total work—amazing unity, throughout his half-century of writing—makes possible one emphasis of this study, that on the interrelationships between his prose and his poetry; just as his skill in the various categories of prose makes feasible the detailed study of each work of fiction, drama, and nonfiction.

Chapter One presents the argument for considering Williams' writing as a unity, the prose fitting into the poetry and allowing Williams to develop as a writer both thematically and technically. His shift from Objectivist poems, for example, came only after he had explored more subjective statement in the Stecher novels and *Many Loves*. Williams' thinking about literature is strangely devoid of comment about genre; the means seem almost incidental to the effect the poet desired. As Emily Wallace points out, among Williams' last papers were notes for *The Complete Collected Exercises Toward a Possible Poem*. Included in this group were both prose and poetry (*Kora in Hell* and *Spring and All,* as well as other prose selections), proof again that, to Williams, all writing was related.[1]

Chapters Two through Six dwell on Williams' first six books of prose, touching briefly on the poems which were written during the same years. The impressionistic *Kora in Hell: Improvisations* (1920) finds Williams searching for a way out of the short, Imagist poem

3

pattern. In *Spring and All* (1923) he imposes more order on his un-ruly freedom by writing in either prose or poems, the poems acting as illustration for the discussions of art which are written here as prose. *The Great American Novel* (also 1923) moves toward longer blocks of prose, with the well-detailed anecdotes of Williams' later fiction appearing. All three of these books show the poet searching for both values and identity, in art, history, personal relationships, and in his pervasive concern with Americanism. Williams' 1925 collection of essays, *In the American Grain,* continues part of his exploration of American history and also shows his versatility in various styles of prose. *A Voyage to Pagany,* his first conventional novel, places the in-genuous American Dev Evans in Europe, but brings him back after all his explorations. The next year, 1929, he translated Soupault's *Last Nights of Paris,* a novel which heightened his interest in the mys-teries of both women and place.

Chapter Seven describes Williams' writing during his two sab-batical years, 1924 and 1927, the last periods of leisure he was to have until 1951. Close examination of his manuscripts for "The Descent of Winter," another prose-poem matrix, provides much information about the way Williams was writing during the 1920's, as well as the way he was thinking. Many of the themes and images of the later writing, including *Paterson,* begin here.

Chapter Eight surveys all his shorter fiction, relating the subjects and methods of his short stories to the writing which both precedes and follows it. In this writing from, largely, the 1930's, Williams is moving restlessly but surely toward the bigger projects which will occupy the fifteen years to come. Chapters Nine, Ten, and Eleven study his longer works of fiction, drama, and poetry: the novels, writ-ten from 1936 and 1952; the plays, written from 1937 to 1960; and *Paterson,* published from 1946 to 1958. In the nearly simultaneous pro-duction of such works as *White Mule, Many Loves, A Dream of Love,* and the five books of *Paterson,* Williams comes to a full statement. The "making," however, is not always technically satisfying. The poems of Williams' last ten years, including the beautiful "Asphodel, That Greeny Flower," are discussed in Chapter Twelve, primarily be-cause his writing in prose as well as in poetry comes to its natural and easy culmination in them. Chapter Thirteen atempts to relate Williams' use of prose to his over-all artistic theory, particularly in *Paterson* and his last prose work, *Yes, Mrs. Williams.*

CHAPTER ONE

The Unity of Williams' Art

"LIFE isn't any more poetry than prose," [1] Williams mused in *I Wanted to Write a Poem*. Prose "emphasizes a metrical continuity between all word use . . . prose and verse are both writing." [2] Stressing the unity between the forms of writing, Williams called for a "prose construction" for his poetry—the use of normal syntax, colloquial vocabulary, and direct statement, with characterization often achieved through monologue or dialogue. As he wrote in 1947, "One must not slip back into the ruts of rhyme and inversion of phrase. Let speech be the rule." [3] And when he spoke of finding a new measure for modern poetry, he concluded, "Speech, nascent prose, holds within it that which measured in more simple fashion might make a verse." [4]

Williams' view of the relationship between poetry and prose—reciprocity if not a complete identity—is of great importance to an understanding of his complete work. For fifty years, Williams' writing has defied easy categorization. His poems are like prose ("Just rearrange the lines," nonpoets say); his prose, like either shorthand or prose poems. *Kora in Hell: Improvisations* is somehow less formal than a prose poem; *Spring and All* alternates prose with poetry; *The Great American Novel* (our American *Ulysses*) relies for its coherence on many poetic devices. The *American Grain* essays show that organic form works as well in prose as in poetry. The culmination of Williams' experiment with the forms of writing is, of course, *Paterson*, written from 1940 to 1958. I think *Paterson*—and Williams' later writing both in the great poems and the businesslike prose—can be understood fully only if they are related to his earlier writing and thinking, especially that writing and thinking about the act of composition.

I have said elsewhere that Williams was a reasonably conscious craftsman—as conscious a workman as a poet can ever be. In the tradition of Coleridge and Emerson, Williams constantly made notes and

5

worried the age-old problems of writing, as any study of his drafts
and work sheets proves. Much interested in *the word* as an identity, a
valuable counter to be used thoughtfully, Williams viewed the poem
(and every unit of prose) as "machine or engine . . . composed of
words to do a certain job," "an engine that needs continual redesigning
in each period so as to increase its capacity to refresh the world." [5]
MAKE IT NEW echoes through Williams' writing. It is not that Williams disliked rhyme, sonnets, inversion, but that he felt them to be
worn-out devices, no longer capable of reaching most readers. And the
poem must reach an audience, so Williams tells us in all his writing:

<blockquote>

It is difficult
to get the news from poems
yet men die miserably every day
for lack
of what is found there.
Hear me out

for I too am concerned
and every man
who wants to die at peace in his bed
besides.[6]

</blockquote>

No poet is more reverent of tradition, of the past, than Williams.
Readers sometimes forget that Williams—like Faulkner and unlike
Eliot and Pound—was not educated in literature. He went from sec-
ondary school directly into the University of Pennsylvania Medical
School. In many ways he wrote from an "anthology" background:
Keats, Shakespeare, a little Poe, even less Greek drama. Williams
seemed not to realize his own affinities to the literature of the past:
perhaps he never knew enough of that literature. (This is some of his
debt to Pound, who frequently suggested and sent books, though Williams often reacted against Pound's suggestions.) Yet, Williams' rev-
erence for the past went beyond Pound's, it seems to me. He saw
himself as one of the great tribe of ancients, the creators, working
in and through the traditions of poetry. It is through Williams' intense appreciation of Homer, Sappho, Theocritus that he came to his
equally intense belief in the local as the source of all viable art. As he

explained it in 1947, "The poem connects the past with the present. And thus we know we are alive for seeing particulars all about us, and being instructed by the poem that the past was no different, we get our sense of continuity and the world becomes real to us." [7]

Williams turns to his local, Rutherford, New Jersey, not because Rutherford is an appropriate subject for great art, but because Rutherford is what he knows. In a 1921 essay, Williams defines "local" as "the sense of being attached with integrity to actual experience." [8] Honesty, involvement, the real—the poet must feel, must know true experience; only then can he write. But only through formal structures can he realize his feelings: "IT IS THE FORM," Williams declares with his usual vehemence; "I have tried so hard to make this clear: it is the form which IS the meaning." [9]

The form of poetry was Williams' primary interest throughout his career, but he increasingly recognized that he needed prose too. To make clear, clean, prose was perhaps more effective than poetry. From 1920 on, Williams wrote at least as much in prose as in poetry; during the twenties and thirties, in fact, he wrote much more prose. After the poems of *Sour Grapes* in 1921, seven books of prose were published before *Collected Poems* in 1934. Work sheets of his poems from the twenties show that most of them were drafted first as prose. Such was his practice in the 1927–1928 "The Descent of Winter," with lines like these written first as prose:

> I make really very little money.
> What of it?
> I prefer the grass with the rain on it
> the short grass before my headlights
> when I am turning the car—
> a degenerate trait, no doubt.
> It would ruin England.[10]

The sheer quantity of Williams' prose—twenty-one published books and much uncollected material—testifies also to his interest in the form. Even though Williams is quick at times to point out differences between the two—that prose is more "factual," "clearer," less demanding —his easy alternation between the forms proves his real confidence in each of them. To Williams, writing a short story or an essay was no less difficult than writing a poem. A novel was not awesome; it was simply another thing to be written.

There is great similarity, too, in Williams' criticism of prose and poetry. In each mode he admired concision, understatement, concentration on the thing itself, and organization which grew from juxtaposition and montage rather than from purely logical order. His comments on Marianne Moore's poetry sound like those on James Joyce's or Kay Boyle's fiction. And one of the few omissions in Williams' literary criticism is mention of genre—Gertrude Stein's stories are not good *stories*. They are good *writing*.

One of the most striking reasons for believing Williams when he stresses the unity between poetry and prose is the applicability of his "poetic" theory to his prose writing. The basic principles of Williams' poetic theory are (1) his insistence on the use of the American idiom as distinct from the British; (2) his devotion to his own local as a means of attaining a valid universal; (3) his premise of "No ideas but in things," the need to communicate through tangible situations and objects; (4) his rationale of organic form, the art object as a machine made of words, searching for its own autonymous shape.

Williams' American Idiom

We are Americans; not only a material future but an unimagined future lies before us. We are a great people in the making. We are a new race, speaking our own language. We do not speak English—remember that. We speak our own language.[11]

Williams' antagonism toward all things British, intensified by the expatriation of Pound and Eliot, was only a small part of his insistence on the use of America in American art. As a doctor, he was surrounded with the vernacular: sometimes crude, sometimes impassioned, but always real. Just as many of Williams' poems aim to re-create lines from speech, so do more of his short stories. In fact, his attempt to catch the life of the episode often forces Williams into a dialogue structure for the entire story: the doctor and his patient, the doctor being told stories by an acquaintance. Stark in its effect, Williams' dialogue is perhaps less "meaningful" but truer than Hemingway's (as Williams himself noted):

She's one of the funniest women I have ever known. Everything amuses her.

What's her name.

Mrs. Weber. She has a son named Frankie and she's always thinking about Frankie. . . . My son Frankie, she says. He's in trouble again.

What's so funny about that?

They won't let him graduate from the school this year. . . .[12]

The rhythms of a person's speech are important to Williams' characterization, especially since his description is usually cryptic and his point of view limited.

There were a coupla guys prowling around here this morning but when they seen me they beat it.

Thanks.

Any luck?

No. Not with these hands.

What are you gonna do, hang around this tub all winter? And, say, where the hell do you keep the key to that booze, anyway? I bet it's around your neck. Scotch ("The Dawn of Another Day," *FD,* 144).

Speech and actions delineate the men as this story moves on. We never know their backgrounds, but we do know their present attitudes and commitments.

Near drama in its directness, Williams' fiction is strongest when it is aimed through active scenes. The failure of some of the stories and parts of the third Stecher novel, *The Build Up,* lies in Williams' turn to recitation rather than re-creation. He is at his best in essentially dramatic forms of fiction. It may well be that much of Williams' best writing, both in poetry and prose, tends toward drama. Indeed, the success of Williams' plays themselves often hinges on his command of dialogue. *A Dream of Love,* for example, is effective because much of the characterization is conveyed through varying speech rhythms: the staccato urgency of the doctor's speech as he searches for his car keys counterpoints Myra's comfortable—as yet unsuspecting—replies.

The idiomatic quality of Williams' other prose—essays, *The Great*

American Novel, the *Autobiography,* the letters—is one reason for its difficulty. Instead of logic, Williams gives us truly personal improvisation.

> Surely there is no poetry so active as that of today, so unbound, so dangerous to the mass of mediocrity, if one should understand it, so fleet, hard to capture, so delightful to pursue. It is clarifying in its movements as a wild animal whose walk corrects that of men.[13]

The numerous qualifying phrases and the esoteric simile illustrate some of Williams' weakest stylistic practices. The control he achieves in much of his fiction is less evident when the poet himself speaks. Williams' painful honesty, his groping, sometimes obscures rational progression, but never the effect of genuine speech—terse, emotional, stubborn, perceptive.

The greatest example of Williams' use of idiomatic American speech is *In the American Grain.* Often praised for its wide range of prose styles, the book is also a showcase for quotation from the characters' writing itself. So great is Williams' trust in the "truth" of a man's speech—the identity of speech and person—that he uses Cotton Mather's words alone in the long essay on the witch trials. It is Mather's own words that damn him. So, too, do Ben Franklin's phrases show his "commonplace" limitations; and it lies in the speech of John Paul Jones and Columbus to create their magnitude.

Williams followed his early insistence on speech as a way to truth in his epic *Paterson.* Most of *Paterson'*s important themes are illustrated best in the excerpts from letters which Williams included so frequently. The frustration of the poetess Cress; the enthusiasm of the young Ginsberg; the stentorian Dahlberg; the comic and reproving Pound—we know these people from their speech rhythms as much as from the content of their letters. In much the same way that he kept Cotton Mather's lines intact, Williams used prose passages from old histories of the area, some dating back more than a century. These rhythms and vocabularies counterpoint the poet's modern idiom elsewhere in the poem in the same way he juxtaposed seventeenth-century speech with modern idioms in his drama *Tituba's Children.*

It is interesting, too, that the idiom of the persona Paterson becomes more varied than one might expect, raised above the common through his multiple identities, mythological as well as real.

The Local

Paterson is the best-known example of Williams' use of the local, one's own place and time, elevated through the imagination into art. Yet while Williams describes the park, the library, the falls that he knows, his concerns with his world have certainly gone beyond geographic matters. His sorrowing lines relate to all of us:

> Minds beaten thin
> by waste—among
>
> the working classes SOME sort
> of breakdown
> has occurred [14]

as do his tranquil descriptions of "the poem/ the most perfect rock and temple, the highest/ falls, in clouds of gauzy spray" (99).

Even Williams' so-called "turn to art" in the tardy Book V (published in 1958 after Book IV in 1950) is no betrayal of his local. He draws on tapestries housed at The Cloisters, a museum in Tryon Park, New York, just across the Hudson from Paterson; on a Brueghel painting from a book in his own library; on references to other painters he has long admired, as his earlier writing shows. So little is "new" in *Paterson* V, except, perhaps, the complacent rhythms of the writing, that one might well consider it an anticlimax rather than a change.

New Jersey as local—the persistent fox sparrow that awakens Paterson (and the world), the equally tenacious pink locust (like the frail asphodel—and Williams—indomitable), Flossie's roses (on ice or in the garden), and Flossie herself, again and again; the sycamore trees, the downtown area of Rutherford (as in "A Negro Woman"), "Stormy" (Williams' Shetland sheep dog), the grandchildren—"Suzy," "Paul," "Erica," "Eloise," "Elaine"; the postcard from Cummings, the old goose on Charles Abbott's farm—all the subjects of Williams' late poems come just as immediately from his local as did the early poems (the green glass between hospital walls, the striped wallpaper, the red wheelbarrow). In fact, the local in the later writings is, if anything, more specific, more easily identified.

The new dimension to Williams' use of his local in later work is that he no longer dodges what has been traditionally the artist's responsibility: the correlation of "thing" and "meaning." How does it fit? Where does it fit? And Williams can tell us now (although he often told us in the earlier poems, too: "so much depends/ upon/ a red wheel/ barrow"). In the later, still local, poems, Williams will more positively assert: "this is/ reassuring," "it is a satisfaction/ a joy," "I persist." The willingness to identify, to place, had long been evident throughout Williams' prose, perhaps because he felt that the purpose of prose was to clarify, to explain.

There is little question that the local is also the source of Williams' prose. Most of his fiction stems from his experiences as a doctor and a man. If his characters are not identified as patients, sooner or later someone calls the narrator "Doc." The three Stecher novels focus on Flossie's family: "White Mule" is Flossie herself. The plays are often too autobiographical to be read in comfort. As Williams wrote in an essay on *White Mule:*

> Of course the story's invented. The principal characters in it are taken more or less from life and the incidents are, in the main, accounts I have heard of past happenings but all the detail is my own. Some of the conversation was put down verbatim from things said by my patients. I tried in every way not to distort anything of this. . . .[15]

Williams' use of these materials is evident in his novels and short stories, but it is interesting that all his other prose also builds from the framework of personal anecdotes to the larger thematic issues. *Kora in Hell, The Great American Novel, A Voyage to Pagany, A Novelette,* many essays, employ reminiscence which might seemingly be more appropriate to autobiography or to *Yes, Mrs. Williams.* Sequences of anecdotes and experiences are described with the careful detail, the idiomatic phrasing, of Williams' clearest fiction.

"No Ideas But in Things," One Way to Organic Form

The doctor's struggles with a stubborn child, a man and wife driving in the rain to see "ferns of three sorts," a young girl's pimply face—"these things astonish me beyond words." The specific detail, the single example, is the core of Williams' approach to art. His many references to Dewey's "universal through the particular" should serve as explanation enough that his single-edged focus is intentional. Sometimes he misses. But when he hits—who can forget "Old Doc Rivers," "Jean Beicke," the slatternly housewife in "Four Bottles of Beer," or the vivid pictures of childhood and adolescence in the Stecher trilogy? Ezra Pound saw *White Mule* as the culmination of Williams' prose style; [16] Fred Miller wrote of it that its style was "bound to color the writing of decades." [17]

His concentration on specifics often gave Williams his rationale for structure. His discontent with Imagism stemmed from its formlessness (although he praised it for its focus on the "thing"). He turned to the Objectivists because they "attempted to remedy this fault by fusing with each image a form in its own right." [18] The whole theory of organic form, a shape for each piece of writing consonant with its subject, tone, and intended impact, grows logically from a writer's real concern with the piece of work before him.

The varying lengths of Williams' short stories show his use of appropriate form. This is not formula fiction: "The Pace That Kills" is two pages long; "The Farmers' Daughters," thirty. "The Use of Force" (four pages) presents one brief incident, in several stages, whereas "Old Doc Rivers" (twenty-eight) is digressive biography. Variation in the shape of Williams' plays is also interesting. Drama, as Williams saw it, was one of the most flexible of forms. *Many Loves* (earlier titled *Trial Horse No. 1*) makes use of both prose and poetry and three plays within the play. *A Dream of Love, The Cure,* and *Tituba's Children* are three-act plays, whereas many of the early plays are single acts. Williams' introduction to the liberetto for his opera about Washington, *The First President,* is one of his most thorough statements on drama. In many ways, Williams seemed to consider drama, poetry, and prose interchangeable. I have written elsewhere about the striking resemblances between *The Great American Novel* and *Paterson*—themes and the sequence of their presentation as well as techniques Williams' play *Many Loves,* in the comprehensive treatment of its theme (the kinds and characters of love), bears equally close resemblance to the novel and the epic.

It is almost as if Williams—confronted as he was with so many things, people, situations, and, perhaps, morals—could not find time to distinguish among his means, in his vehement effort to speak truly. As Frederick J. Hoffman writes in *The Twenties:*

> The problem of what to make of this detail, how best to signify its importance, how to order it without losing sight of it, has preoccupied Williams throughout his life. It is both a formal and a moral problem: as a formal problem, it involves a choice of poetic means; as a moral problem, it considers the behavior of man (and his history) in terms of the barriers he has set, unwittingly or maliciously, to natural communication and understanding.[19]

Although there are many other facets to Williams' theory of art, these are the major, stable principles. For underlying each of his technical premises is Williams' passionate belief that one begins with the real in life and, through the imagination and the shaping processes of art, raises the subject past "fact" into "truth."

How one accomplishes this is never a mandate: the artist must be free to use whatever is at his command. The poet must be free to write fiction, drama, essay, just as a "poem" must be free to include "prose" if necessary. These are the means, and only the means, to truth.

"The business of the writer is the study of language," Williams wrote in 1937. "Poetry and prose are alike in this."[20] The work of William Carlos Williams is important in its totality because Williams so early recognized that good writing was writing that worked and that a man might need *both* poetry and prose to say all he was compelled, through the years, to say. It is that spirit of innovation which so many younger writers have emulated, not the specific way Williams did one thing or another. It is the same spirit of innovation that prompted Williams to say, "Modern verse and prose may, in some measure, be complements one of the other." As his half century of writing shows, to Williams, "It is all writing. It is all one."[21]

CHAPTER TWO

Williams' "Nude": *Kora in Hell*

Kora in Hell: Improvisations (1920) was Williams' first break from the poetry he had been writing since 1904 or before, when he was a student at the University of Pennsylvania Medical School. As the progression within his poetry indicates (*Poems*, 1909; *The Tempers*, 1913; and *Al Que Quiere*, 1917), he moved quickly away from the "Keatsian" mode of his first, unfinished epic and the romantic poems addressed to fire goddesses and Apollo toward a more common subject matter, housed in a natural "speech rhythm" line, a blunt phrasing and diction which gave readers a sense of clarity and statement not unlike those of prose. The famous "Tract" with its opening "I will teach you my townspeople/ how to perform a funeral"[1] is one of the more didactic poems from his third book, *Al Que Quiere*. Its sharp commands mimic speech ("Knock the glass out!/ My God—glass," "For Christ's sake not black," "No wreaths please"). Even more representative of the change occurring in his poems from 1915 on is the idiomatic "Promenade,"

> So. We'll sit here now
> and throw pebbles into
> this water-trickle . . .
>
> But—
> It's cold!
> It's getting dark.
> It's going to rain.
> No further.
> (*CEP*, 132–133)

It takes Williams only a few years to become more interested in the language of the poem than in its imagery. Lines like "I am ready for bed," "We walked/ in your father's grove," "I wanted to write a poem/

that you/ would understand" illustrate his reliance on clarity rather than metaphor in many poems from the 1917 collection. It is then, in the years of 1917 and 1918, after progressing to an easy use of prose rhythms in his poetry, that Williams writes the free-form passages of *Kora in Hell: Improvisations.*

As he recounted, every night for a year he wrote something, "Nothing planned . . . anything that came into my head."[2] One assumes there would be 365 entries, but when the year was over, Williams deleted many of the passages. The published *Kora* includes only twenty-seven selections, most comprised of three sections each. To some passages Williams then added, in his words, "notes of explanation, often more dense than the first writing."[3] The format of the small book was taken from the 1795 edition of Metastasio's *Varie Poesie,* which Ezra Pound had left long before at Williams' home.

Why a book of "improvisations," seemingly more prose than poetry? Williams had never published prose. He had won some recognition as a poet with the three books published before *Kora,* but no financial success (each book cost him at least fifty dollars to have published). As much of his writing around 1917 shows, Williams was discouraged. When would recognition come? For a man of thirty-five, with a wife, children, and parents to support, the whims of an unpredictable literary world were often disheartening. His bitterness during this period is evident in the titles of his current books: *Al Que Quiere (To Him Who Wants It),* with its implications of a limited audience; *Kora,* Persephone gone to hell for the winter; *Sour Grapes,* the group of diffident poems to follow. In his *Autobiography,* Williams wrote about this period,

> It was Persephone gone into Hades, into hell. Kora was the springtime of the year; my heart, my self was being slaughtered. . . .
> Damn it, the freshness, the newness of a springtime . . . was being blotted out by the war. The stupidity, the calculated viciousness of a money-grubbing society such as I knew and violently wrote against (158).

Perhaps Williams felt also that he needed change artistically, a turn to prose. More likely, with the excitement of the 1913 Armory Show (and Duchamp's "Nude Descending a Staircase") still very much alive, and, in a sense, counteracting the depression after World

War I, Williams felt himself less bound by former literary conventions. Just as pictures no longer needed to be "about" a thing, so the need to identify writing as "poetry" or "prose" was also less pressing. In *Kora* Williams refers to the excitement of the times, to the fact that *The Little Review* was publishing *Ulysses* in 1918; in his *Autobiography* he speaks of "my chance. . . . There had been a break somewhere, we were streaming through, each thinking his own thoughts, driving his own designs toward his self's objectives. Whether the Armory Show in painting did it or whether that also was no more than a facet . . ." (138). In a conversation twenty years after the period in question, Williams is more specific, as Constance Rourke reports his saying,

> "As I look back I think it was the French painters rather than the writers who influenced me and their influence was very great. They created an atmosphere of release, color release, release from stereotyped forms, trite subjects. There was a lot of humor in French painting, and a kind of loose carelessness. Morals were down and so were a lot of other things. For which everybody was very happy, relieved." [4]

Williams evidently responded to this aura of change, release, but he too was searching for the stability of guidelines, as he questioned in his prologue to the reissue of *Kora,*

> But what was such a form to be called? I was familiar with the typically French prose poem, its pace was not the same as my own compositions. What I had permitted myself could not by any stretch of the imagination be called verse. Nothing to do but put it down as it stood, trusting to the generous spirit of the age to find a place for it (6).

"What I had permitted myself," "The generous spirit of the age"— Williams' phrasing suggests his view of the artist as newly free agent and of the postwar culture as receptive to any and all innovation.

The theme of change is pervasive throughout Williams' writing; yet even in his early enthusiasm there is a tempering perspective. In his 1918 prologue to *Kora,* he describes a conversation with Walter Arensberg about the "cubists" of the day: Man Ray, Gleizes, Demuth, Duchamp. Arensberg's concept of good art was that "anything in paint that is truly new, truly a fresh creation, is good art." Man's strength lies almost singly, according to Arensberg, in "his ability to improvise novelty." [5] In *Kora,* Williams echoes this premise: "Nothing is good save the new." He damns artists who are "content with the connotations of their masters" (21). In his enthusiastic overstatement, Williams stresses what is for him the touchstone of twentieth-century art: purposeful innovation, the power to write as one dares with no consideration for the critics, the establishment. Yet a few pages later, he modifies his statements by quoting these more balanced axioms from Kandinsky's *Ueber das Geistige in der Kunst:*

> Every artist has to express himself.
> Every artist has to express his epoch.
> Every artist has to express the pure and eternal
>   qualities of the art of all men (23).

Again and again, Williams refers to the "ancients," to the power of the man of imagination to "rise into comradeship with the grave and beautiful presences of antiquity" (17). "Ancient harmonies" are Williams' ideal, his concept being that what is truly related to modern times will echo classic art in its own correspondence to its era.

"An artist has to express himself"

"Why go further?" Williams asks early in his journey to hell. (His use of the Persephone legend and the journey motif is not unlike Pound's technique in the *Cantos* or Eliot's in *The Waste Land* to come.) Why not "perfect" rhythm and form, the poet asks, instead of trying new approaches? Much as in "Portrait of a Lady" and other of his half-ironic poems, Williams mocks himself: "One might conceivably rectify the rhythm, study all out and arrive at the perfection of a tiger lily or a china doorknob. One might lift all out of the ruck, be a worthy successor to—the man in the moon." Any optimism is grudging: "Perhaps we'll bring back Euridice—this time!" (11).

The second part of this passage continues with a discussion of the artist's means of expression—and his frustration in choosing a means. *"Ay dio!* I could say so much were it not for the tunes changing, changing, darting so many ways" (11). The frustration of multiple choices gives way to a revitalization, however, and one of the pervasive themes of *Kora* appears: a man's desire is also his torment. And more broadly, what is desire? what is truth? what is honesty when life changes momently? Williams is to write throughout his life of apparent dichotomies: virgins paralleled with whores, the just opposed by the corrupt, the ascent defined by the descent (It's hard to tell loss from gain anyway" [43]). As he was to write in the 1950's, "No defeat is made up entirely of defeat." [6]

One reason for Williams' move from poetry to the improvisations comes, I think, from his own changing stance toward reality. Williams' early poems and letters show his dogmatism. Being both vehement and positive, he was inclined to "mother" his "townspeople" with all the answers possible. Although there are still some "townspeople" poems to come, the poet in *Kora* vacillates between his hearty, bluff courage and a deep anxiety about his life and his work, a mood nothing short of despair at times. (The poems entitled *Sour Grapes,* published just after *Kora* in 1921, share this latter tone.) He speaks of his thirty-fourth birthday and his "unsettled life"; he poses defensively ("The trick is never to touch the world anywhere" [39]). "Their half-sophisticated faces gripe me in the belly" (42), he writes of virtuous girls and their mothers—and one must think of the poem "Apology,"

> Why do I write today?

> The beauty of
> the terrible faces
> of our nonentities
> stirs me to it

contrasted with colored women's faces ("like/ old Florentine oak"),

> the set pieces
> of your faces stir me—
> leading citizens—
> but not
> in the same way
> > (*CEP,* 131)

Of the sins of hypocrisy and selfishness, Williams writes in *Kora,* "How deftly we keep love from each other" (56). "A man's carcass has no more distinction than the carcass of an ox," he muses, speculating on the qualities that make man: desire, love, purpose. Williams' answers border on being platitudes, but the reader is convinced that these are *his* truths because of his constant use of personal anecdotes. One of the most striking passages in *Kora* is Williams' soliloquy on being a doctor (in tone and style, much like Kafka's descriptions in "A Country Doctor"):

> He comes to do good. Fatigue tickles his calves and the lower part of his back with solicitous fingers, strokes his feet and his knees with appreciative charity. He plunges up the dark steps on his grotesque deed of mercy. In his warped brain an owl of irony fixes on the immediate object of his care as if it were the thing to be destroyed, guffaws at the impossibility of putting any kind of value on the object inside [the patient]. . . . So one is a ridiculous savior of the poor (58–59).

Yet the paradox of Williams' situation as poet-physician, a man who is forced to see too much not to know the real world, is that he can conclude a passage like the one above with a stoic "one must dance nevertheless as he can."

Throughout his career, the dance is Williams' answer to the inert "set pieces," the apathetic parasites of his culture. Repeatedly, the dance appears, its prose shaped to fit a more broken, exuberant motion: "Dance! Sing! Coil and uncoil! Whip yourselves about! Shout the deliverance!" (46). An early passage re-creates the moment of the dance, the preparation for it, as it were.

> how will you expect a fine trickle of words to follow you through the intimacies of this dance without—oh, come let us walk together into the air awhile first . . . Hark! it is the music! Whence does it come? What! Out of the ground? . . . . —and I? must dance with the wind, make my own snow flakes, whistle a contrapuntal melody to my own fuge! Huzza then, this is the dance of the blue moss bank! Huzza then, this is the mazurka of the hollow log! Huzza then, this is the dance of rain in the cold trees (13).

Williams' emphasis on dance as the poet's means of finding expression—and its source in the "ground," the local—is reflected in his own somewhat musical organization of these improvisations: the use of the coda as an ending summary; the use of the dash and, more significantly, of vertical space between words—sometimes three spaces, sometimes more—visually giving a tempo to the line: "But—well—let's wish it were higher after all these years staring at it deplore the paunched clouds glimpse the sky's thin counter crest . . ." (25).

Usually the dance is equated with fulfillment, but Williams does occasionally employ the image for a negative effect, as when he says the music is "beyond them all"; they are "faultily listening" (26); or more emphatically, "There's small dancing left for us any way you look at it" (32).

The dance and the alert imagination are dominant themes throughout *Kora*. Section XV is characteristic in both its content and style, beginning as it does with a rhythmic denotation of a dance: " 'N! cha! cha! cha!" This gay opening is followed with an ironic near cliché, "destiny needs men, so make up your mind." We see here juxtaposition in operation, the principle Williams described in the 1918 prologue to *Kora:*

> By the brokenness of his composition the poet makes himself master of a certain weapon which he could possess himself of in no other way. The speed of the emotions is sometimes such that thrashing about in a thin exaltation of despair many matters are touched but not held. . . .[7]

The speed of rapid progress through images, emotions, the things of a culture can create effects impossible in a passage using more complete transitions. This juxtaposition is one of the principal techniques in *Kora* and in Williams' poems being written during the same period, as well as later.

> My whisky is
> a tough way of life:
>
> The wild cherry
> continually pressing back
> peach orchards.
>
> I am a penniless
> rumsoak . . .
>
>   ("Drink," *CEP,* 140)

The alternating images—the speaker's lines phrased expertly in a conversational idiom—provide a frequent kind of juxtaposition in Williams' poems. "Drink" also illustrates Williams' ideas about the sources for poetry. He describes the value of "things under their noses," things to be expressed in "a language of the day." To this concept, Williams devotes the ending section of Passage XV. He has begun with the reference to the cha-cha, gone through a discussion of the descent-ascent theme, reflected—colloquially—on a dying man as "an old sinner," and ended with a long passage describing April as a Scotch landlady (one of the more surreal excerpts). Williams moves, evidently through his own memories, from boys jumping in the hay of the Scotswoman's establishment to a girl's "being virtuous, oh glacially virtuous" and writes one of his most bitter indictments of man's present condition: "Love, my good friends has never held sway in more than a heart or two here and there since—" (48). (He echoes this in his poem "Memory of April": "Hagh!/ Love has not even visited this country" (in *CEP,* 207).

Selection XV circles finally to "I confess I wish my wife younger" and the poet's reflection on lewdness and chastity, all phrased in idiomatic language. His note to Part 3 discusses the poet's diction and is, in a sense, a rationale for the passages just written.

> That which is heard from the lips of those to whom we are talking in our day's-affairs mingles with what we see in the streets and everywhere about us as it mingles also with our imaginations. . . . This is the language to which few ears are tuned so that it is said by poets that few men are ever in their full sense since they have no way to use their imaginations. . . . But of old poets would translate this hidden language into a kind of replica of the speech of the world with certain distinctions of rhyme and meter to show that it was not really that speech. Nowadays the elements of what language are set down as heard and the imagination of the listener and of the poet are left free to mingle in the dance (49).

A more active participation. The word "dance" suggests it, as does the principle itself. The poet presents; he does not interpret or condition. His arrangement of language, objects, motifs may heighten a reader's response, but the poet cannot create the response for him. He is "free," just as is the poet, "to mingle in the dance."

It is freedom, ebullience, that shouts through most of Williams' lines about the dance—and foreshadows some of the lively passages in *Paterson*'s "A Sunday in the Park."

> Hey you, the dance! Squat. Leap. Hips to the left.
> Chin-ha!—sideways! Stand up, stand up *ma bonne:*
> you'll break my backbone. So again!—and so forth
> til we're sweat soaked (44–45).

And with masterful juxtaposition, Williams follows this section with a clear statement about his quandary as a poet:

> Some fools once were listening to a poet reading his poem. It so happened that the words of the thing spoke of gross matters of the everyday world such as are never much hidden from a quick eye. Out of these semblances, and borrowing certain members from fitting masterpieces of antiquity, the poet began piping up his music, simple fellow, thinking to please his listeners. But they getting the whole matter sadly muddled in their minds made such a confused business of listening that not only were they not pleased at the poet's exertions but no sooner had he done than they burst out against him with violent imprecations (45).

Unity in the *Improvisations*

"The imagination leads and the deed comes behind," writes Williams (57). "That which is known has value only by virtue of the dark" (71). Despite Williams' insistence on the primary faculties, on the values of the sub (or supra) conscious, his writing in *Kora* seems far from surreal. As André Breton defined surrealism in 1924: "Pure psychic automatism, by which it is intended to express, verbally, in writing, or by other means, the real process of thought. Thought's dictation, in the absence of all control exercised by the reason and outside all aesthetic or moral preoccupations." According to Breton, surreal writing can be distinguished by "a very high degree of immediate absurdity." [8]

Most of Williams' improvisations can hardly be termed "absurd." In nearly all the numbered sequences, the relationship among the parts is clear (keeping in mind the common modern practice of juxtaposition). Passage XVI, for example, has to do with the figures of classic mythology: the poet as satyr, Zeus ("country doctor without a taste for coin jingling"), and Homer, with references to "giants in the dirt" and to a human variation on the theme of giant appetites, the story of Lizzie Anderson (also, see the poem "To a Friend," *CEP,* 205). The mention of weak-minded Lizzie and her seventeen lovers helps give point to the sad tone of the passage: "They are the same men they always were—but fallen. Do they dance now, they that danced beside Helicon? They dance much as they did then, only, few have an eye for it, through the dirt and fumes" (51).

Passage XXI is one of the most tightly related, although it has three parts and a coda, each having a note in italics. Part I begins, as so many of the opening sections do, with a personal, more or less physical observation: "There's the bathtub. Look at it, caustically rejecting its smug proposal" (66). The self-abasing fun in Williams' admission, "Fresh linen with a dab here, there of the wet paw serves me better," parallels his tone in so many of his "self-portraits" in poetry. Honesty—with an edge to it. The note comments matter-of-factly on the modern practice of wasting an entire room for "the relief and washing of the body."

Part II moves to "Neatness and finish; the dust out of every corner." As the poet considers his wife's laborious house cleaning, as important to her as his writing is to him, he turns to gentle irony: "The house may now be carefully wrapped in brown paper and sent to a publisher." This second note deals with the hesitancy, the mistrust, between man and wife. Although the poet has sympathy for her and her life, he dare not express that, "knowing she will never understand" (67).

Part III brings the poet to the house itself, the house as entity. The note expands the idea that the house belongs to no one, that it forces the architect to form it as *it* will. Man is never in control.

Back to the human element with the Coda. In the midst of a storm, "we my dear sit stroking the cat stroking the cat and smiling sleepily, purr" (68); with the note, "A house is sometimes wine," because it is protection, benevolence. It lulls anxieties just as wine does.

In this passage, as in others, Williams moves from physical observations to much more subjective reactions, almost as though freeing himself from the demands of a "truthful" or "factual" observation.

As well as having unity within the parts of each passage, Williams also has arranged the passages meaningfully. Many of the first excerpts are related in some way to technique, to the artist's problems and to his means of solving them. Increasingly come the recurring themes: dance as a way of finding imagination, love, the promise of a new world, the fallacy in "fact" and in "history." As each theme is presented and then discussed, the reader collects groups of associations about each one, enriching the single word or image whenever the poet chooses to use it.

This larger method of interrelating ideas gives Williams maximum content in relatively small space. By the end of *Kora,* the reader feels as though he knows the poet and his concerns (a great many of which are to appear for the next forty years of Williams' writings). He also feels as if he has been pointed in some direction, rather than just rambling through the poet's effusions. The concluding passages, XXVI and XXVII, do not disappoint him. Williams closes with an extension of the ascent-descent idea, "Doors have a back side also." And, later, "There is no truth—sh!—but the honest truth" (80), moving into another dichotomy of "truth":

> All that seem solid: melancholias, *idées fixes,* eight years at the academy, Mr. Locke, this year and the next and the next—one like another— whee!—they are April zephyrs, were one a Botticelli, between their chinks, pink anemones (80).

Whee! a typically Williams' confrontation with "fact." The passage closes with a picture of the poet himself, a rarity in *Kora*—a picture which is to appear thirty-five years later in Williams' poems "The Pink Locust" and "The Sparrow,"

> Often it happens that in a community of no great distinction some fellow of superficial learning but great stupidity will seem to be rooted in the earth of the place the most solid figure imaginable   impossible to remove him (81).

The concluding Passage XXVII resembles the opening of *Paterson,* I think, in that it lists the components of poetry, musically.

> The particular thing, whether it be four pinches of four divers white powders . . . or say a pencil sharpened at one end, dwarfs the imagina-

tion, makes logic a butterfly, offers a finality that sends up spinning through space, a fixity the mind could climb forever, a revolving mountain, a complexity with a surface of glass; the gist of poetry. *D. C. al fin.* (82).

Williams' punctuation here invites the reader to telescope: "The particular thing; the gist of poetry." And then, in conclusion, on to that most dominant of themes, "There is no thing that with a twist of the imagination cannot be something else" (82). The power lies within the mind itself, the power even to create the seasons. So Williams concludes, after much concern throughout *Kora* with the season of a man's life: "this day of all others is the one chosen." Seasons provide only "a mockery of the warmth or frozenness which is within ourselves" (83). It comes back again to man, to the poet, not to mythology or to weather. Williams has learned—almost in the writing of *Kora,* it seems —that he must make his own fortune, his own place, his own art.

"Its pace was not the same . . ."

In Williams' comment about the rhythm of his improvisations, he compares his prose with the nineteenth-century French prose poems—those of Baudelaire, Rimbaud, Mallarmé—and concludes that "its pace was not the same." Undoubtedly, some of Williams' passages would resemble the writings of these poets, but, taken collectively, his improvisations lack the finish of any artificial form; they seem to grow into a unit rather than being completed segments in themselves.[9] *The Encyclopedia of Poetry and Poetics* defines a prose poem as having "more pronounced rhythm, sonorous effects, imagery, and density of expression. It may contain even inner rhyme and metrical runs."[10] As close reading shows, Williams' improvisations cover a wide range of subjects; yet the rhythms and forms do not, for the most part, differ strikingly within the book. The rhythm of many of the passages suggests the poet—impetuous, emotional: short exclamations accenting long, qualifying sentences.

Once again   the moon   in a glassy twilight. The gas jet in the third window is turned low, they have not drawn the shade, sends down a flat glare upon the lounge's cotton-Persian cover where the time passes with clumsy caresses. Never in this *milieu* has one stirred himself to turn up the light. It is costly to leave a jet burning at all. Feel your way to the bed. Drop your clothes on the floor and creep in. . . . (54).

The comparatively long opening sentences modulate to the faster, shorter phrasing midway through the excerpt (thirty-four words per sentence coming down to thirteen, ten, six, and nine). The pose of the poet as persona, as active observer-participant, helps vary the phrasing easily. Again,

> The words of the thing twang and twitter to the gentle rocking of a high-laced boot and the silk above that. The trick of the dance is in following now the words, *allegro,* now the contrary beat of the glossy leg: Reaching far over as if—But always she draws back and comes down upon the word flat-footed. For a moment we—but the boot's costly and the play's not mine. The pace leads off anew. Again the words break it and we both come down flatfooted.

Whether Williams opens with a long sentence (as above, twenty-two words) or a short one (he likes maxims: "Truth's a wonder" [36], "It's all one" [45], "Giants in the dirt" [50]), he usually moves into a longer sentence pattern before coming back to a midpoint of sharper, more emotional sentences, often written with exclamation points: "But all's right now . . . Haia!" (53); "Solitary poet who speaks his mind and has not one fellow in a virtuous world! I wish for youth! I wish for love—! . . . Heigh-ya!" (48); "And you'ld be right too. The path's not yours till you've gone it alone a time. But here's another handful of west wind. White of the night! White of the night" (36).

As pointed out on page 24, the progression in each improvisation is from an objective lead-in description to the poet's personal involvement with the situation. The sentence rhythms reinforce the kind of expression being given. Somewhat surprisingly, many of Williams' short poems of this period evince the same kind of structure (*surprisingly* because the characteristic short lines of his poems suggest that all sentences are short). "The Cold Night" is similar because of its rhythms and also because of its images of whiteness:

> It is cold. The white moon
> is up among her scattered stars—
> like the bare thighs of

the Police Sergeant's wife—among
her five children . . .
No answer. Pale shadows lie upon
the frosted glass. One answer:
It is midnight, it is still
and it is cold . . . !
White thighs of the sky! . . .

(*CEP*, 203)

Williams' use of ellipsis to indicate pause and of the exclamation mark, dash, and colon shows his struggle to create exactly the right rhythm in his writing. When he is able, much later, to accomplish rhythmic control through line position and division, as in the poems of the 1950's, the rhythms have themselves modulated into smoother, more restrained patterns. These earlier writings, however, show that his recollections in *I Wanted to Write a Poem* are, for the most part, accurate: "I didn't go in for long lines because of my nervous nature. I couldn't. The rhythmic pace was the pace of speech, an excited pace because I was excited when I wrote." [11]

Several principles of Williams' rationale for writing are evident here. Of the idea of organic form, of the poem—or any piece of writing—creating its own shape, he writes in *Kora:*

It is nearly pure luck that gets the mind turned inside out in a work of art . . . it's a kind of alchemy of form, a deft bottling of a fermenting language. Take Dante and his Tuscan dialect—It's a matter of position. The empty form drops from a cloud, like a gourd from a vine (72).

And, in the prologue to *Kora,*

XIII. No. 3. A poet witnessing the chicory flower and realizing its virtues of form and color so constructs his praise of it as to borrow no particle from right or left. He gives his poem over to the flower and its plant themselves. . . . [12]

Williams' four flower poems, written during this period and chosen by the poet for inclusion in Whit Burnett's *This Is My Best,* illustrate the difference in rhythm and tone evoked by the daisy ("weeds stand high in the corn"), the primrose ("Yellow, yellow, yellow, yellow!"), the beloved Queen Anne's lace, and the strident great mullen. In the rhythms of the latter poems, Williams creates very different tones by changing his usual sentence patterns. "Queen-Ann's-Lace" builds through sentences of seventeen to twenty words to two shorter images (sentences of nine and eleven words) to the stately yet erotic closing:

> Each part
> is a blossom under his touch
> to which the fibers of her being
> stem one by one, each to its end,
> until the whole field is a
> white desire, empty, a single stem,
> a cluster, flower by flower,
> a pious wish to whiteness gone over—
> or nothing.
>   (*CEP*, 210)

In contrast, the gruff burlesque of the great mullen is achieved through abrupt punctuation and small sentence units, but especially through the device of dialogue, as in "Portrait of a Lady,"

> Liar, liar, liar!
> You come from her! I can smell djer-kiss
> on your clothes. Ha! you come to me,
> you—
>   (*CEP*, 211)

These poems also show another of Williams' means of writing in any tone/pace he chooses: the use of persona. Though most of the improvisations are the poet speaking for himself, Williams does on occasion create other characters. These personae are identified not through the author's naming them or describing their traits, but through the rhythm and diction of their speech. Notice, for example, the hesitancy in this bored woman's lines,

> You would learn—if you knew even one city—where people are a lit-
> tle gathered together and where one sees—it's our frontier you know—the
> common changes of the human spirit: our husbands tire of us and we—
> let us not say we go hungry for their caresses but for caresses—of a
> kind. Oh I am no prophet. I have no theory to advance . . . (34–35).

The almost desperately simple language contrasts greatly with the poet's few patches of humorous writing, where rhythms again reflect the accents of the diction. Williams' passage "When beldams dig clams their fat hams balanced" is the same kind of word play as Wallace Stevens' "Chieftain Iffucan of Azcan in caftan/ Of tan." [13] This love of the word itself—what it is capable of creating in character as well as in mood—shows also in Williams' inclusion of foreign phrases and lines. The opening of Passage XXIII, for example, provides a humorous re-creation of the rhythms in the "words" of both the sheep and the Spaniard,

> Baaaa! Ba-ha-ha-ha-ha-ha-ha-ha! *Bebe esa purga.* It is the goats of Santo Domingo talking. *Bebe esa purga!* Bebeesapurga! And the answer is: *Yo no lo quiero beber!* Yonoloquierobeber! (72).

This excerpt is followed by the discussion of form as a gourd, quoted on page 28, and then Williams breaks into another example of very different organic form, using vertical space to help in suggesting rhythm:

> The   red   huckleberry   bushes   running miraculously along the ground among the trees everywhere, except where the land's tilled, these keep her from that tiredness the earth's touch lays up under the soles of feet. She runs beyond the wood follows the swiftest along the roads laughing among the birch clusters   her face in the yellow leaves the curls before her eyes   her mouth half open (72).

It is interesting to notice that Williams' style and rhythm in most of the added notes differ from the general form of the improvisations proper. Sentences in the notes are sometimes quite long, often unwieldy to the point of awkwardness, because Williams is using a single sentence to make a fairly complete statement:

> Between two contending forces there may at all times arrive that moment when stress is equal on both sides so that with a great pushing a great stability results giving a picture of perfect rest (11).

Passive verbs, delayed structures, an absence of personal pronouns—one thinks in contrast of Williams' direct poem "Arrival," written during this period, which opens with the same image of arriving,

And yet one arrives somehow,
finds himself loosening the hooks of
her dress
in a strange bedroom—
                    (*CEP*, 215)

Concise, immediate, clear, the lines move easily from one active verb construction to another. It is the awkwardness of much of the phrasing in these prose notes that leads to many of the charges about Williams' confused prose style. The improvisations themselves seldom suffer from the hesitant syntax and pretentious diction of the notes. On page 29, Williams writes

> In great dudgeon over the small profit that has come to him through a certain companionship a poet addresses himself and the loved one as if it were two strangers, thus advancing himself to the brink of that discovery which will reward all his labors but which he as yet only discerns as a night, a dark void coaxing him whither he has no knowledge.

Great dudgeon, thus advancing himself, brink, void, whither—Williams' diction here is at best self-conscious, "poetic." One thinks of his earliest poems, nearly ten years before, where such phrasing was also used. Passages such as this are probably the reason for Joseph Bouma's comment that Williams' prose is "behind" his poetry in this period and in the 1920's.[14] In many respects, it is as though Williams has to work through imitation in both poetry and various kinds of prose before he can attain the simplicity of a colloquial diction and a natural syntax.

CHAPTER THREE

Spring and All: The Unity of Design

IN 1921, William Carlos Williams included a prose piece, "The Delicacies," among the poems of *Sour Grapes*. The study alternates between descriptions of the food at a dinner and of the people there; "The hostess, in pink satin and blonde hair" is set against "the great silent bald head of her little-eyed husband!" [1] Then Williams describes the herring salad: "delicately flavoured saltiness in scallops of lettuce leaves." Some of the food demands as much exuberance as the pretty women at the festivities (Salz-roles; exquisite!"), although there is no question that his title relates as much to the woman with "hair like some filmy haystack" as to the "masterly caviare sandwich."

Williams' inclusion of this prose in a book of poems sets the key for his writing practices in the 1920's. Between 1921 and 1934, Williams was to publish no books of poetry. The seven books and several shorter selections published in magazines were all either prose or mixtures of poetry and prose, extending the techniques he had introduced in the 1920 *Kora in Hell: Improvisations. Spring and All,* the collage of prose commentary, typographical jokes, and untitled poems, appeared in 1923, as did Williams' attempt at a stream-of-consciousness novel, *The Great American Novel* (Joyce's *Ulysses* had been published in 1922). In 1925 appeared the twenty essays of *In the American Grain,* Williams' great testimony to the efficacy of organic form in prose as well as in poetry. In 1927 and 1928 he published mixed selections in the two volumes of *American Caravan,* prose and poetry coupled and titled as one piece of writing. Work sheets show that he was also writing *as prose* the poems which later appeared in "The Descent of Winter" (1927). In 1928 Williams published *A Voyage to Pagany,* his first novel, and in 1929, his translation from the French of Philippe Soupault's *Last Nights of Paris*. Not until 1934 were the poems of the period published as *Collected Poems, 1921–31,* following the 1932 *A*

Novelette and Other Prose and Williams' first short stories, *The Knife of the Times.*

Surely this was a decade of prose for Williams. Yet the question remains, why? *Kora in Hell* had not received so much attention that Williams felt compelled to continue with prose. True, it was a period of great interest in fiction: Fitzgerald had published *This Side of Paradise* in 1920, *The Beautiful and Damned* in 1922, and *The Great Gatsby* in 1925; Hemingway's short stories had achieved much notice even before *The Sun Also Rises* appeared in 1926; Gertrude Stein's 1914 *Tender Buttons* and 1925 *The Making of Americans* were exciting writers in much the same way the Armory Show had aroused painters in 1913. In 1921 Sherwood Anderson won the Dial Award for his two collections of short stories, *Winesburg, Ohio,* in 1919 and *The Triumph of the Egg* in 1921. Dos Passos' experimentation in his 1921 *Three Soldiers* and the 1925 *Manhattan Transfer* helped to emphasize the innovation in technique, used also by e. e. cummings, not only in his poetry but in his 1922 novel *The Enormous Room.* Joyce's *Ulysses* in 1922; Dreiser's *An American Tragedy* in 1925; D. H. Lawrence's *Lady Chatterley* in 1928; Sinclair Lewis' news-making novels, six or seven in the decade—the affluent public was buying books, and the books they were buying (and talking about) were novels.

Set against these (for the most part) exciting works of fiction (technically exciting as well as thematically), the production in poetry during the twenties was most disappointing—to Williams, even defeating. Eliot was the central figure: *The Waste Land* in 1922 created as much furor in one way as did *Ulysses.* Williams said of "the great catastrophe to our letters," *The Waste Land* "gave the poem back to the academics. We did not know how to answer him." [2] Then in 1925 came Eliot's *Collected Poems* and the same year the first book of Pound's *Cantos* (1–16), followed with Numbers 17 to 27 in 1928. It was a dismal showing for poetry—dismal because, in Williams' words, much of it was a "looking backward." Of Eliot, a "conformist," Williams writes,

> I felt he had rejected America. . . . I knew he would influence all sub-
> sequent American poets and take them out of my sphere. I had en-
> visaged a new form of poetic composition, a form for the future. It
> was a shock to me that he was so tremendously successful; my con-
> temporaries flocked to him—away from what I wanted. [3]

In one sense, Williams' writing throughout this decade is an exploration of his comment about Eliot, that he had rejected America. Like *The Great Gatsby* and Hart Crane's *The Bridge,* many of Williams' books attempt to define the spirit of America. (As Williams acknowledged in his *Autobiography,* "Mencken's *The American Language* [1919] stood in the background as a sort of formal liturgy" [147]. Art was everywhere concerned with the newness of this land and its promise—a promise dimmed if not tarnished by World War I and the disappointing peace.) The essays of *In the American Grain* study some of the best-known figures of American history—some good, more evil (see Chapter Five); *A Voyage to Pagany* is almost Jamesian as the American Dev Evans searches abroad for his identity, his allegiance (see Chapter Six). Though less patently "explorations," *The Great American Novel* has many passages dealing with history, and the title makes any discussion of American art relevant. *Spring and All* deals in large part with the art and thought of Williams' contemporary America. Just as *Kora* seemed to be a working out of many personal and technical problems for Williams, so do his writings of the 1920's.

It may be misleading to place so much emphasis on Eliot's poems as a negative force in Williams' writing. Yet the times were in upheaval: Williams himself spent two years (1924 and 1927) in Europe during this decade, leaving his medical practice and, during the first absence, his two sons, and facing the disapproval of Rutherford and the loss of his patients. As well as seeing Pound when he was abroad, Williams corresponded with him frequently. In 1922, in fact, Pound had asked Williams to send fifty dollars for Eliot's personal use: "The point is that Eliot is at the last gasp. . . . Too tired to write, broke down; during convalescence in Switzerland did *Waste Land,* a masterpiece." [4]

Williams the poet-physician was even more conscious than usual of the world of literature during the early 1920's, because he had become a magazine editor. With Robert McAlmon, he edited *Contact* for three years, from December of 1920 to June of 1923. Publishing such writers as Marianne Moore, Kenneth Burke, Marsden Hartley, Wallace Stevens, H. D., Ezra Pound, and Kay Boyle, he worked to bring the new into focus. As he wrote in the second issue of *Contact:* "In answer to all criticisms we find the first issue of *Contact* perfect, the first truly representative American magazine of art yet published." [5]

An American magazine, Williams continues, must emphasize "an indigenous art." Based on Williams' deep-rooted belief that an artist must "become awake to his own locality" before he can join "the main body of art," *Contact* was established to "develop among our serious writers a sense of mutual contact" and to " emphasize the local phase of the game of writing." [6]

By the fourth issue of *Contact* (1923), Williams was more defensive. He realized that not all young talents mature into "major" ones, but even that premise was to him essential to American art and criticism:

> It is young. It is not necessarily inexpert . . . but it is necessarily young. There is no long chain of sophistication to engage us. . . . Our processes are for the moment chaotic but they have the distinct advantage of being able to claim no place of rest save immediacy. [7]

Issue V brought a further clarification of Williams' artistic rationale:

> *Contact* has never in the least intimated that the American artist in preparing his position "should forget all about Europe." On the contrary the assertion has been that he should acquaint himself with everything that he can gather from European sources. [8]

Immediacy and the local; the great unity of all art; "naked attention to the thing itself"—the principles Williams had emphasized in *Kora in Hell* and in his frequent writing for *Contact* grew to even fuller expression in the 1923 *Spring and All*. Kora had returned from her winter sojourn in hell; the prose and poetry of *Spring and All* testified to a new mood, a new theme, for the poet.

Art as NEW

Dedicated to Charles Demuth, *Spring and All* reads in its opening paragraphs like a continuation of Williams' *Contact* essays. The appreciation of experiment, the need for contact, the artist's realization that he will not be understood:

> If anything of moment results—so much the better. And so much the more likely will it be that no one will want to see it.

> There is a constant barrier between the reader and his consciousness of immediate contact with the world. . . .[9]

The predicament: that men are out of touch, with themselves as well as with art. The artist's solution: to write for the imagination rather than for himself or for others. The dedication: "To refine, to clarify, to intensify that eternal moment in which we live there is but a single force—the imagination. This is its book" (3).

Spring and All is no "beautiful illusion," Williams tells us, but a book of violence. How else to make the world new (*Kora in Hell*'s pervasive theme)? How else to make art new, but to start from the beginning? The real theme of *Spring* lies in this idea of violence, expressed so forcefully in the eleven-page opening essay:

> The imagination, intoxicated by prohibitions, rises to drunken heights to destroy the world. Let it rage, let it kill. The imagination is supreme. . . . To it now we come to dedicate our secret project: the annihilation of every human creature on the face of the earth. This is something never before attempted. None to remain; nothing but the lower vertebrates, the mollusks, insects and plants. Then at last will the world be made anew. Houses crumble to ruin, cities disappear. . . . A *marvellous serenity* broken only by bird and wild beast calls reigns over the entire sphere. *Order and peace abound.*
>
> This final and *self inflicted* holocaust has been *all for love, for sweetest love* . . . . and it is spring—both in Latin and Turkish, in English and Dutch, in Japanese and Italian; it is spring by Stinking River where a magnolia tree, without leaves, before what was once a farmhouse, now ramshackle home for millworkers, raises its straggling branches of ivorywhite flowers (5–6; italics mine).

The results are worth the catastrophe, Williams' emphasis seems to prove, as he brings his proposal down to the specifics of the local (Stinking River, millworkers, straggling branches). The obvious parallel with spring's violence as a season is the apparent unrest of innovation in modern art. Later in the essay, Williams concentrates on the new in painting: Charles Demuth and Juan Gris seem to take the lead, to break with pictorial reality and find imaginative truth.

Again and again Williams returns to this point: the artist's responsibility to create the new, the meaningful. Again and again his practices in the book show the value of innovation, as he uses the poems of *Spring and All* to both illustrate and substantiate his prose theories. Frederick J. Hoffman describes *Spring and All* as "one of the most important volumes of modern poetry published in the 1920's. It is a veritable 'book of examples' of the principles (implicit and explicit) that governed the making of it." [10]

The first poems in the book are vivid evocations of the title. "By the Road to the Contagious Hospital" and "Pink Confused with White" represent both the spirit of spring and the even less concrete spirit of art. Williams leads into the poems with a grand affirmation of newness, intensified by spacing and capitalization:

> . . . at last SPRING is approaching . . .
>
> THE WORLD IS NEW.
>
> I.
>
> By the road to the contagious hospital
> under the surge of the blue
> mottled clouds driven from the
> northeast—a cold wind. Beyond, the
> waste of broad, muddy fields
> brown with dried weeds, standing and fallen
> patches of standing water
> the scattering of tall trees . . .
> (11)

This poem, with its more than realistic detail ("clouds driven from the/ northeast," "muddy fields/ brown with dried weeds"), emphasizes not the "beautiful illusion" of spring, but the tortuously slow awareness: "Lifeless in appearance, sluggish/ dazed spring approaches—." The process of growth is presented almost as if an artist—a graphic artist—were drawing the poem. "One by one objects are defined—/ It quickens/ clarity, outline of leaf. . . ." Just as the the prose leading to the poem has been slowed by Williams' positioning of the lines, so does his word choice and line arrangement help maintain the sedate tempo of the conclusion:

> But now the stark dignity of
> entrance—Still, the profound change

has come upon them: rooted, they
grip down and begin to awaken.

"The Pot of Flowers," the poem paired with "By the Road," is another picture; in fact it seems to be a literal "painting" of a painting. Much as he is to do forty years later with Pieter Brueghel's pictures, Williams at least starts with his own description of the model painting:

Pink confused with white
flowers and flowers reversed
take and spill the shaded flame
darting it back
into the lamp's horn . . .

(14)

Progressing as would the eye, Williams' poem moves, in meaningful rhythm, down the picture to the leaves of the plant and, finally (and perhaps not too "poetically"), to the pot:

petals radiant with transpiercing light
contending above
the leaves
reaching up their modest green
from the pot's rim

and there, wholly dark, the pot
gay with rough moss.

The prose which follows these two picture poems opens with a phrase that relates quickly to the opening of "The Pot of Flowers," its motif of confusion. "A terrific confusion has taken place," Williams begins, speaking once again of the need for genuine art in modern man's life (one of Williams' pervasive themes). "No man knows whither to turn. . . . Emptiness stares us once more in the face." And the image of the hoop snake, later to appear frequently in *Paterson,* "Has life its tail in its mouth or its mouth in its tail?" (14).

The poet's despairing tone modulates in a comment that hope "long asleep" is now "aroused once more," and Williams gives his purposely earthy description of the imagination—a description consistent with the two "unpoetic" poems already presented:

> The imagination, freed from the handcuffs of "art," takes the lead! Her feet are bare and not too delicate. In fact those who come behind her have too much to think of. Hm. Let it pass (15).

The next section concerns "Demuth and a few others" who "do their best to point out the error [of tradition], telling us that design is a function of the IMAGINATION" (16). Before the next two poems, Williams comments that he is joining the "battle" now, with "these few notes jotted down in the midst of the action, under distracting circumstances. . . ."

"The Farmer in deep thought" does seem to be almost a "note." It ends with a brief descriptive phrase (linking Demuth, Williams, and the idea of battle with the farmer):

>   . . . Down past the brushwood
>   bristling by
>   the rainsluiced wagonroad
>   looms the artist figure of
>   the farmer—composing
>   —antagonist

Just as this is not the "typical" picture of a farmer, neither is its companion poem the usual re-creation of a spring night. "Flight to the City" opens traditionally enough:

>   The Easter stars are shining
>   above lights that are flashing—
>   coronal of the black—

before the poet breaks in

>   Nobody
>   to say it—
>   Nobody to say! pinholes

"Coronal" is poetic; perhaps "pinholes" is more nearly truth. Williams goes on later, "Burst it asunder/ break through to the fifty words/

necessary" and then in the poem comes the "breakthrough" itself, the poet, free, letting his imagination "see" the night as it wants to, the images juxtaposed grotesquely, in the immensity of the poet's view:

> a crown for her head with
> castles upon it, skyscrapers
> filled with nut-chocolates—
>
>   dovetame winds—
>
> stars of tinsel
>
> from the great end of a cornucopia
> of glass.

Despite the fact that these may not be finished poems, as Williams' prefatory comment suggests, each one accomplishes what the poet's immediate aim in *Spring and All* seems to be; here, to break with the traditional associations, the usual poetic views of a subject. What more common subjects for poetry than night, a farmer, spring, or flowers? Williams' choice of topics seems to parallel some of his typography (the opening of *Spring and All* is numbered Chapter 19, followed by Chapter XIII, which is printed upside down). Critics had been objecting to the topics for his poems (a few years later Wallace Stevens is to make the "antipoetic" statement [11]); now Williams is meeting an even greater challenge, proving he can make *new* poetry from the most worn of poetic subjects.

In the next section of prose, Williams makes the point that the farmer and the sky might "rediscover or replace demoded meanings" (20). He questions the practice of equating objects on a one-to-one basis. Why does anger have to be represented by lightning? Why do flowers have to connote love? As the following poems illustrate, "the word must be put down *for itself,* not as a symbol of nature but a part, cognizant of the whole—aware—civilized" (22).

> Black winds from the north
> enter black hearts. Barred from
> seclusion in lilies they strike
> to destroy—

Trying to break the usual associations, Williams moves into more didactic comment, "Hate is of the night and the day/ of flowers and rocks. Nothing/ is gained by saying the night breeds/ murder—it is the classical mistake." At the end of "Black Winds," admittedly difficult to follow without reference to the prose, Williams lapses into a more traditional image, only to bring himself up short with the observation, "How easy to slip/ into the old mode, how hard to/ cling firmly to the advance—." The following poem, "To Have Done Nothing," seems to answer "Black Winds." Despair about his work sets the tone, in a Gertrude Stein-like pattern of repetition,

> No that is not it
> Nothing that I have done
> nothing
> I have done
>
> is made up of
> nothing
> and the diphthong
>
> ae

To clarify Williams' meaning would require italicizing the phrases in lines 3 and 4, 6 and 8. Words used as words. Williams is taking his own advice, to put down the word "for itself." This grammatical study "proves" that "everything/ I have done?" is the same as "nothing/ I have done," leaving the poet in "confusion/ which only to/ have done nothing/ can make/ perfect."

Back to art, this time to a concentration on Juan Gris and his use of "things" presented imaginatively rather than realistically. As Williams writes just before his poem "The Rose," "The attempt is being made to separate things of the imagination from life, and obviously, by using the forms common to experience so as not to frighten the onlooker away but to invite him" (30). Williams' re-creation of Gris's rose ("metal or porcelain," as the poet describes it) begins with the dogmatic, "The rose is obsolete." In much the same way, "At the Faucet of June" describes a scene using the same artistic techniques. Williams' sly references to "a Veronese or/ perhaps a Rubens?" help the reader keep his place—it is art we are speaking

of—and bring the poem back in its conclusion to a restatement of
Williams' basic artistic principle, "no ideas but in things":

> Impossible
>
> to say, impossible
> to underestimate—
> wind, earthquakes in
>
> Manchuria, a
> partridge
> from dry leaves.

Williams, like Gris, is concerned with things, familiar and simple,
and at the same time with detaching them from ordinary experience.
As he writes in the prose which follows the poem.

> Thus they are still "real"; they are the same things they would be if
> photographed or painted by Monet, they are recognizable as the things
> touched by the hands during the day, but in this painting they are seen
> to be in some peculiar way—detached. . . .
>   Here is a shutter, a bunch of grapes, a sheet of music, a picture of sea
> and mountains (particularly fine) which the onlooker is not for a
> moment permitted to witness as an "illusion." One thing laps over on
> the other, the cloud laps over on the shutter, the bunch of grapes is
> part of the handle of the guitar. . . . All drawn with admirable sim-
> plicity and excellent design—all a unity (34).

Williams does, in fact, run the poem directly into uncapitalized prose,
a device which emphasizes vividly the continuity between the poems
and prose in *Spring and All* (a practice much like his later technique
in *Paterson*).

The Artist and His Medium

Edgar Allan Poe is the next subject for the prose of
Spring. As Williams' *In the American Grain* was to show, Poe was
one of his favorite artists because of his "close identity with life . . . .
Poe could not have written a word without the violence of expulsive
emotion combined with the in-drawing force of a crudely repressive

environment" (36). Recurring themes for Williams—the tortured artist as involved man, the alienating culture—lead the poet into more personal statements ("No man could suffer the fragmentary nature of his understanding of his own life" [38]) and his poem "Young Love":

> What about all this writing?

> O "Kiki"
> O Miss Margaret Jarvis
> The backhandspring
> I: clean
>   clean
>   clean: yes . . New York

> Wrigley's, appendicitis, John Marin:
> skyscraper soup—

> Either that or a bullet!

This is the opening of the longest poem from *Spring and All,* a poem admittedly autobiographical. This poem recounts truly, *cleanly,* the montage of the poet's experience: the model; the young nurse; New York, where Williams interned at Old French Hospital, with its dime stores, skyscrapers, and the painter John Marin (to whose work Williams wrote a tribute in 1956). It must be "clean" or—"a bullet." As the poem continues later

> Pah!

> It is unclean
> which is not straight to the mark—

The love scene that follows makes use again of the *things* involved in the emotion:

> Your sobs soaked through the walls
> breaking the hospital to pieces
> Everything
> —windows, chairs

obscenely drunk, spinning—
white, blue, orange
—hot with our passion
wild tears, desperate rejoinders
my legs, turning slowly
end over end in the air!

The poem ends with an ambivalent contrast. Williams repeats the central word "clean" in the next-to-the-last stanza; then introduces the last five lines with "but" to imply that the love scene was only supposition.

Clean is he alone
after whom stream
the broken pieces of the city—
flying apart at his approaches

but I merely
caressed you curiously
fifteen years ago and you still
go about the city, they say
patching up sick school children

(41)

The earlier theme of poetic violence comes to mind again, as well as the later image of Paterson approaching his city, before Williams dwindles, rhythmically at least, into *truth*. The prose which follows this poem states simply: "Understood in a practical way, without calling upon mystic agencies . . . it is that life becomes actual only when it is identified with ourselves" (41).

With few exceptions, many of the remaining poems from *Spring and All* have to do with Williams' concern with this real experience and with the things of the poet's local as ways into those real experiences (this theme also dominated many of McAlmon's writings in *Contact*). "The Eyeglasses" (which opens with a line about "the universality of things"); "The Right of Way" ("The supreme importance/ of this nameless spectacle"); the red paper box of "Composition"; cathedral spires; a conversation with a barber in "Death the Barber." In "Light Becomes Darkness" Williams reiterates the theme, "destruction and creation/ are simultaneous."

Three of the most popular poems from this collection—"To an Old Jaundiced Woman," "Shoot it Jimmy!" and "To Elsie"—are prefaced with the comment that art "places a value upon experience" (61). The idea of the imagination raising everyday experiences to art underlies the next group of poems, which includes "Horned Purple," "The Sea," "Quietness," and the much-anthologized, much-maligned wheelbarrow poem. Prefacing these poems with his usual emphasis on "a new world" and its "freedom of movement and newness" (69) in contrast to the present "stale" age in literature, Williams is free to write

> so much depends
> upon
>
> a red wheel
> barrow
>
> glazed with rain
> water
>
> beside the white
> chickens.

Many critics have made ambitious defenses for this poem, though perhaps the best defense is that it is so similar to many other of the poems in *Spring and All* that it evidently suits what Williams wants a poem to be at this time, as the prose statement following it would suggest: "The same things exist, but in a different condition, when energized by the imagination" (75). And, further on, "life is absolutely simple" (76). In this simplicity of his real experiences, Williams has again and again found the materials for his poems.

Williams' concern toward the end of *Spring and All* is increasingly with the form best suited to his writing. He frequently touches on the differences between poetry and prose: "Prose has to do with the fact of an emotion; poetry . . . with the dynamisation of emotion into a separate form" (67); prose and poetry are not by any means the same *in intention* (78). Williams, here, in the midst of writing each form, comments that prose has a single purpose, "to clarify, to enlighten the understanding . . . . There is no form to prose but that which depends on clarity. Poetry is something quite different" (78). Then, a note that he is to repeat later in his career, that there is little metrical difference in the two, that poetry and prose may be "both, phases of the same thing" (83). And finally, back to an earlier theme, the freedom of words (in poetry more than in prose) to act as separate entities, without "impositions." The closing poems of *Spring and All* seem to illustrate this freedom; every word is somewhat unexpected, though apt. In "Rapid Transit," slogans and maxims are juxtaposed ("Cross Crossings Cautiously"); "At the Ball Game" pictures an "Alive, venomous" crowd; and "The Wildflower" presents a unique image of the black-eyed susan,

> rich
> in savagery—
>
> Arab
> Indian
> dark woman.

The stark expression of these poems, the intense focus, the care in choosing the single word—in 1924 Williams won the Guarantor's Award from *Poetry* and in 1926 *The Dial* award. The working out of his theory—and his years of thinking about and scrutinizing poetry for *Contact*—had brought Williams to some of his strongest, least derivative poems. No Ezra Pound, no Keats; just Williams, a local and, yet, not parochial Williams, now writing with what Marianne Moore was to call "authoritativeness" and "wise silence" (also "compression, colour, speed, accuracy and that restraint of instinctive craftsmanship").[12]

Yet, taken without the prose that so fittingly accompanied them, the poems of *Spring and All* are very different in effect than Williams intended. Like halves of any book, any painting, the poems cannot be separated from the prose without reducing the whole to fragments. As conscious as Williams was about the unity of design in modern art, it seems grossly unfair to have disregarded the unity of his design in *Spring and All*.

CHAPTER FOUR

"Like Stroke of Sunlight"

> I want to write. It does not drug my senses, it sharpens them.
> It is the holy ghost of that trinity: The Senses, Action, Compo-
> sition. I am damned only when I cannot write.[1]

AGAIN and again Williams states his primary ambition, this time
in an autobiographical sketch published in 1918. Many such comments
testify to William's dedication as a writer. Many more statements,
and the great volume of his "experimental" writing, prove that he
was, from the beginning of his career to its end, a practicing and
innovative craftsman.

Williams frequently complained about his own writing and that
of others; about the imperfection of a line, a title, an ending. His
comments during the 1920's show that he was as critical about prose
as he had earlier been about poetry. In *Spring and All* Williams
voiced his dissatisfaction with the earlier *Kora in Hell: Improvisations:*
"their fault is their dislocation of sense, often complete: But it is the
best I could do under the circumstances."[2] Judging the *Improvisations*
technically, Williams found their structure weak, transitions lacking.
Of the themes of the book, however, he wrote, "I began there and
then to revalue experience, to understand what I was at."

In *Spring and All* he continued to explore the themes of the artist
as creator of a new world, just as he continued his search for an
effective mode, this time a reasonably conventional prose mixed with
poems. That he was fascinated by the differences between poetry and
prose is clear from his many distinctions between the two. His
interest in prose as a viable, a forceful, writing form had been evident
as early as 1921 when he wrote admiringly about the work of James
Joyce,

> the underlying fact which has impressed me is that by the form of his
> thought he has forced the reader into a new and special frame of mind

favorable to the receipt of his disclosure. By his manner of putting down
the words it is discovered that he is following some unapparent sequence
quite apart from the usual syntactical one. That is of course the power
behind all good writing but Joyce has removed so many staid en-
cumbrances that his method comes like stroke of sunlight today.[3]

"Like stroke of sunlight" comes the artist's power to cut through to
meaning, to dislocate conventional understandings and build new
reactions into old patterns. As he continues, "Joyce forces me, before
I can follow him, to separate the words from the printed page . . .
the words are no more than titles under the illustrations."

Excited by the writing of particularly Joyce and Stein,[4] Williams
was intrigued by the forms of fiction and, one cannot but think, by
the interest of the reading public in them. It is not surprising that the
poet turned next to his own fiction. "Three Professional Sketches" had
appeared in *The Little Review* even before *Kora in Hell* was published; "The Accident," a brief story, and "The Three Letters," the
genesis of *A Voyage to Pagany,* had been published in *Contact.* Then
in 1923 came *The Great American Novel.* As American as Joyce's
Ulysses was (to Williams' mind) British and Irish, the novel was an
"answer" for the poet. As he wrote in 1924, "I *am* trying to speak,
to tell *it* in the only way possible—but I do want to say what there is.
It is not for me merely to arrange things prettily." [5] Again, the arrangement, the form, is one of Williams' primary concerns. His emphasis
here suggests his many comments in *Spring and All* about Juan Gris
and Charles Demuth, with his insistence on the local source of art.

Then, too, Williams is a child of the twenties. The furor of Cubism
and Dadaism, the excitement of stream-of-consciousness and other
literary innovations, create a heady atmosphere which further experimentation reflects and, probably, in turn, fathers. So far as the novel
form is concerned, no mere chronology can, in such times, "say what
there is." Instead of using sequential order, Williams arranges his book
in a kind of impressionistic recall pattern. Transitions are implicit; the
better the reader knows Williams, the clearer his associations become.
Language is neither so playful nor erudite as Joyce's; tone is not
that of parody, as Williams later suggests. Indeed, tone is closer to that
of prayer in many sections. The themes, vivid in their cyclic recurrence,
are once again those of *Kora, Spring and All,* the rest of Williams'

early writing. It is interesting that although the form of prose fiction was new to Williams, his subjects were either the preoccupations of his earlier writing or the as yet undeveloped concerns which were to appear again in the *American Grain* essays (1925) and the novel *A Voyage to Pagany* (1927). Williams' themes were relatively constant. It was with the urgency born of desperation that he investigated every kind, every method, of writing: "I *am* trying to speak."

The Great American Novel

Besides his excitement over modern fiction, Williams had an even stronger personal motivation for writing the novel. Late in 1922 Ezra Pound wrote that he had found another publisher for Williams, this one interested in prose. As Pound described it, Williams would join Eliot, Lewis, Hueffer (Ford Madox Ford), Hemingway, and Pound in "a prose series. General success or point of the thing would lie in its being really interesting." [6] For the first time in his literary career, Williams would not have to pay any of the publishing costs; in fact he was offered one hundred dollars for "fifty pages of prose." The following year William Bird published *TGAN* at his Three Mountains Press in Paris.

Years later (1958), Williams described the novel as "a travesty on what I considered conventional American writing. People were always talking about the Great American Novel so I thought I'd write it." [7] Reading the book, however, is a very different experience from the one Williams suggests. Rather than a travesty, a burlesque, the novel has its own kind of honesty. The fact that its structure is cyclic instead of chronological only intensifies the feeling of urgency. Not satire, but almost tiresomely repeated axioms (of virtue, honesty, love, art) create the main impression of *TGAN*.

> I'm new, said she, I don't think you'll find my card here. You're new; how interesting. Can you read the letters on that chart? Open your mouth. Breathe. Do you have headaches? No. Ah, yes, you are new. I'm new, said the oval moon at the bottom of the mist funnel, brightening and paling. I don't think you'll find my card there. Open your mouth—Breathe—A crater big enough to hold the land from New York to Philadelphia. New! I'm new, said the quartz crystal on the parlor table—like glass. . . . Turned into the wrong street seeking to pass the

power house from which the hum, hmmmmmmmmmmmmmmmmmmm-sprang. Electricity has been discovered for ever. I'm new, says the great dynamo. I am progress. I make a word. Listen! UMMMMMMMMMM—Ummmmmmmmmmm—Turned into the wrong street at three A. M. lost in the fog, listening, searching—Waaa! said the baby. I'm new. A boy! A what? Boy. Shit, said the father of two other sons. Listen here. This is no place to talk that way. What a word to use. I'm new, said the sudden word.[8]

The early chapters of *TGAN* complement this excerpt from Chapter II. Working from doctor-patient scenes which have the semblance of reality, Williams develops his theme of newness: new patient, new perspective, new quartz, new power, new child, new word. That many of his observations accrue from "wrong turns" reminds one of his interest in paradox (descent-ascent, knowledge-ignorance). "The new" consistently fascinated Williams; as he wrote in his essay on Gertrude Stein, "Writing, like everything else, is much a question of refreshed interest." [9]

Like much of his other work from the 1920's, *TGAN* is here concerned with words, with forms, with the materials and the techniques of the act of writing: "There cannot be a novel. There can only be pyramids, pyramids of words, tombs . . ." (308). Williams' rather characteristic despair at the writer's predicament leads him in several directions, to the easy formula for fiction ("catch up a dozen good smelly names and find some reason for murder, it will do") and to the optimism of the writer who thinks he *can* "progress" ("Break the words . . . Awu test grang splith graphagh ag him—Yes, one can break them. One can make words" [10]).

The excerpt above shows that Williams has transferred some of his poetic techniques to his prose. The specific scene, the concrete detail, the thing—the abstract theme of newness is accented with these details of Williams' experience. The picture of the disappointed father recurs in the novel, as does the poet's view of the moonlike object. Another such vivid episode is that of the men leaving the Mosquito Extermination Committee meeting, driving home in the fog, one lending the other his handkerchief to wipe the glass. The male companionship here presented is much like the scene Williams is to use several times in *Paterson* and "Asphodel," of Marsden Hartley and the poet watching, wistfully, the "fast freight" ("That's what we'd all like to be, Bill").

Juxtaposed with the instances of masculine expression are scenes between the poet and his wife, the poet and other women. The depiction alternates between secure understanding ("she had penetrated his mystery" [309]) and deep personal isolation:

> He went in to his wife with exalted mind, his breath coming in pleasant surges. I came to tell you that the book is finished.
>
> I have added a new chapter to the art of writing. I feel sincerely that all they say of me is true, that I am truly a great man and a great poet.
>
> What did you say, dear, I have been asleep? (312).

In his essential limitation, in this selection of the most relevant of details, Williams foreshadows the techniques which make the best of his short stories highly effective. The anguish of two long chapters about writing comes to a close with the wife's ironic answer to her husband's radiant satisfaction. The scene "proves" what Williams has earlier tried to say, that writing, words "must become real, they must take the place of wife and sweet-heart. They must be church—Wife" (312).

This vacillation in the poet's view of his relationships—with art, with wife, with friends—is in turn counterpointed early in the novel by his reflections about his car, a small Ford. In 1958, in fact, Williams said, "The heroine is a little Ford car—she was very passionate—a hot little baby." [11] Unfortunately, many critics seem to have taken Williams' word for the content of the novel. Perhaps the poet was not intentionally misleading the reader, but the novel is far from the Ford's story. *The Great American Novel* is a man's book. It has many heroes, ranging from the poet himself to a number of men from American history and art. There are fewer women; but Elena (as she is called in this text), Williams' mother, and Flossie, his wife, are central. The car appears early, primarily to get the doctor around from meeting to call, much as the bus conveys Paterson twenty years later. I do not mean to discount the Ford entirely, however. Williams draws an interesting comparison between wife and car, as he thinks enviously of the car's simple life:

The owner groped his way to the little door at the back and emerged into the moonlight, into the fog, leaving his idle car behind him to its own thoughts. There it must remain all night, requiring no food, no water to drink, nothing while he, being a man, must live. His wife was at the window holding the shade aside (313).

Williams' great concern for effect is evident in the inclusion of the last sentence. The juxtaposition of the waiting wife, with whom an ambivalent relationship has already been suggested, and the simple presence of the car is masterful. Earlier Williams has shown the empathy that exists between poet-doctor and personified car; in the following chapter he again invests "the little dusty car" with the kind of unpretentious response he admires.

There drawn up at the gutter was a great truck painted green and red. . . . The small mechanism went swiftly by the great truck with fluttering heart in the hope, the secret hope that perhaps, somehow he would notice—HE, the great truck in his massiveness and paint, that somehow he would come to her (314).

Open desire, honest response: in most of his writing, Williams presents these attitudes as virtues. Just as much of the action in *TGAN* takes place in the relentless New Jersey fog (as in *Paterson* the setting is noise and separation, divorce), so are there barriers among most of the people Williams draws. The Ford runabout may in some sense be an admirable "figure" because she at least represents a desire for emotional contact. Once Williams has made this initial presentation, however, the car disappears from the book; she is scarcely its "heroine."

"What then is a novel?" Williams asks at the opening of Chapter V. Previously he has discussed the particulars of writing style. Now he comes to the total art form, the somewhat awesome shape of the writing he is attempting. True to his style in the previous four chapters, Williams arranges a collage of subjective impressions rather than an erudite definition of the novel. The very range of his scattered recollections, and the incorporation of colloquial phrases from three languages, gives one the feeling that, contrary to his seeming informality, he is drawing on many resources. Defining the novel is an unwieldy prospect.

What then is a novel? *Un Novello,* pretty, pretty Baby. It is a thing of fixed form. It is pure English. Yes, she is of Massachusetts stock. Her great grandfather was thrown out of the Quaker church for joining the Continental army. Hates the English. Her life is a novel—almost too sensational.

The story of Miss Li—so well told.

Qu'avez-vous vu? Or they that write much and see little. Not much use to us.

Speak of old Sun Bow pacing his mesa instead of Felipe Segundo in the barren halls of El Escorial—or asleep in his hard bed at one corner of the griddle.

My mother would have a little nigger boy come with a brush and sit at her feet and brush her legs by the hour.

Expressionism is to express skilfully the seething reactions of the contemporary European consciousness. Cornucopia. In at the small end and—blui! Kandinsky.

But it's a fine thing. It is THE thing for the moment—in Europe. The same sort of thing, reversed, in America has a water attachment to be released with a button. That IS art. Everyone agrees that that IS art. Just as one uses a handkerchief (315).

As the progression in this passage shows, the question shifts from "what is a novel?" to "what should an American novel be?" Apparently it should be something unpretty, unfixed, unsensational, un-English; something sharply seen through ordinary but expressive details, yet not a push-button version of European expressionism. Williams' concern in much of his writing—what *is* it to be an American artist? what *is* it to be an American?—becomes primary in this middle section of the novel. As David Ferry wrote of Williams in 1965, "He is, of the *most* respectable figures in modern American poetry, perhaps the most thoroughly concerned with what it means to be an American poet." [12] And as Williams mocks himself in the novel proper, using the ironic persona of many of his dialogue poems, "In any case it all seems to preoccupy you so" (316). Thus his tone vacillates now between despondency ("America is a mass of pulp, a jelly, a sensitive plate ready to take whatever print you want to put on it—We have no art, no manners, no intellect" [316]) and elation: "I am an American. A United Stateser. Yes it's ugly, there is no word to say it better. I do not believe in ugliness. I do not want to call myself a United Stateser but what in—but what else am I?" (316)

Williams next explores the identity of one such United Stateser through vivid description of an abortive romance with a high-school girl. In her purity and youth, she represents some elusive spirit of the *new* to the older man; "this is romance: to believe that which is unbelievable. This is faith: to desire that which is never to be obtained" (319). Immediately following the long sequence comes "Nuevo Mundo!": the cry of Columbus' sailors as they disembark on American soil. Then comes a montage of descriptions in which historical figures, brought amazingly to life in Williams' quick recounting of detail and idiomatic phrasing, are juxtaposed with Williams' contemporaries to show that "the American background is America" and not Europe. Yet instances of sadistic cruelty mix with simple nobility: concrete episodes support Williams' critique of American life: that there is too much restraint, niggardliness, malice; too little openness, honesty, love. "Property is sacred and human liberty is bitter, bitter, bitter to their tongues" (329).

Although the persona of the poet has dominated *TGAN,* he has been less in evidence midway through the novel. Now, toward the end of Chapter XI, Williams appears again: "But he was an outsider. He was new to all" (329). Charity and love, the earnest desire to help people—the hero of *TGAN* is less an actor than a spokesman (almost a medicine man) for such homilies. In one scene he quotes Vachel Lindsay, "America needs the flamboyant to save her soul," and then cites the circus (a recurring image), the *Follies,* jazz, the flapper, and movies as examples of fulfillment of this need. The speaker's tone will range from irascibility to empathy in the last eight chapters; now his compassion breaks through.

> Human souls who are not living impassioned lives, not creating romance and splendor and grotesqueness—phases of beauty's infinite variety—such people wistfully try to find these things outside themselves; a futile, often a destructive quest.
>
> The imagination will not down. If it is not a dance, a song, it becomes an outcry, a protest . . . if it is not art, it becomes crime (329–330).

The next few pages offer an interesting series of excerpts from contemporary print and speech: blurbs about a new novel, a label from a new drug, an announcement from a stockbroker, a "story" about a narrow escape, a notice from a collection agency (threatening action over a one-dollar debt). Waste, violence, usury (à la Pound). Then the poet interrupts, with delightful ambivalence, "At this, De Soto, sick, after all the months of travel, stopped out of breath and looked about him" (331).

Such arrangement is typical of Williams' care in *The Great American Novel*. He had criticized *Kora in Hell* for its formlessness, its carelessness; there are both intention and skill in every passage of this book. Seen in the continuum of Williams' other writings, *TGAN* shows not only his constant interest in the themes already discussed but also his increasing care to make his writing accurate and coherent. As he wrote earlier in the novel about Dadaism, "It has no value for ME" (315). In contrast, of Joyce's work ("his real, if hidden, service"), Williams said, "He has in some measure liberated words, freed them for their proper uses. He has to a great measure destroyed what is known as 'literature.' For me as an American it is his only important service" (313). By "their proper uses" Williams means easy communication, and one of the most direct routes to clear understanding is the illustration. The remainder of *TGAN* is a collection of stories (one might be tempted to call them fables, were they not so real in their impact). Williams takes more time with most of these: the Esquimau Indians; the bleeding of George Washington to his death; Nettie Vogelman and her child; the ancient sages ("See they return," a refrain from Pound's poem); the long sequence on the Cumberland mountain women, Lory and Ma Duncan. This series of Cumberland portraits (Chapter XVII) gives the reader a pause. Its pace is slower, its tone, sad, almost reverent, as it is narrated presumably by a Cumberland resident.

> We settle down on the doorstep probably on straight chairs with seats of cornhusks twisted into a rope and then interwoven. There is a sound to which the mountains have accustomed me—the sharp jolting thud when a mother, if she possesses neither cradle nor rocker, puts her baby to sleep by jerking forward and backward on two legs of a straight chair (338).

Such acute details build the forceful picture of the mountain women as "sharp and sane," "untouched by all modern life," "the typical Americans" (340). They are admittedly short on sanitation, as Williams points out with the perceptive humor that runs through the novel. Speeches like old Ma Duncan's, however, show their sensitivity, love, and almost stoic acceptance of life—an acceptance tempered with flamboyance, as when they take a day's journey to see a field of "yaller lady slippers":

> "I wish you could have seen the great old trees that used to be here. If folks wasn't so mad for money they might be here and a preachin' the gospel of beauty. But folks is all for money and all for self. Someday when they've cut off all the beauty that God planted to point us to him, folks will look round and wonder what us human bein's is here fur—" (340).

The following chapter, XVIII, seems to illustrate "what us human bein's is here fur." Williams' collection of Horatio Alger tales has been called by Hugh Kenner "surer-footed parody" for which Williams borrows "the journalists' congratulatory accents to suggest the apotheosis of commercial dreams." [13] But Kenner fails to note that the success stories Williams tells concern immigrants whom he treats with gentle seesaw humor. Thus he concludes the life of an immigrant scientist with: "America, besides breeding great men, imports them"; immediately notes an export: "Claude Monet was born in Columbus, Ohio"; and follows this blithely with: "In industry and commerce the stories of many of the successful immigrants read like romances" (340).

Taking things as they are—immigrant millionaires, emigrant artists—and presenting them more or less "factually" is Williams' usual mode of presentation in prose as well as in poetry. From the facts, he builds to the emotional ramifications of the situation, as when we see business "success" juxtaposed with literary success (the *Atlantic Monthly* described as the mecca of modern art) and with advertisements for both. With devastating irony, Williams mourns such uses of the word,

> Now when Christmas bells ring clear
> Telling us that love is here
>   And children sing
> Gifts that speak of thoughtful love
> Just like angels from above
>   Glad tidings bring (341).

From ads for thirty-dollar footrests and Oriental rugs, Williams turns to California and Spanish history and the reminiscences of a colorful speaker who grew up on a farm but now runs a factory. In the progression from rural to urban, in the fifty years that have molded one man's life, changes have come rapidly. When he speaks of the present business, Williams introduces a concept central to *Paterson* thirty-five years later: "Our main specialty is shoddy" (343).

By the close of *TGAN,* there exists little virtue, little love of doing a job well; only the love of money, at whatever cost to a man's heart. The ethical idea relates, of course, to everything Williams has touched upon in *TGAN*—from the way the mountain mothers live to the poet's struggle to create meaningful art. With his usual restraint (more evident when he needs to condemn his culture than when he can praise it), the poet closes the novel with three short paragraphs, the first two showing the modern preoccupation with "shoddy"; the third, a Spanish irony for such life.

> He took any kind of rags just as they were collected, filth or grease right on them the way they were and teased them up into a fluffy stuff which he put through a rolling process and made into sheets of wadding. These sheets were fed mechanically between two layers of silkolene and a girl simply set there with an electric sewing device which she guided with her hand and drew in the designs you see on those quilts, you know.
>
> You've seen this fake oilcloth they are advertising now. Congoleum. Nothing but building paper with a coating of enamel.
> *'O vida tan dulce!*

Styles and Similarities

"It is Joyce with a difference," writes Williams in Chapter III of *The Great American Novel,* in what well may be the best critical comment yet made about the style of this book. He continues, "The difference being greater opacity, less erudition, reduced power of perception" (312). Admiring Joyce as he does for his courage to innovate, Williams still objects to much of his writing:

> But Joyce. He is misjudged, misunderstood. His vaunted invention is a fragile fog. His method escapes him. He has not the slightest notion

what he is about. He is a priest, a roysterer of the spirit. He is an epicurean of romance. His true genius flickers and fails (313).

No jokes or puns, no neologisms, no portmanteau words—Williams' novel asks nothing from the reader except the seriousness of mind to shape the fragmented parts into a whole, to supply the transitions, to align the virtues. There is no external framework like a Ulysses journey, no intricate time scheme to relate characters; there is only one man's mind, one man's memory, trying to sort through the things, the happenings, of his world, to find value rather than shoddy. In an age of relative literary sophistication, it may be that the musings of one heart are of small interest. As Eli Siegel pointed out in 1952, the value of Williams' work is its honesty. Williams "has added one new way of seeing the world, that arose from him, that without him wouldn't be . . . the honesty is something that makes work seemingly different, similar." [14]

Technically, Williams follows the approach, already familiar in his poetry, of presenting salient details and accurate portraits as objectively as possible. There is little "interference" from the poet, except in his phrasing. Long, reassuring rhythms create one impression; short, staccato lines, another. Plosive words add to urgency or unpleasantness; somnolent sounds, to the opposite effect. Organic form operates as much in *TGAN* as in any of Williams' poems. And as in the prose of *Spring and All,* some of Williams' sentences in *TGAN* are awkward, especially when he has a great deal to say (usually about the art of writing). But for the most part, the reader feels a new unity in the prose sections—in both rhythms and images—as in the passages about the doctor and his patients, the women of Cumberland. Williams seems more at home with prose. One might almost say of him, as he did of his personified car,

It seemed glad to be at home in its own little house, the trusty mechanism. The light continued to flare intimately against the wooden wall as much as to say:

And what is good poetry made of
And what is good poetry made of
Of rats and snails and puppy-dog's tails
And that is what good poetry is made of (313).

And good novels? Even great novels? Williams' *TGAN* has usually been written off as an experimental oddity—if not entirely ignored—except by R. P. Blackmur, who included it in a 1960 anthology of American short novels. In his introduction to the collection, Blackmur pointed out about *TGAN* that it reveals Williams' own concept of order:

> He asks us to listen to a tumult of fragments, selected only because it is impossible to put everything that appears in lively revery into handy words, and given in minimum order only because everything looked at gains an order by the act of looking. Order is a human invention to account for what the senses perceive in sequence. Williams seems to hold that the best orders are the most fortuitous, least human, and those we can be the most nearly careless of (13).

Blackmur further gives Williams' novel critical respectability by answering the question, Is it a novel or an autobiographical essay?

> This is a fiction the reader must write as he reads. But it is a fiction, not an essay, at one of the extremities that fiction can reach: the extremity of expressionism which says that things mean whatever we would have them mean and that the structures we make will carry any weight we put upon them, even the weight of the real world. It is the sort of fiction that tugs at us to put our own reality in to see what will happen to it. After all, this is how most of us actually look at the world, and not alone in our daydreams, and there is every reason why there should be a form of fiction to correspond to a deep habit (15).

Perhaps Blackmur is right in labeling this writing *expressionism,* but when *TGAN* is seen in relation to Williams' other prose and poetry, the virtues of its arangement are more apparent. In everything he writes, Williams builds from sharply outlined pictures of real objects to more subjective impressions. Notice this same technique in a critical review of Kay Boyle's stories:

> The phenomenon of our attitude toward the work of George Antheil . . . ; the brilliant newspapers actively trembling under a veil; the work of the poet H. D.; the young wife that walked six blocks asleep in her husband's pajamas one winter's night, the pant's bottoms trailing in the mud; the boy that, thinking himself in an airplane, dived from

a window in a dream head down upon the gravel path—this is America accurately delineated. It is the School Board which made a rule that forbids themselves smoking at their evening meetings in the School building in order that they may prevent the janitors from smoking. . . . Fear to vary from the average, fear to feel, to see, to know, to experience—save under the opacity of a mist of equality, a mist of common mediocrity, is our character.[15]

Besides this progression, Williams also moves in many works from discussions of literary technique to themes of deep humanistic concern; and, in association, from comparatively bare language to passages of symbolic and imagistic interplay. Changes in theme and perspective usually require modifications in style; the interesting point about so much of Williams' writing, in both poetry and prose, is that it follows the same kinds of patterns, regardless of when it was written.

So far as the themes of Williams' work are concerned, Eli Siegel has already pointed out that there is "continuity between what is said in *Kora in Hell* and what is said even in *Paterson*. There is a trying to see. The best thing about Williams is that he's not given up seeing." [16]

An even closer correspondence in both content and style exists between *The Great American Novel* and *Paterson,* the five books of which were written from twenty to thirty-five years later than the novel. Critics frequently have asked of *Paterson:* when did it really begin, Williams' need to assess his culture in a big work? Many have traced the origins to "The Wanderer," the poem Williams wrote perhaps as early as 1909. The lewd and violent she-wanderer, the roaring Passaic, the powerful birds and protective trees—many of the later elements are here, as well as that paradoxical tone of excited sadness that pervades and, in a sense, confuses *Paterson.* Then came the shorter poems titled "Paterson" or "Detail," from 1925 and after.

These poems are certainly important in Williams' progression toward *Paterson,* but perhaps more important than these short units of poetry are the long prose pieces in which Williams attempts to do the same things he ultimately does in *Paterson:* "Notes in Diary Form," which opens "I will make a big, serious portrait of my time," has many elements of the later epic, but on a smaller scale than does *TGAN.* In many ways, the novel is similar to *Paterson.*

Williams opens both with some discussion of technique. It is as if he were presenting his "defense of poesie," his "preface to the novel," at every opportunity. In *TGAN,* it is words, structure, the novel as a whole. In *Paterson,*

> To make a start,
> out of particulars
> and make them general, rolling
> up the sum, by defective means—
>
> (11)

In each book the technique is the same: details (particulars); progress (sum); and the attitude, the abashed "defective means," much like his earlier admission, "There cannot be a novel" (308). Williams uses the persona of a dog early in *Paterson,* the complacent "just another dog/ among a lot of dogs. . . . The rest have run out—/ after the rabbits./ Only the lame stands—on/ three legs." The simplicity of the dog's view (*Paterson*'s lusty dogs contrast vividly with its sterile people) is much like the attitude Williams assigned in *TGAN* to the Ford coupé.

In the Introduction to *Paterson* I, Williams speaks of "design" in much the same way he spoke of "progress" in *TGAN.* In 1923 the poet is to write "of what he sees"; in *Paterson,* he observes, "walking up and down." And the two books also contain Williams' emphasis on paradox: "The beginning is assuredly/ the end—since we know nothing . . . . In ignorance/ a certain knowledge" (*Paterson,* 12).

Once the action in *TGAN* begins, Williams first shows us men going home to the wife already in bed ("Her right arm was under her head" [309]). Part I of *Paterson* depicts, first, the sleeping Paterson; then the low mountain of a woman ("facing him, his arm supporting her" [17]). Immediately after the cast is introduced in each book, Williams begins his juxtaposition of seemingly unrelated passages. In *Paterson,* he turns first to a prose account of finding the "Queen Pearl"; in *TGAN,* to the new patient–new word passage (see p. 0). Next he describes Mr. Paterson (and locates him "inside the bus"), much as he associates the doctor with his car in *TGAN.* The sewer images and the use of the new word "shit" in the novel have their counterpart in *Paterson* ("the giant lets fly!"), just before more unifying themes are introduced (the *new* and the obliterating fog in *TGAN;* the miraculous in *Paterson*).

Paterson continues with a lament for the failure of language:

> The language, the language
> fails them
> They do not know the words
> or have not
> the courage to use them. (20)

That setting is coupled with the strange *Geographic* picture of the nine African wives, bringing us to women, to marriage, and to the same dissatisfactions Williams has portrayed in *TGAN:* man, "no matter/ how much a chief he may be," is destroyed by his women "at home."

While a line-by-line comparison of *Paterson* and *TGAN* is not practical, the two books are strikingly similar in their subjects and in Williams' attitudes toward those subjects. Most interesting of all the correspondences is the order of the subjects in appearance. The arrangement of items in Chapters I and II of *TGAN* is very close to that of sections of Paterson I, Part I. Part II of *Paterson* Book I covers the same dichotomy of beauty and ugliness that Chapters III and IV of *TGAN* do: the same ambivalent mixture of elements, the same despair on the part of the poet. Although the texture of *Paterson* is richer because of the blending of poetry and prose, both books treat a wide variety of subjects, yet with nearly the same themes emphasized. *TGAN* and *Paterson* both end on the sad note of "shoddy," with *Paterson* V redeemed somewhat by the poet's own sheer energy, expressed through images of the spirit, the dance.

There are technical similarities too. The letters in *Paterson* which provide such fitting, vivid contrast have their limited counterparts in *TGAN* as various speakers tell their characteristic stories. And in the earlier book, also, Williams was using prose alternated with poetry. In *Paterson,* of course, the basic mode is poetry, with the many prose passages used for illustration and rhythmic variety; in *TGAN,* the basic vehicle is prose, but rare lines of poetry act as accent and illustration.

Most important of all correspondences is the wide use Williams makes of narrative, of personal history, in each book. As the poet has decided in his earlier long poems "March" and "History," factual history is comparatively worthless beside the account of one man's life. History is a lie unless it is tied to a human force (Williams' approach in the *American Grain* essays is further proof of his belief). So in *TGAN*, Williams does not give us a discussion of immigration in the nineteenth century, but rather the words of Professor M. I. Pupin ("I had five cents in my pocket and a piece of apple pie in my hand" [340]); in *Paterson* we hear the long, dramatic sequence of Klaus Ehrens, the preacher in the park, who made his money and then gave it away. In *TGAN*, the simple mountain women declare their joy in beauty; in *Paterson,* the old woman in the park dances, drinks, incites the younger people: "Come on! Wassa ma'? You got/ broken leg? (73)" Williams' description of old Mary leads to his definition of a term he uses only twice in his many poems, once in reference to Ford Madox Ford, again to Mark Anthony: "Heavenly man."

> Remember
>
> the peon in the lost
> Eisenstein film drinking
>
> from a wine-skin with the abandon
> of a horse drinking
>
> so that it slopped down his chin?
> down his neck, dribbling
>
> over his shirt-front and down
> onto his pants—laughing, toothless?
>
> Heavenly man!
>
> (74)

A passage such as this—detailed, explicit, passionately earnest—certainly ties history to human forces.

As both *Paterson* and *TGAN* show, Williams' interest in history, in the relevant American past, was far more than passing. In the years after *TGAN*, the poet would go abroad (1924 and 1927) looking for answers to the quandary of an American identity. He would write the questioning *A Voyage to Pagany* and the exploratory essays of *In the American Grain*. But he will move very little from the point he makes so positively in *TGAN:* "The danger is in forgetting that the good of the past is the same good of the present. That the power that lived then lives today. That we too possess it" (334). Indeed, lines from *Paterson* sound almost as an echo: "This is the old, the very old, old upon old,/ the undying: even to the minute gestures" (73).

It comes as no surprise, then, that the draft for *Paterson* Book VI, dated July 1, 1961, speaks of Li Po, of "an obscure Montezuma," of "a forgotten Socrates or Aristotle," and of Washington. As he had written in 1923, Williams still believed, "The American background is America" (327). His view had only deepened to include "the old, the very old."

CHAPTER FIVE

Williams' Search: "To Have a Country"

IN 1925, William Carlos Williams' first book from a commercial publisher appeared, the twenty essays on American history titled *In the American Grain*. A few years later, the books were remaindered and Williams went about, sadly, picking up copies for friends. The apparent failure of this, his eighth, book discouraged Williams even further (he was disheartened already—nearly a literary unknown, past forty, trying through poetry, drama, and prose to express his "fervent, fierce, anger to have a country"[1]). The proposed second volume of essays was never written.

That Williams was preoccupied with America as theme particularly during the twenties is evident from his work as well as from his own admissions. His purpose in planning the *Grain* essays, he recalls in his *Autobiography,* was "to try to find out for myself what the land of my more or less accidental birth might signify."[2] As he explained later to Horace Gregory,

> Of mixed ancestry, I felt from earliest childhood that America was the only home I could ever possibly call my own. I felt that it was expressly founded for me, personally, and that it must be my first business in life to possess it; that only by making it my own from the beginning to my own day, in detail, could I ever have a basis for knowing where I stood.[3]

In 1924 from Paris he wrote to Kenneth Burke, "I have heavy bones, I am afraid—there's little here for me . . . only America remains where at least I was born."[4] In 1927, after the essays had been published, and generally ignored, he spoke of America as "my country that I strive so wildly to possess."[5]

Williams was hardly alone in his search for the meaning of America. Interest reawakened with Van Wyck Brooks's *Wine of the Puritans* (1909); the *Seven Arts* magazine (from 1916 on); H. L.

Mencken's *The American Language* (1919); and D. H. Lawrence's essays in both the *English Review* (1918–1919) and *Studies in Classic American Literature.* All these investigations were eclipsed, however, by Eliot's dramatic queries in *The Waste Land* (1922). Contrary to the view that Williams' *Grain* essays are a response to Lawrence's studies,[6] evidence is conclusive that these essays, as well as much other American writing in the twenties, existed at least partly as answer to *The Waste Land.* Williams' reaction to the poem is well known— that, technically, it set poetry back twenty years; that what he considered its despair was not representative of the times. In seeking to confront Eliot, Williams began the writing which culminates in the *Grain* essays: his 1923 *Spring and All* defends modern America even while questioning some of her present ideals. *The Great American Novel* testifies more specifically, and with fewer reservations, to the elements of greatness in America. History here provides many of Williams' characters—Burr, De Soto, Washington, Arnold, the Mormons; the past juxtaposed throughout with the present.

From the vignettes of *TGAN,* Williams moves to the full-dress portraits of *In the American Grain.* He is still searching, but the essays show an awareness, both technical and thematic, born of his earlier writing. Just as he has come from expressing his own thoughts, undisguised, in *Kora* and *Spring and All* to giving those thoughts a more concrete illustration in *TGAN,* so he has learned to vary technique to suit theme. As he recalls in his *Autobiography:*

> The Tenochtitlan chapter was written in big, square paragraphs like Inca masonry. Raleigh was written in what I conceived to be Elizabethan style; the Eric the Red chapter in the style of the Icelandic saga; Boone in the style of Daniel's autobiography; Franklin was in Franklin's words; and John Paul Jones I gave verbatim. Thus I tried to make each chapter not only in content but in the style itself a close study of the theme (183–184).[7]

Many critics have emphasized the virtuosity of Williams' prose styles in the essay collection; what is more significant, I think, is that what Williams has learned technically makes the book an integrated whole rather than a collection. Indeed, the real themes of *In the American Grain* are cumulative, emphasized and enhanced by the arrangement of the essays themselves. The impact of the book is dramatic because momentum rises and falls, pace builds, as in any well-structured piece of writing. Williams' transitions between essays also show that the sequence of the book was important to him.

Preliminary Studies: The First Four Essays

How much of himself Williams saw in Eric the Red is perhaps relevant in considering this first essay. In *The Great American Novel,* the poet wondered as he walked along "if it were too late to be Eric. What a new world they had made of it with their Cortezes, their Pizarros, yes, and their Lord Howes, their Washingtons even." [8] Eric the Red stands in contrast to the other conquerors named because of his selfless motives. A loving man, separated from his family through duplicity and an odious, unloving Christianity ("Eric the bedless, the sonless"), Eric lives to reunite his family, his people. Williams' admiration of a strong man, chosen for a task, yet never rewarded, only abused, begins here ("Myself in the teeth of the world"): "I, then, must open a way for them into the ice that they follow me even here—their servant, in spite of myself." [9] Raleigh, Columbus, Boone, Jones, Lincoln—Williams sees them all in this perspective: chosen, in spite of themselves, yet repressed, even murdered, by the very men they care for.

Throughout *In the American Grain,* Williams mourns this treachery, as well as the promise of a man's strength, physical and moral, shattered against the very society he has helped to create:

> But they have marked me—even to myself. Because I am not like them, I am evil. . . . Because their way is the just way and my way—the way of the kings and my father—crosses them: weaklings holding together to appear strong (1).

"Because I am not like them" might well be the refrain for Columbus, the subject of the second essay in the book. Again, his country against him, "more and more alone," "heroically but pitifully," "this straw in the play of the elemental giants" was betrayed (10). Here Williams' emphasis shifts to America itself—a "bitter fruit," an "acrid and poisonous apple" (7). America, too, betrays Columbus.

The reader admires Columbus because he is sensitive and loving, ready to champion the New World rather than fear it. After the long account of his voyage, much of it taken from Columbus' journal, Williams ends abruptly with a brief description of the native trees as "the most beautiful thing which I had ever seen . . . ." (26). The "beautiful thing" motif which is to figure importantly in *Paterson* begins here, in Columbus' simple acceptance of a natural wonder.

Although Williams refers to Columbus frequently in other writings (and calls him "Christ-over" in a later essay), Columbus as a persevering yet bewildered man is overshadowed by the majestic though conquered Montezuma. "The Destruction of Tenochtitlan" is perhaps the best known of these essays—lush description presented in equally ornate prose—but its significance to the book as a whole lies in its emphasis on man's unity with the earth. Montezuma's people had a "primal and continuous identity with the ground itself" (33); even their human sacrifice seemed justified as Williams viewed it.[10]

Opposing such an "earthward thrust" came the conqueror Cortez, demanding change, capitulation. The New World as something to be used rather than as a prize to be understood and revered on its own terms: this is the tragedy of the exploration of America as Williams saw it. And "yet it was no man's fault." "They do not fathom the forces which carry them." Even Cortez, violent and insistent, is caught up in his concept of "duty." The sadness of the destruction of Tenochtitlan is, perhaps, not the great physical waste so much as it is the inevitability of the outcome. Men are this way, as Williams' essays on Eric and Columbus have already shown. The fourth study, "The Fountain of Eternal Youth," opens with a summary of the situation:

> History, history! We fools, what do we know or care? History begins for us with murder [Eric] and enslavement [Cortez], not with discovery [Columbus' short-lived joy] . . . . the spirit, the ghost of the land moves in the blood (39).

Ponce de León fits the pattern of Cortez in that he fails to understand; he only deprecates the natives, while searching for his own sensual satisfactions. In contrast to their conqueror, the natives— unchristian, uneducated—have remarkable dignity. As Williams describes their enslavement:

The Indians having no souls knew what freedom means. . . . They took them in droves, forced them to labor. It was impossible to them—not having been born to baptism. How maddening it is to the spirit to hear:—Bands of them went into the forests, their forests, and hanged themselves to the trees (41).

One cannot help but think of a line from Williams' 1955 poem "Asphodel, That Greeny Flower": "Waste, waste!/ dominates the world." [11]

These four essays, then, with their themes of love and promise, cruelty and disappointment, seem to be the setting for Williams' exploration of his America, his purpose stated as being "to establish myself from my own reading, in my own way, in the locality which by birthright had become my own." [12]

The Central Arc: De Soto to Boone

With his essay on De Soto, Williams begins developing a major theme, in this book and later ones. The concept of "female principle," of a creative force which ennobles man even while challenging him, is introduced here in the feminine person of the Mississippi River. De Soto is destined to be buried in this water; the river has been luring him ever since he first saw it. In *The Great American Novel* Williams has described De Soto's fascination ("the river alone could give him rest" [331]); here, he chronicles it using the voice of the provocative river at intervals. [13] In its use of the sporadic refrain, this essay anticipates the one to follow, "Sir Walter Raleigh."

"Sing, O Muse" is the refrain throughout the short lyric praise of Raleigh, a man like Columbus, yet even more tragic, betrayed as he was by his love. Yet again, in Williams' view, Elizabeth is not to blame: "Sing! O Muse and say, he was too mad in love, too clear, too desperate for her to trust upon great councils . . . . He was not England, as she was" (60). Williams' description is almost of types: Elizabeth (and Muse) as woman in power; Raleigh as self-sacrificing and noble lover—of both Elizabeth and America, neither love consummated.

Williams uses this essay as more than incrementation of theme. The impact of the refrain, the rhythmic power of the long sentences, composed of short, resurgent phrases, helps to give the feeling of climax. Ironically, and with calculated effect, Williams follows this essay with the dour description of the Pilgrims, "hard and little," "stripped and little," "surrounded by winter's cold." "If they were pure it was more since they had nothing in them of fulfillment than because of positive virtues" (63). Niggardliness, repression, hatred—cardinal sins to Williams—all can be counted among the Puritan "virtues." In the sharp contrast between the beloved Raleigh (nominally a "traitor") and Williams' scathing picture of the Pilgrims lies the first sense of climax in the book. Williams' hatred of the imposed "right" religion had been implied from the beginning, with his sympathy for Eric the Red. Here it comes to a full release. Emotionally, Williams blames America's ills in the 1920's on just these people:

> The result of that brave setting out of the Pilgrims has been an atavism that thwarts and destroys. . . . Today it is a generation of gross know-nothingism, of blackened churches where hymns groan like chants from stupefied jungles, a generation universally eager to barter permanent values (the hope of an aristocracy) in return for opportunist material advantages (68).

Williams' view of the Pilgrims stated here and in subsequent essays parallels his aversion to the Mormons in *The Great American Novel*. His description of Joseph Smith's wild search for truth (in the episode he recounts, of the theft of one apple) is phrased sedately: "Joseph Smith shook where he stood and fell frothing at the mouth. He was of Vermont mountain stock" (332). The channels of Mormon cruelty—torture, forced polygamy, murder—are described vividly through Williams' simple prose, perhaps more effectively than if he had used less restraint in the telling. The poet's verbal techniques as he builds toward the climax of *In the American Grain* (the Mather and Rasles essays) are no less well done. From the unrestrained vituperation of the Pilgrim essay, Williams breaks abruptly into the most personal account in the volume: a loving tribute to Samuel de Champlain, phrased in the shorter, staccato rhythms characteristic of Williams' prose. "The Founding of Quebec" opens:

> Why cannot I sit here lovingly, quietly and simply thinking of that most delightful man, Champlain, without offending you? . . . . Here

was a man. Here *is* a man after my own heart. Is it merely in a book?
So am I then, merely in a book. You see? Here at least I find the thing
I love (69).

"The perfection of what we lack here," Williams describes the gentle
Champlain, comparing his manner of living to that of a woman's,
especially in regard to his "tenderness" (70). The tone of the essay is
mournful from the start, however, because gentleness without accompanying violence ("Rebellion, savagery") will never work in the New
World. The themes of the feminine principle and the violence-
gentleness dichotomy (so prevalent in both *The Great American Novel*
and *Paterson*) are here reiterated before Williams reaches toward his
strongest outburst against the repressive forces in America.

"The May-Pole at Merry Mount" illustrates in itself Williams'
opening statement, "A most confusing thing in American History
. . . is the nearly universal lack of scale" (75). This episode of
Thomas Morton's selling guns and liquor to the Indians, himself
sympathizing with the Indians and their women, and being punished
"with fantastic violence—and some duplicity" shows once again the
Puritan fault of intolerance. Their vengeance operates not only
against Morton but against the Quakers and the Salem "witches." This
essay ends with a transition into the Cotton Mather study: "Trustless
of humane experience, not knowing what to think, they went mad,
lost all direction. Mather defends the witchcraft persecutions" (80).

In his Introduction to *In the American Grain,* Williams speaks
of the difficulty of finding the truth as it is "lost in a chaos of borrowed titles," of the necessity to search through the written words
"under which the true character lies hid." "In letters, in journals,
reports of happenings I have recognized new contours suggested by
old words . . . . Thus, bits of writing have been copied into the book
for the taste of it." Williams' belief that a man's speech reveals much
of his character, evident in his poems and short stories, also has
determined much of his technique in these essays. He is to use the
device of the persona's words again and again, in *Paterson* and the
later poems as well as in his fiction, but never to better effect than
in the Mather essay. Not one word of the twenty-two-page essay is
Williams'. Excerpts from the *Wonders of the Invisible World* tell the
story and reveal poignantly the mind that brought further savagery

upon America's head. Reading Mather's words today is far from pleasant. That Williams quotes at such length shows that he recognizes the agony of Mather's calmly "factual" approach, doing his best to prove, through testimony and detail, the reality of bedevilment.

> All I shall Report Nothing but with Good Authority, and what I would invite all my Readers to examine, while 'tis yet Fresh and New, that if there be found any mistake, it may be as willingly Retracted, as it was unwillingly Committed (100).

"Waste, waste," Williams echoes; and we appreciate the artistry of letting Mather's own words damn him.

In contrasting style comes the Père Rasles essay, as complete a summation of all positive values as Mather's essay is of the negative. We have been prepared for this black-to-white movement by Williams' earlier juxtaposition of Raleigh and the Pilgrims; the difference between Mather and Rasles is further heightened by Williams' shift from objectivity to autobiography. As he recalls his six weeks in Paris (1924), he includes a conversation with Valery Larbaud. Always the dramatist, Williams repeats the dialogue of Larbaud comparing the English and the Spanish colonization of America:

> The English appraised the New World too meanly. It was to them a carcass from which to tear pieces for their belly's sake, a colony, a place to despise a little. They gave to it parsimoniously, in a slender Puritan fashion. But the Spaniard gave magnificently, with a generous sweep, wherever he was able (108).

Emphasizing his earlier themes, Williams agrees with Larbaud, saying that Puritanism stinks about him like a "ghostly miasm," "an atrocious thing, a kind of mermaid with a corpse for a tail" (115).

His praise of Père Rasles, the French priest who lived for thirty-four years among the Canadian Indians, beloved by them, grows easily from the preliminary discussion with Larbaud. In contrast to the smallness of the Pilgrims, Williams describes Rasles as "a spirit rich, blossoming, generous, able to give and to receive, full of taste, a nose, a tongue, a laugh, enduring" (120). Then, encouraged by Larbaud's agreement, he concludes, "All that will be new in America will be anti-Puritan." Williams establishes the polar extremes of

Mather as the stingy, repressive force and Rasles as the loving, expansive one: "It is *this* to be *moral:* to be *positive, . . .* to be sure, generous, brave—TO MARRY, to *touch*—to *give* because one HAS, not because one has nothing" (121).

As if in illustration of this definition, the following essay presents Daniel Boone, "a great voluptuary," a man working "against the niggardliness of the damning puritanical tradition" (130). The violence of an Eric the Red has modulated to the quiet sobriety of the mild hunter, whose explorations are prompted more by "the peace of solitude" than by any acquisitive impulse (131). Such men as Boone are not passive or weak, however, as Williams' recurring use of sexual images (and the metaphor of marriage) suggests.

Boone, like Columbus, Champlain, and Rasles, humbles himself to the New World—and Williams picks up the theme of "descent-ascent" which has figured in his earlier writings. What appears to be a descent to primitive conditions may well be the ascent to a true understanding. Williams aligns Boone with Columbus in this image: "like an Indian, the ecstasy of complete possession of the new country was his alone. In Kentucky he would stand, a lineal descendant of Columbus on the beach at Santo Domingo, walking up and down with eager eyes while his men were gathering water" (137). By the position of this essay, Boone serves as application of the principles Williams has established earlier; and we are reminded of Williams' claim in *The Great American Novel:* "The real empire builders of our colonial period were not the statesmen, the men of wealth, the great planters but the unknown pioneers" (332).

Illustrations

In the American Grain seems to fall into three distinct parts. The first four essays tend to present the first explorers and to define their approaches toward America. Williams is able here to explore virtue, love, the position of the good but alienated man. The second group of essays clarifies his original concerns and adds the themes of feminine giving and Puritan repression. The rapid alternation of loving men and hating Pilgrims leads to the crescendo of the Mather-Rasles pairing, Williams' most explicit commentary on American culture. The third set of essays, for the most part, presents the expected historical figures—Washington, Hamilton, Franklin, Lincoln—but in the perspective already established by the earlier writing. Thus, with little direct comment from Williams, we can see the immense difference between Franklin's "common" approach to life and the stoicism of John Paul Jones. Because we have been, in a sense, building Williams' rationale through the earlier essays, we know, too, that his concluding five-hundred-word essay on Lincoln, often overlooked because of its brevity, is the highest possible praise.

Williams' treatments of Washington and Franklin show the suspicion he felt for their conservatism. Washington is much less the hero than Boone, "in a great many ways thoroughly disappointing," because of his great restraint. "Resist and protest." "Resistance was, I believe, his code" (141). Washington did his duty, but, Williams felt, never with passion; seldom, in fact, with interest. Less noble than Washington, Franklin represents to Williams the acquisitive, play-it-safe American, incapable of "sufficient strength for the open assertion." Williams chose to show Franklin's timidity in the same way he showed Mather's perversity, through direct quotation ("with Franklin, the tone is frightened and horribly smug" [154]). His essay opens with excerpts from Poor Richard's descriptions of America; later Williams says of this "small, hard" wisdom: "it keeps the attention fixed so that the eyes shall not see" (156).

Immediately following the Franklin essay comes John Paul Jones's account of the battle between the *Bonhomme Richard* (named for Franklin) and the *Serapis,* written as a letter to "His Excellency Benjamin Franklin." Beset by treason, beaten by superior forces, Jones maintains his proud yet self-effacing spirit. That this patriot, writing clearly, reasonably, looks to Franklin for advice is another of Williams' ironic comments on the men involved.

In the essays "Jacataqua" and "The Virtue of History," Williams elaborates on the dichotomy hinted at in the Franklin-Jones essays. Williams feels that the man who is true to himself, emotionally as well as morally and intellectually, is greater than he who lives by someone else's standards of virtue. Ostensibly about one of Aaron Burr's lovers, the Indian Sachem Jacataqua, the first essay is Williams' tribute to the pioneer women who lived and died under all the repressions of "virtue." Williams' understanding of women is unusually accurate. Yet, sadly, he shows them vulnerable to the failing of all Americans: unable to give, to "serve" others. The result of years of instruction in "morals," they offer nothing to modern men. Most of them. Then there are the Jacataquas. Closing with Burr's meeting with the Indian, the essay leads directly into Williams' praise of the hero-traitor.

Burr is a tragic figure, in Williams' eyes, because he has been the victim of prejudiced history: "it's the malice I decry," Williams writes; "Burr's account in history is a distortion. The good which history should have preserved, it tortures . . . . This is my theme" (197). In an almost Socratic progression, Williams considers each slanderous view of Burr and answers the objection. Against Burr, history has set Hamilton, "a balloon of malice" (190), a man interested only in harnessing men to a treadmill (a view Williams makes more explicit in *Paterson*). The "good" Americans, according to history, use their fellow men (since one of Poor Richard's virtues is to get, to save); a man who does not share this motivation is, at best, misunderstood; at worst, a traitor, "They feared him. He was out of their control; out of their understanding most likely" (191). Rather than brotherhood, the "good" American believes in exploitation. Burr was destined *not* to be good.

The next essay seems to be a corollary to Williams' criticism of politic behavior. In "Advent of Slaves," he stresses the Negroes' solidarity as a people, a trait which "gives them poise in a world where they have no authority" (210). Unity and fellowship are their virtues, accompanied by a "rich," honest language.

The concept of humility, of going back to beginnings, connects the slaves with Sam Houston in the following essay titled "Descent." Trying to reach "the frail genius of place," Houston, in Williams' account, lives several times with the Cherokee Indians. Alan Holder has commented on the one-sidedness of Williams' picture of the Indians and of Houston's relationship with them, but I think this distortion in perspective is explained by Williams' emphasis throughout the book. For example, his stress on Houston's "descent," his degradation, as it were, is an implied defense of Williams' own artistic themes and techniques. Notice in this section how he moves from discussing Houston to defending his own poetic practices in relation to, probably, *The Waste Land*.

It is imperative that we *sink*. But from a low position it is impossible to answer those who know all the Latin and some of the Sanskrit names, much French and perhaps one or two other literatures. Their riposte is: Knownothingism. But we cannot climb every tree in that world of birds. . . . I would rather sneak off and die like a sick dog than be a well known literary person in America (214).

In the American Grain never presumes to be "history" or "fact," as Williams defines them with derogation (see his poem "History"). It is rather Williams' attempt, as he states in his Introduction, to "rename the things seen," "to draw from every source one thing, the strange phosphorus of the life, nameless under an old misappelation." The role of the artist is, then, implied: he is, first of all, one who *sees;* second, one who *names* (and, more important in modern literature, *renames*) in order to re-create life where only dust has survived.

Earlier, I suggested the unspoken similarity between Williams the isolated poet and Eric the Red, lonely and betrayed in his own Greenland. The parallel becomes clearer as we read what would have been the last essay in the book (had not the publisher insisted on including Lincoln), that of Edgar Allan Poe. The only writer in the collection, Poe speaks directly for Williams' beliefs. As Williams presents the unhappy poet, he becomes an amalgam of images and themes used in the earlier portraits. The Houston essay closes with Williams' statement that "we must go back to the beginning; it must all be done over; everything that is must be destroyed" (215). The Poe essay opens with a description of Poe's criticism as being "a single gesture . . . to sweep all worthless chaff aside. It is a movement, first and last, to clear the GROUND" (216). Not only is Poe aligned with Houston; he also parallels the Negroes in what Williams calls his "legitimate sense of solidity which goes back to the ground" (216). And more: "Poe was a new De Soto" and also a new Eric, " 'Rather the ice than their way' " (22).

Williams sees in Poe much to admire. His language was fearless, new, words used *as* words, Stein-like, as bare of connotation as his art could make them. Form was correspondingly free, shaped from the impetus of the thing being written, but a tension, a form to stave off sentimentality. Rather than using "local color," Poe wrote of his knowledge of place and people: "What he wanted was connected with no particular place; therefore it *must* be where he was" (220). And Williams' last note of applause is his description of Poe as he "turned his back and faced inland, to originality, with the identical gesture of a Boone" (226).

Any artist is tempted to think that his art should have the last word, that the answer to many questions of living can be given in a metaphor about art. *In the American Grain* is a stronger collection, I think, because it ends with the Lincoln essay than it would have been, ending with Poe. Williams chooses several familiar details from Lincoln's life, describes them graphically, and adds brilliance to them through his impressionistic comments about Lincoln as a Brancuşi sculpture or as a symphony performance conducted by Mengelberg. Much like "The Gettysburg Address" in its surprising brevity, this essay builds toward two evocative images—images which can be fully meaningful only after one knows what the feminine principle means to Williams:

> It is Lincoln pardoning the fellow who slept on sentry duty. It is the grace of the Bixby letter. The least private would find a woman to caress him, a woman in an old shawl—with a great bearded face and a towering black hat above it (234).

Lincoln, to Williams—in his grotesque appearance, his charity, his rude death—represents both the "brutalizing desolation" and the perverse "flowering" of life in America. That life does include both elements—and that *In the American Grain* so fully presents them—seems somehow to erase any hint of apology from these essays. Williams' final image of Lincoln is a masterful synthesis of the spirit of America, as he saw it—and charted it—so consistently throughout this book, "Failing of relief or expression, the place tormented itself into a convulsion of bewilderment and pain—with a woman, born somehow, aching over it, holding all fearfully together" (235).

CHAPTER SIX

In Pagany and Paris

MAN as voyager, man on quest, is Williams' theme in his second novel—and his translation of a third. Just as he has made American history his ground for investigation in the early 1920's, so now he explores foreign culture: more expressly, the impact of a foreign culture on an American. In *A Voyage to Pagany,* the American Dev Evans confronts Europe in all the richness of her traditions; in *Last Nights of Paris* by Philippe Soupault, the observer-hero is intrigued by, and subsequently involved in, the mysteries of Paris. Both novels are reminiscent of early James in that they present the comparatively passive central character surrounded, and often bewildered, by his experiences abroad. As Williams noted in *I Wanted to Write a Poem,* "I hadn't read much of Henry James, but possibly he influenced me." [1]

Increasingly in the twenties, with many of his friends leaving America, Williams was subjected to the kind of deflating comment he records in *The Great American Novel*:

> This stuff that you have been writing today, do you mean that you are attempting to set down the American background? You will go mad. Why? Because you are trying to do nothing at all. The American background? It is Europe. It can be nothing else. . . .
> As far as I have gone it is accurate.[2]

"The Three Letters," one of Williams' first prose pieces, rebels against this overriding assumption. In this story, Williams traces his relationship with a vile, syphilitic woman who, to the impressionable young poet, represents the finest of Europe. Imprisoned for petty larceny, La Baronne usually lives "in the most unspeakably filthy tenement in the city. Romantically, mystically dirty." [3] Williams' sentimentalization of the slum is evident in this description also: "Close up, a reek stood out purple from her body, separating her forever from the clean muslin souls of Yankeedom. . . . There she lived with three dogs and her clean soul. Let America be damned or do better."

Awed by La Baronne's response to life, Williams (Evans Dionysius Evans is his fictional name here) writes the first letter, a declaration of his love. The Baronne answers that she also loves him.

The second letter from Evans is a translation of some Latin, sent after his ardor has cooled but hers has grown until she is a literal ball of frenzy. In her passion, she tries to strike him, provoking the poet's later question, "What in God's name *does* Europe want of America." Angered at her demands, Evans began the third letter: "You damned stinking old woman . . . you dirty old bitch—"

The fact that the story has opened with the sentence, "America, since his boyhood, had stood before the heated imagination of Evans Dionysius Evans as a virginal young woman" only substantiates his equating Europe with La Baronne.[4] From "The Three Letters" with its poet-hero, it is only a step—and a few years—to *A Voyage to Pagany* and its doctor-hero, Dev Evans. The surreal descriptions of the short story have given way to romantic re-creations of place and mood (one critic considered the novel a travel book); somewhat overly symbolic characters; and enough comments on art to place the novel in direct line from Williams' 1923 *Spring and All*.

A Voyage to Pagany, in part, recounts Williams' 1924 experiences in Paris and elsewhere in Europe. In his *Autobiography* some twenty-five years later, Williams again describes the visit (working largely from his journal) and acknowledges his use of the real material in the novel: "It is, in fact, the opening chapter of my first (limping) novel, *A Voyage to Pagany*, following the complete itinerary of the same trip Floss and I were now on, though the chief characters were not ourselves" (186). Although the similarities are clear, the differences are perhaps even more striking. One of the most apparent is Williams' change in attitude toward Paris, symbolic in his novel as well as Soupault's of mysterious fulfillment, both physical and artistic. In the 1920's, as a man nearing forty, Williams feels himself the gauche provincial, attracted to the city, yet defensive about his curiosity. In the 1951 *Autobiography*, he is more nearly objective in his recitation. Remarks like *"Everyone* was in Paris—if you wanted to see them. But there were grades too of that cream" (190) and "I had nothing in common with them" (195) show the older man's distance from the experiences recounted earlier with enthusiasm.

The quality of Williams' prose has also changed greatly between 1928 and 1951. In his *Autobiography,* Williams writes, "Huge waves from behind the ship, lifting up the stern. The wind howls and drives the spray ripping the foam to lace" (186). The novel begins with the same scene, but Williams uses it to introduce Evans' romantic nature, his love of the fierce sea, Nature personified, "home of the wild gods in exile." Williams achieves his dramatic tone by using numerous phrases in one sentence and by selecting charged, almost musty language:

> At once the great sea, never calmed by divine feet, came from astern, a northwest gale that caught the old *Rochambeau* on her starboard after-quarter in sleet and rain. The wind shrieked as the whipping spray struck the ship's cabins momently all day long for three days; while from the sheltered foredeck the clouds and stars—for the middle sky remained often clear in spite of the storm—could be seen to circle and zigzag overhead. Evans, standing in whatever shelter he could find, was thrilled by that ferocious might of Nature, the ancient antagonist and begetter, green, protean, slippery, yet pointed and personal as a god, while he thought, watching—lace white, spinning among the waves—of white flowers, bunches of them, yarrow, boneset and of the epithet "privet white."—How apt that is for seafoam.[5]

The pervasive god imagery, with its accompanying tone, is one reason several critics have characterized the novel as "romantic." Coming as it does in Williams' writing career—after *Kora in Hell, The Great American Novel, Spring and All,* and *In the American Grain,* and before the cryptic short stories and novels of the 1930's and 1940's—*A Voyage to Pagany* is an interesting transitional book. Williams' exploration of America, its history and its art, changes for the first time to an implied defense of American culture. For the first time, too, he admits Europe and its very real attraction; earlier he has only hinted about that supposedly irrelevant "other" culture.

To Pagany

Perhaps because Williams claims ignorance about the form of a novel,[6] he chooses a simple chronological shape for *A Voyage to*

Pagany. Since the book follows Evans' European tour, the progression
is natural, and also effective in that it allows a series of isolated characters to interact with Dev. It is from the differences in these peoples'
views of life (and of art and America) that Evans determines his own
judgment about life and country. True to Williams' earlier tendency to
equate nationalistic traits with women, most of Evans' friends are
women. But it is interesting that Dev's first encounter is with Jack
Murry, a character reminiscent of Robert McAlmon, the coeditor of
Contact. In scenes much like Lambert Strether's waiting for Way-
marsh, Dev waits for Jack and enjoys his lonely freedom in Paris. Once
Jack arrives, Evans' response is ambivalent, yet heavily sensual. Jack is
a man who knows Europe, knows art, yet has written little. Evans dis-
trusts men of inaction. But his primary question is with himself. Why
does he admire Jack? After a chapter of sorting through his feelings,
Williams concludes that their friendship lies in their respect for writing, for art. Evans' alienation from America results chiefly from its lack
of response to art, to love, to any humane activity; his anger with his
medical profession stems from its usurpation of his "free" time. Williams' initial presentation of this familiar hero has also been highly
charged: Evans is alone, in the prow of the ship, almost like a god,
coming in to his country—his pagany—where, supposedly, love and
freedom to love exist. Williams establishes early the theme that dominated so much of his earlier writing: the ugly force of Puritan repression in American life, the fact of generosity tainted with reproof
or guilt in every area of life. Niggardliness, Williams had called it once.

The strained scene to follow between Evans and his little sister
Bess, a girl seemingly in her mid-twenties, after an absence of a year
and a half, points up again Evans' pervasive loneliness. There is a deep
love here (in the *Autobiography* Williams gives the source for what
he calls "the brother-sister incident" [7])—a love complicated by Evans'
remaining a bachelor even though he is nearly forty. Bess has not been
free to love other men, although she asks his help now in arranging
a rendezvous with a would-be lover. Heartsick, Evans agrees to help.
For him, Bess symbolizes all truth, beauty (and "America," we learn
in his story "The Venus," an excerpted section of the original novel
published separately because the book proper was too long [8]). Because
Bess's chastity represents the same kind of American innocence James
identified, it is important that her lover is not American, but European.

In each romantic situation in the novel, and in the many descriptive images of gods and goddesses, Williams seems trying to define any impulse, whether in art or in emotion, as *pagan,* and any grudging restricted response as Christian. Bess, with her attempts at self-determination, illustrates the best a conscious America can produce; Delise, in the party scene to follow, represents America loosened from its inhibitions, largely through European example and through drink.

> What a delightful thing—drunkenness. He grew furious at the damned stupidity of his people. Whose people? Look, he thought, at this beautiful girl, this armed, able woman. Look! compare her with that, that God damned hell hole of a country.—He wanted to be profane. (63).

Williams' criticism of Christianity, organized, formal, is new here. In the past, he has been interested in Puritanism and what he sees as its damning aftereffects, but he has not labeled its aftermath so explicitly "Christian." The older culture of this novel gives him a way to compare the classic and the Christian, and he frequently does.

On visiting the old cathedrals of Paris, Evans comments: "The pagan strength is in them. When the Christian spirit conquered the world, the pagan gods were turned into these stone images" (51). In Carcassonne, he concludes that Christianity has "wasted" modern man (73). In Florence, he is deeply moved (and "cleansed") by "the Greek beauty—a resurgent paganism, still untouched" (140). Again and again, new beauties prompt Evans' bitter recoil from America. His passion reaches its climax in Rome when his oblique comments turn to outright vituperation: "And religion, that childish horror of misapplication, that stewing and stewing of the stale sauce. . . . That insult to death—that might be at least clean and not craven" (152). A few pages later he speaks of the church as it "lays waste nine parts of the light, the major part of morals, to have its penny's worth of clammy candle-promise of eternity. There must be in Rome a greater thing, inclusive of the world of love and of delight; unoppressive— loosing the mind. . . ." (153).

It is because of this building unrest that Evans' recognition of the statue Venus comes as such a relief. Vacillating between "the stone-like reality of ancient excellence and the pulpy worthlessness of every day," Evans is amazed at the purity of the statue, the "quietness and fulfillment" of its beauty. Frequently in the novel, Williams compares the sea or a beautiful woman to "Venus." Here his imagery is crystallized in the tranquil figure; and with Evans' torment resolved, the tone of the novel changes. Criticism of America—some of it scathing—will come from other characters in the book, but never again from Evans.

Since *A Voyage to Pagany* is constructed as a series of encounters between Dev and various young women, the critical comments now come from women, a situation well in keeping with Williams' view expressed in *TGAN*: that American women are not using their resources and beauties with any understanding of themselves or of their country or with any relevance to either their American pasts or their historic roles as women. Each of the American women in the novel seems, in one way or another, to illustrate this failure, from the almost inarticulate Lou, who marries an Englishman for "stability," to the most nearly wise Bess, Evans' sister. It is with Bess that Williams makes the strongest statement: Bess saying passionately, "I hate America" (52) while she plans her liberating affair; then coming full circle at the end of the novel—although disappointed in that liberation—urging Evans to stay abroad. America, to her, has no honor, or only a "starved, thin, lying one" at best. And Dev owes it to himself, she cants, as does every person, "to use well what one has, that's all. . . . to make a beginning" (329). The ironic effect of her argument is clearly seen as Evans returns to America, precisely for Bess's reason: "to use well what one has." America *is* what Evans has. He can recognize his shortcomings, as his earlier writing has declared; but he can also recognize his commitment to his country. The last line of the novel, as Evans approaches the coast of Maine, is "So this is the beginning."

The clearest statement of why Evans returns home lies, unfortunately for the impact of the novel as published, in the excerpted chapter, "The Venus." This short story focuses on the most interesting of Williams' women characters, the elusive yet searching Fräulein von J. who plans to enter a convent in lieu of finding peace in her own country. Interrogating Evans, she uncovers his feelings about America. "It is like . . . a badly trained voice. It is a world where no man dare learn anything that concerns him intimately—but sorrow . . ." (214). Some of these same reactions appear during Evans' second affair in the novel, that with the pseudo musician Grace Black, but not with the clarity and succinctness of the dialogue in "The Venus." Cutting the Venus chapter from the novel was probably a mistake, because the German woman is also the personification of the statue which so moves Evans. A European, she comes closest to understanding life. At least she does not condemn it before she knows it. Since Evans is hardly a picaro, this kind of encounter lends a rationale to his adventures more in keeping with the ostensible theme of the book. Each of his love affairs is a search for self-identity; but only this dialogue with Fräulein von J. gives him any such realization.

Including the young German woman as the living Venus would also emphasize Evans' reaction to the mystic statue. Anyone familiar with Williams' later writing will recognize this early use of the "feminine principle." For Williams as poet and doctor, all life resolved itself in the mystery of birth; he never ceased to believe that women, at least the best of them, knew the answers. His almost exclusive use of women characters in this novel is a new technique, one that suggests his turn away from a single interest in a man's relationship with his country. Just as he has described Lincoln as a woman in the last of the *American Grain* essays, so Williams is to find his peace of mind—fictionally, at least—through relationships with wise women.

A Voyage to Pagany, despite its skimpy dramatic hold and its occasional travel-book chapters, is an important book in Williams' writings. We have seen earlier that after World War I Williams was a troubled man, both personally and professionally. His writing of the early 1920's, from *Kora* to *IAG,* helped him establish his rationale for art as well as for a kind of virtue. He tests this rationale in *Pagany.* When Evans encounters Europe and comes to terms with his own American culture and, as a result, with himself, Williams feels that the somewhat nebulous principles have been tried. These same principles are to appear over and over, in the later fiction, in *Paterson,* and beyond. Touch, acceptance, love—Williams' ethic becomes simpler and simpler as his search comes closer home. Although he still tends to rely on what he can learn from "history" (witness all the historical accounts in the early books of *Paterson*), he comes ultimately to himself. By Book V of the epic, De Soto has given way to

> Paterson has grown older . . .
>   And went on
>   living and writing
>   answering
>   letters
>   and tending his flower

garden, cutting his grass and trying
to get the young
        to foreshorten
their errors in the use of words . . .[9]

It seems fair to say, considering all Williams' writing, that his search—for meaning, for truth—remained the same throughout, but that his interest no longer lay primarily in American history, rather in his own. *A Voyage to Pagany* is the beginning of *that* exploration, as, indeed, Williams has said.

Interestingly, the novel is also a kind of casebook for much of Williams' later writing. Many of the impressions that play a minor role in the novel reappear years later in more complete form. The description of Evans as a "sparrow" suggests the 1954 poem of that name, just as the scene of a woman "fixing her hair with arms raised in classic style" leads to the 1955 "Classic Picture." The long description of the jiggling priest at Amalfi is recast in Part III of "The Clouds," many years later, in the same tone of shocked amusement. Brueghel's paintings, asphodel, the ocean—many of the later poems and stories seem to begin here. Another interesting description is of a river, with Evans thinking of it as a "prototype of art" and commenting that one doesn't have "to describe everything that's in a river" (132), a comment Williams brought to life in *Paterson*.

As casebook and as notebook, as montage of some good dialogue and some erotic but effective travel descriptions, *A Voyage to Pagany* deserves the attention it has recently received. The obvious identity of Evans-Williams as he makes "a wife of his writing," attempting to "free himself from his besetting reactions by transcribing them—thus driving off his torments" (145), holds a necessary place in Williams' lifelong struggle to write, to "shoot a clarity through the oppressing, obsessing murk of the world" (155). That he chooses a much straighter narrative style, and that he is not afraid to use himself at least partially as protagonist, is evidence of his struggle for that clarity.

And Paris

It is no accident that Williams translated Philippe Soupault's *Last Nights of Paris* (*Les Dernières Nuits de Paris*) just after his own novel was published. A woman, a haunting city, a search for meaning far beyond the literal mystery—in brief, Soupault's novel is almost a better-defined statement of Evans' search than was *Pagany* itself.

Soupault's novel opens with the kind of thematic intensity which Williams admired. "She smiled so curiously I could not keep my eyes from her pale face." [10] Georgette, the discreet whore who seems to symbolize the mysterious Paris, attracts Soupault from the moment he sees her. Then the fusion begins, first by equating Georgette with Paris and then by personifying Paris at every turn: "Paris was confiding to me another secret" (57); "the breath and gestures of Paris, Paris and her supple and silent nights" (144); "a hidden cry loosed by Paris, Paris who wanted me and who, once more, had chosen for this mission the name of a friend" (62).

The intrigue which surrounds Georgette throughout this mood piece is never explained. The narrator is drawn in simply because he knows the woman, but he never resents his entanglement. The restraint of the many weird characters, even the sinister Volpe—whether they are hiding bodies or lighting fires—is nightmarish. Soupault's corresponding understatement, suggestive description, and limited (outside) point of view help to keep the focus of the novel on Georgette's seemingly innocent role (in the various gang mysteries, as well as in her own life) rather than on the acts of violence themselves.

> Georgette resumed her stroll about Paris, through the mazes of the night. She went on, dispelling sorrow, solitude or tribulation. Then more than ever did she display her strange power: that of transfiguring the night. Thanks to her, who was no more than one of the hundred thousands, the Parisian night became a mysterious domain, a great and marvelous country, full of flowers, of birds, of glances and of stars, a hope launched into space (73).

As a result of Georgette's transfiguring presence, Soupault sees Paris as "surely not the same city. It lifted itself above the mists, rotating like the earth on its axis, more feminine than usual. As I looked at it, it contracted. And Georgette herself became a city" (74). Williams has used this kind of progression himself in the fusion of the old woman and the river in "The Wanderer"; he is to use it again and again in

Paterson, here the city as man; the river, again, as woman. One of Williams' great unspoken sadnesses about *Paterson,* I think, was that the industrial city was more nearly masculine than it was feminine. As he had written in his 1950 *American Scholar* essay,

> Women are more sensitive to what Ezra Pound once called "the purring of the invisible antennae". . . . Life still interests me, and not because of any masculine competition. Let my sex take care of themselves. But the gentleness and tenderness and insight and loyalty of women . . . keep me plugging.[11]

As Soupault presents her, Georgette is the essence of these characteristics Williams admires. Her loyalty is directed to her slow-witted artist brother Octave, who eventually attempts to burn down Paris. To support him, she turns streetwalker ("we grow accustomed to the strangest circumstances"), yet Soupault shows that she has never lost her tenderness or gentleness. He describes her as typifying "the tenderness" of Paris (120); he speaks of her as "certainty, clarity, and truth" (118). In some respects a Gatsby, Georgette's fault is her unquestioning simplicity. She conspires to save Octave; she whores to support him. As she explains to the narrator:

> We had to live. . . . I know Paris; and we are placed on this earth to live. Everything is so simple when one knows all the streets as I do, and all the people who move in them. They are all seeking something without seeming to do so (118).

Reinforcement for Georgette's rationale, and for her effect on the narrator, comes from the most intellectual of the characters, Volpe. Even he can say only, with admiration, "Georgette is a woman. That's all I can say. She lives and that's all" (165).

Since most of the novel occurs at night, Soupault's constant shadowy scenes do not seem bizarre, but necessary. Against the pervasive darkness, the red of explosions and fires, the images of lust serve as effective contrast. Otherwise, the painting is unrelieved—and the novel, much clearer, much less surreal technically than Soupault's earlier writing. As Williams had written in 1928, when he was just beginning the book,

The first few pages of Soupault, by the way, are delightful reading. Easy, deceptive, accurate to the rules of conversation (which I am afraid Hem doesn't at all understand, since it is rarely as expressive as he makes it and almost twice as succinct), just batting the air effectively and swimming in it—like an airplane. I like the Soupault better than anything of his that I have encountered. Perhaps it will grow foolishly fantastic later in the book—as much of the little modern French stuff that I have seen does.[12]

That it does not grow "foolishly fantastic" is certainly part of the novel's appeal in this stage of Williams' writing (where even his montage poems have a clearly defined focus in title or first lines). Clarity, clarity is the dictum that runs through much of his prose, and he is turning increasingly to prose. Williams' many essays and reviews are evidence of the impulse to teach, to explain, that is to prompt much of his writing in the future. Whether in Pagany or Paris or Rutherford, Williams has no choice but to speak to his "townspeople."

CHAPTER SEVEN

Genesis at Mid-Point

THE year 1927 was a climactic one for Williams. Impressed with the quantity of his writing, a reader will sometimes forget that Williams was an incredibly busy man. Although he had specialized in pediatrics, his medical practice was general and heavily obstetrical as well. His early life was a composite of the interminably ringing telephone, tiring night calls, and, in the midst of it all, his voluminous writing.[1] Considering the kind of life he lived, I think it reasonable to view his two sabbatical years of 1924 and 1927, the only breaks in his medical practice until his retirement in 1951, as highly formative. The leisure to write, to travel, and, not the least, to talk [2] forced Williams into definite commitments to the future of his art.

Much of *In the American Grain* was written before and during the 1924 experience, in Europe and in New York during the earlier months of his sabbatical. Many poems, with his increasing fascination for the moving images of Objectivism, appear now also, including an early "Paterson." Essays and reviews were published as Williams, misread and misunderstood for nearly twenty years, tried to explain the principles of his poetry. By 1927, when he and Floss took young Bill and Paul abroad for a year's study, he was deeply interested in many kinds of writing: drama, novel, short story, translation, as well as the poem and the essay. Returning home in September 1927 to face nearly a year's separation from his family, Williams expressed natural misgivings in several letters to his wife.[3] But his anticipation about his writing was running high, as he wrote in a September 25 letter to Floss: "I'm crazy, more or less, to get at my writing again. This year I'm going at it differently than usual. I'll write something every day but I'll keep five or six things going at once." [4]

The immense amount of writing which he did during his family's absence testifies to his tireless production. As he recalls in his *Autobiography,* "During that year I wrote furiously at *White Mule,* at the poems, and at the short stories that later made up *The Knife of the Times,* as well as many prefaces and critical essays of various complexions" (258). In addition, *A Voyage to Pagany* was finished and polished for its publication later in 1928. Williams, with his mother, who was in charge of 9 Ridge Road during Floss's absence, began translating the Soupault novel; and the poem sequences "Della Primavera Transportata Al Morale" and "The Descent of Winter" were written (the latter originally appeared in a prose form, later modified to the prose-poem matrix published in 1928). "The Descent" must have been some of Williams' first writing when he returned home in September 1927, because the opening section is dated "9/27"; it seems to continue in the vein of his long letters written on shipboard to his wife.[5] Art, nature, the facts of his life, feelings, subjects poetic and antipoetic—all appear in the free-form writing. And in this rush of effort came materials enough to last him nearly a lifetime. Just as *A Voyage to Pagany* contained many glimpses of later poems, so did the montage of "The Descent of Winter" introduce what were to be continuing themes for Williams, among them the early Dolores Marie Pischak–Fairfield stories foreshadowing both *White Mule* and *Paterson.*

"The Descent of Winter"

As it was originally published in thirty-nine pages of Pound's *The Exile* (1928), "The Descent of Winter" consisted of dated prose passages and poems, most of them short and highly objective. Similar in effect to *Spring and All,* this selection also emphasizes the role of art in contemporary life. But its concern is generally much more humane than that of Williams' earlier writing. Art in the abstract has been supplanted by art based in the human condition. Opening with reactions on board ship as he returns to America, Williams quickly moves to the declaration, "I will make a big serious portrait of my time." [6] The theme in the passage which follows is freedom, abandon to record whatever is present—shop windows, trees, but particularly love: "love is my hero." Williams' beloved freedom, however, is immediately blocked (paralleling *Paterson*'s blockage images) as he sees the "barred windows, wavy opaque glass . . . STOP in black letters." Yet from this seeming obstacle comes birth:

Blistery, prickly heat red midget face, Wagh! lying there helpless in its
too heavy clothes and blankets. Write a novel about that? Realism about
that. Christ. Its little hands have all the markings in the palms. Read
its horoscope. Tell its fortune. Life line says it will live to be 650. Same
as the Wop kid that survived that pneumonia. . . . Its hands stuck up
in the air like prongs. . . . Bow legged. Feet purple red, scrawny. The
whole thing only 6½. Pukes up a little thin milk. . . . Wagh! This—
this—this. Good God. What in hell is this. Humanity. Plays never tell
the right things . . . No one writes the plain scalding, shell cracking
truth.[7]

The birth of the "hero," Dolores Marie Pischak, pervades much of the
original "Descent," with its images of birth and growth, as we see
her in various erratic glimpses throughout her life. These early versions
of the montage include much more biography. True to his acknowledged rationale in 1927—that the poet has to work from "truth," has
to be content with the objectively knowable—Williams seems to be
focusing here on one person who would synthesize the spirit of her
locale, the town named first Garfield and then Fairfield, presumably
Rutherford. The child of the migrant workers Williams knows so well,
Dolores Marie (or Veronica Magdalene as he suggests in another
work sheet) is to be a way into the "serious portrait" Williams finally
draws twenty years later in *Paterson*.

His early notes suggest the process of combining the concrete detail
with the historic background:

She said to the doctor: I wish you'd examine her. His people have
tuberculosis. She's so thin I thought she might have a touch of it.

A chapter now on the history, in the confluence of the Saddle and the
Passaic rivers. . . .

Then, as if in explanation to himself, Williams justifies this use of
history in the present, a practice he is to employ throughout his later
epic: "Her history comes in where it comes in, ONLY her history and
poetry, and HER fields, HER school, HER parents, HER needs, HER
ecstatic, me-enkindling life of her in Garfield—MY poems, MY
thoughts, MY writing."[8]

Although she is born to a bootleg saloon owner and his wife, Dolores Marie's story is not sensational (once in the work sheets, Williams seems to suggest her murder, but that ending was evidently dropped). The emphasis he intended to give the Fairfield story is positive, as suggested in this long opening description, with his comments, "This is the world. Here one breathes and the dignity of man holds on" and "in Fairfield men are peaceful and do as they please—and learn the necessity and the profit of order" (66, 67).

Because life is good, especially as these simple people live it, the artist does not need to elaborate on the given fabric, "That's the feeling of Fairfield" (65). To recapture it, with all its moral relevance, one has only to select and describe the salient particulars. For this Williams uses the poems in "The Descent of Winter" framework: the black boy in the doorway, dead weeds, "men at the bar/ talking of the strike/ and cash," freight cars, billboards, dahlias. Like the poems in *Spring and All,* these also gain from their arrangement in the prose passages; the spirit of the entire work—that of both questing and proving—connects the short poems and gives them a cumulative impact. One of the most typical of these poems is the "11/10" entry, which Williams in an early draft opens with "someone/ should write of their front rooms,"

> The shell flowers
> the wax grapes and peaches
> the fancy oak or mahogany tables
> the highbacked baronial chairs
>
> Or the girls' legs
> agile stanchions
> the breasts
> the pinheads—

Once he has placed the girls in their setting, he moves to their speech:

> —Wore my bathing suit
> wet
> four hours after sundown.
> That's how. Yea?
> Easy to get
> hard to get rid of.

Again, "truth" of character is achieved through the spoken word. As Williams' choice of words during this period shows, sometimes the plainer the word, the better. (A belabored defense of the expression "piss" appears in a draft of dialogue from a playlet with the poet-doctor as hero, trying to give a testimony in court, but being censured for his word choice. Similarly several poems, never published, are concerned with the words "fart" and "piss." As Williams had written in his work-sheet description of Dolores Marie, "Her pukes and shits are important." [9])

The poem continues with other images, nearing its end with the poet's pointed if cryptic observation, "Someone should summarize these things/ in the interest of local/ government" (*CEP*, 309–310). This purpose of art—to serve, to recapture, and hopefully to refocus—usurps the Fairfield story, once Williams opens the prose of "The Descent of Winter" to it. He comments at length on Shakespeare and the drama and the immediate life necessary to that form. These remarks are apt introduction to his own plays, as well as a defense of his technique in these 1927 writings. Poetry must, Williams says, strive for "vividness" like that of the best drama—vividness that has its roots in the actual and, more important, in actual people, actual dialogue. Shakespeare's greatness lies not in any personal characteristics, Williams feels, but in his ability to understand people: "he is a woman, a pimp, a Prince Hal. . . . Such a man is a prime borrower and standardizer—no inventor.[10] He lives because he sinks back, does not go forward, sinks back into the mass" (70).

"A Morning Imagination of Russia," the longest poem from the sequence, also has as theme man's identity with the mass, the earth. Russia throughout Williams' life symbolized a hearty, sensual, if non-intellectual life (his concepts of the country seem to have come from Eisenstein films rather than from contemporary political accounts). "The sky and the earth were very close," the poem opens. Later the poet equates Russia with rural traits, "There were no cities/ between him and his desires. . . . Nothing between now." The Russian peasant typifies for Williams the same kind of instinctive wisdom he has found in some of his own patients, as this graphic passage from the poem indicates:

> He would go
> out to pick herbs, he graduate of

> the old university. He would go out
> and ask that old woman, in the little
> village by the lake, to show him wild
> ginger. He himself would not know the plant
> *(CEP,* 306)

Once the intellectual poet's search has begun (by talking with and listening to his people), he will find "touch." (It is interesting that the only magazines Williams edited were both called *Contact.*)

The prose passage accompanying the poem, later omitted from "Notes in Diary Form," continues with this excited discussion of Russia, the Soviet. Williams thinks the country is strong because it has not separated its riches, because it is a collective economy, and therefore everyone still has his roots in a mass culture. Williams uses as a parallel the fact that "Henry Ford has asked Charles Sheeler to go to Detroit and photograph everything. Carte blanche."[11] Williams again pleads for the real in art, for identity of place, or person:

> I know a good print when I see it. . . . It is the neck of a man, the nose of a woman. It is the name Shakespeare. It is a photograph by Sheeler. It is. It is the thing where it is. So. That's the mine out of which riches have always been drawn.[12]

Ostensibly about Russia as a more favorable place for art, this long passage also makes reference to Dolores Marie Pischak and the sterility of New York ("New York is a blight on my heart, lost . . ."). Few sections in the early versions of "Descent" are without some mention of the Pischak-Fairfield theme. Such recurrence seems to indicate that Williams was working as much from internal necessity as from abstracted theory. Here it is—all this story, all this town, all Williams' life to date, and his knowledge after the forty years of living it. Like his struggle to determine a structure for *Paterson,* Williams' artistic problem here becomes how to present the material to touch the reader as it touches him. Williams does not pretend to know. He states the problem on November 16, 1927, "to make the stores of the mind available to the pen—Wide! That which locks up the mind is vicious." On November 10, he has tried to specify: "Arrange it all in proper paragraphs, with poems—if striking—on a page by themselves as in Villon's *Testament.* The 'Life' as I planned it." He generalizes on November

20, "What I seek and what I see is a clear new light dawning over the whole broken book . . . . the *things* coming into the clear light." December 9 finds him still collecting the "facts." As his work sheets show, sometimes his material is a two-line name and address; again, the synopsis of a possible story; again, a comparatively detailed description. Williams notes on that day, "What I am seeking is a correlation between the imagination and the fact."

A few days later, in a typescript dated December 15, he seems to be considering the novel form for his story of Fairfield.[13] And then, silence—or lost manuscripts. When Pound published the prose and poem "The Descent of Winter" the following year, Williams' agonies about his writing attempts had been deleted, as well as at least half of the poems and prose passages. Whether Williams himself cut the manuscript, saving the sections that dealt more specifically with Dolores Marie and other characters of the town, or whether Pound exercised his editorial prerogative, there is no way of telling. At any rate, much of the original material went unpublished.

The various versions of "The Descent of Winter" provide much information about the genesis of a great deal of Williams' future writing: the brief episodes lend themselves to the short story, a form he had only begun working with in 1927. Williams' lifelong desire to portray the spunky lower-class heroine reaches culmination in several later stories, in *Paterson,* and to some extent in the trilogy of Stecher novels. The most compelling of Williams' desires—to create the all-encompassing picture, of man's past as well as his present, anchored in recognizable people and places—reaches fruition in *Paterson.* Even in these early drafts, Dolores Marie Pischak eventually came to that city: Williams wrote on October 29, 1927, that "Paterson is really a part of it. She ends in the Hotel in the fields. Fascinating to me."[14]

Theory and Practice

In "Della Primavera Transportata Al Morale," the 1928 spring poem sequence which follows "The Descent of Winter," Williams speaks again and again of man's need for love. Whether as sea animal, tree, or rain, the spirit of love offers a way out, a way to fulfillment. Perhaps this group of poems is the collection Williams had promised his wife during their ten-month separation.[15] At any rate, these poems continue several primary themes of "Descent" and also illustrate the poetic theories Williams was developing during the 1920's:

> the beginning—or
> what you will:
>   the dress
> in which the veritable winter
> walks in Spring—
>
> Loose it!
>
> Let it fall (where it will)
> —again

"April," the first poem in the closely knit sequence,* opens with Williams' insistence (by now, characteristic) on freedom to love. "Loose" is a recurring word in these poems, as is the idea of beginning. "April" includes many effective lines as Williams, reaching to include numerous incidents, jumps effectively from rakish juxtapositions like

> trees—seeming dead:
>   the long years—
>
> *tactus eruditus*
>
> Maple, I see you have
> a squirrel in your crotch—
>
> And you have a woodpecker
> in your hole, Sycamore
>
> —a fat blonde, in purples (no trucking
> on this street)
>   POISON!
>   (*CEP,* 63)

to lists from an ice-cream parlor menu to the more stentorian "I believe" and "moral" passages:

---

* Work sheets indicate, in fact, that many of these poems were originally part of one long work.

Moral
>> I can laugh

Moral
>> the redhead sat
>> in bed with her legs
>> crossed and talked
>> rough stuff
> . . . .
>> and the eyes see
>> and see starvation, it is

>> useless to have it thought
>> that we are full—
>>> (*CEP,* 60)

The sobering conclusion to the passage above, signaled by the monosyllabic words and the slower lines, is typical of Williams' concern for his culture, evident throughout this group of poems.

In the great variety of spacing and line formation here and in the other poems of this selection (subtitled WORDS SANS LINES) lies the key to Williams' new critical interest during the late 1920's. His insistence that something new be done with the words grows partly from his admiration for the writing of Joyce and Stein and partly from his own sense of stalemate in the extremely short quatrains and tercets of "The Descent of Winter." These spring poems technically follow the thematic dictum of "looseness." Many lines are double-spaced; some lines are comprised of single words. These are the poems of an extravagant man, no longer chary of either space or emotion.

>> Loose your love
> to flow

> Blow!
>> (*CEP,* 68)

The humor evident in the intentional rhyme and in the "what you will"/ "where it will" echo of page 96 is also a new, more expansive mode for Williams. Dev Evans (*A Voyage to Pagany*) could never have viewed his country's dearth of love with the wit evidenced here.

Part of Williams' use of actual speech is probably occasioned by his need for a humorous tone: "(In/ a practical voice) They/ ought/ to put it back where/ it came from" says the modern woman about the sea monster, love. "Blouaugh!" comes the answer, much in keeping with the comments of the wise trees ("Christ, the bastards/ haven't even sense enough/ to stay out of the rain"),

> Wha ha ha ha
>
> Wheeeeee
> Clacka tacka tacka
> tacka tacka
> wha ha ha ha ha
> ha ha ha

In contrasting these proponents of "Loose desire" with restrained men, Williams pulls the poem down suddenly to describe the latter:

> —ghosts
> sapped of strength
>
> wailing at the gate
> heartbreak at the bridgehead—
>
> desire
> dead in the heart
>
> haw haw haw haw
> —and memory broken
>
> wheeeeee . . .
>
> (*CEP*, 66–67)

Juxtaposing the voices of the trees with the mournful (and effete) description of man is a masterful device, pointing without belaboring to the initial contrast and humorously alleviating the latter comment. The wide range in language here (from the terse "Christ, the bastards" to the maudlin "heartbreak" line) also shows Williams' willingness to employ all his language resources.

Concentrating on the power of each word a writer uses, Williams

wrote of Pound that "the principal move in imaginative writing today
[is] that away from the word as a symbol toward the word as reality." [16] Joyce's portmanteau words, his puns and jokes, his obscenities,
all were justified, to Williams, if they were effective in making the
reader respond to the word. In 1927 Williams described Joyce's style
as "truth through the breakup of beautiful words . . . . If to achieve
truth we work with words purely, as a writer must, and all words are
dead or beautiful, how then shall we succeed any better than might a
philosopher with dead abstractions?" [17]

Williams' lengthy reply to Rebecca West's criticism of Joyce shows
his anger at the reception anything new receives and points irately to
Miss West's mistaken idea that "sentences originate before words." [18]
Although Williams is later to temper this view of the importance of the
single word, he praises Stein because "she has completely unlinked
them [words] from their former relationships in the sentence." [19]

Along with this emphasis on the individual word, Williams admires
"speed," the omission of dull or slowing transitions. Marianne Moore's
"rapidity of movement" brings him to the juxtaposition which dominates so much of his own writing, both prose and poetry. He uses a
geometric principle to describe the effect of images thrown, with seemingly little order, at the reader: "from all angles lines converging and
crossing establish points . . . . there is a multiplication, a quickening,
a burrowing through, a blasting aside, a dynamization, a flight over—"
and so the modern poem.[20]

Much of Williams' own writing in the late 1920's reflects his interest
in this experimentation with words, none more obviously than the
prose poems which were published in little magazines but never collected. THEESSENTIALROAR, WELLROUNDEDTHIGHS,
THAT POEM JAYJAY—running the title words together sets the
mood of these mock stream-of-consciousness pieces. His selections for
the 1927 and 1928 *American Caravan* anthologies are more sedate mixtures of poetry and prose, but they still depend for their effects on juxtaposition and speed.

January, A Novelette

That Williams' most patently "surreal" writing comes in
1928 and 1929 is understandable. He is influenced by his recent trip

abroad, by his interest in and translation of Soupault, by his chagrin with American attitudes (see his essay "George Antheil and the Cantilene Critics"), and by his characteristic readiness to experiment. His interest in the "loose" surreal approach is particularly evident in *January, A Novelete,* written in 1929, published in 1932.[21]

January 11, 1929, finds Rutherford in the midst of an influenza epidemic and Williams in the midst of a renewed love for his wife. In a fragmented montage reminiscent of *Kora in Hell* and *TGAN,* Williams sets forth another of his prolegomena about life and art. As he has written to Floss in 1928,

> the firmness of the written word is a great thing. It is becoming more and more the center about which this small piece of protoplasm revolves —that and his distracting lady—and all that she means, and will mean in the days, and I hope years to come.[22]

One of his primary principles here is that structurally the broken and disordered is the way to true order. The artists must strive for "piecemeal excellence"; the "composed is inadequate" (10). The novella opens with scenes in the Congregational Church yard juxtaposed with cats stalking mice, an injured steer, an old woman, the new moon, Byrd's expedition. The effect is admittedly broken. Yet through it all Williams opts for the discernible, the objective, arranged as if unarranged, as it would be in surreal art. He refers to the Surrealist movement as an "epidemic" (19), changing the connotation of the word to praise when he says of the influenza epidemic itself:

> the stresses of life have sharpened the sight. Life is keener, more pressed for place—as in an epidemic. The extraneous is everything that is not seen in detail. There is no time not to notice (8).

In "An Essay on Virginia," also published in the 1932 collection, Williams continues his explanation of dispersal:

> Unity is the shallowest, the cheapest deception of all composition . . . . ability in an essay is multiplicity, infinite fracture, the intercrossing of opposed forces establishing any number of opposed centres of stillness (74).

Similarly he praises Surrealism for allowing language to revolt against being "enslaved, raped, made a whore by the idea vendors . . . . Language is in its January" (18).

Williams' antipathy for philosophy, logic, other "uses" of language is pervasive throughout this period. Almost defiantly he includes many single phrases (fragments, suspended on the page, separate from context) as he tries to give words a meaning for themselves: "Not pea-NUT, peCAN"; "Phaugh, hougfh, pfaugh, kewoof! said the fat dog" (23).

Rather than a structure based on logical progression, Williams demands "design." Chapter V of the novella, titled "Conversation as Design," implies that recurring ideas, images, even phrases, create the kind of pattern Williams thinks would work in literature—a pattern once again modeled on the "real."

> You are copying.
> Always.
> But that's not original nor is it design.
> Purely.
> Purely what?
> Conversation of which there is none in novels and the news.
> Oh, yes, there is.
> Oh, no, there is not. It is something else. To be conversation, it must have only the effect of itself, not on him to whom it has a special meaning but as a dog or a store window. . . . It must have no other purpose than the roundness and the color and the repetition of grapes in a bunch, such grapes as those of Juan Gris which are related more to a ship at sea than to the human tongue. As they are. . . . It takes writing such as unrelated passing on the street to rescue us for a design . . . (28).

That there may be no ostensible pattern is also possible. One remembers Williams' criticism that Hemingway's dialogue is inaccurate because "it is rarely as expressive as he makes it and almost twice as succinct." [23] "The thing is," Williams writes, "that the actual sentences of conversation simply do not exist in literature"; then he gives the following excerpt as illustration of that actual: "The trouble was that she was run down. You see, they made her an angel just before Christmas and she did quite a little running around in her bare feet and she's not used to that" (30).

As a corollary to the notion of design, Williams adds that any design should be composed of real objects (words, as he defines them, would be included with *objects*). In *January,* he describes leaves, influenza, trees, and rocks and then concludes, "These and other things have a relationship with each other simply because both [*sic*] are actual" (41). As his admiration for Juan Gris indicates, the objects of art must be recognizable; there is to be no "obscure allusion" or "involved symbolism" (35). What a man says should be as clear as what he sees.

Despite its fragmentary appearance (short paragraphs and non-existent transitions), there are several pervasive themes in the novella. One is that of beginning, of "January," whether in season, writing, or love. A second is that of the energy needed for that beginning—energy Williams describes as "fierce singleness." The writer has but one ambition, to make contact: "At 45 there is no quitting. Now especially must the thing be driven through" (37). "Kindly note that all I have ever done has been the one thing" (25). And in his earnestness about his writing, Williams moves to perhaps the most important theme of the novella, that of his love for his wife.

> That singleness I see in everything—actual—which has been my life, because of haste due to the epidemic, I see in you and so you become beautiful partly because you are so but partly because of other women (23).

All sections of *January* have been pulled together by the presence of a beloved woman. Williams at times fuses woman with language, so that the metaphor of writing as "wife" takes on renewed meaning, as in this humorous *non sequitur,* "Theirs is a simplicity of phrase emphasizing the elusive reality of words. Mine is in pink pants, she hanging my coat in the closet . . ." (19).

"Of love, abiding love it would be telling,"[24] Williams was to write twenty-six years later in "Asphodel, That Greeny Flower." But the song begins here, however obliquely. The opening section of the novella contains the timeless interchange of school children: "Buddy loves Eleanor./ You shut up" (9). Chapter I introduces the laughing woman who urges the doctor on in his writing. We meet "her nude pinkness and familiar sex in the icy air"; we hear her compared, once again, to "Venus from the confused sea. Summing all the virtues. Single. Excellence. Female" (20).

The fusion of art and love which is evident in *January* (and may be the gloss for Williams' statement to Pound that the book "contains something I have been trying for half my life"[25]) culminates in the poet's explanation of his art to his wife:

> Would you consider a train passing—or the city in the icy sky—a love song? What else? It must be so.
> And if I told you the dark trees against the night sky and the row of the city's lights beyond and under them—would you consider *that* a love statement?
> This is what my poems have been from the first.
> It is simple. There is no symbolism, no evocation of an image (44).

Loose, fragmented as this novella may appear, *January* has its structural rationale, its familiar techniques. Detail after detail, anecdote building on anecdote—the principles of organization here are very similar to those of Williams' other writing in this period. Initiate the reader, then interest him through the immediacy of the particular. Deluge him with a montage of such specifics. Yet arrange those seemingly unarranged (and "unselected") episodes so there is a sense of progression, an order toward meaning. No matter what his genre, Williams works in this manner.

One reason Williams needed a "composite" organization was the tremendous amount of material available to him. Many writers record their glimpses of life in notebooks for future use; for Williams the stuff of living spilled over him a hundred times a day. His need was to get rid of the abundance of it, not to hoard it. And this atmosphere of freeing himself, of "catching up" during 1927 and 1928, when he could selfishly devote himself to that most unselfish of avocations, his writing, filled his work with an even greater freedom. His belief that he could "make a big, serious portrait of his time" would be shaken during the next decade, but the optimism of this period proved to be indomitable. The sabbaticals of 1924 and 1927 truly provided for Williams' later writings many important beginnings.

[CHAPTER EIGHT]

"The Shapes of Men's Lives"

WILLIAMS' short stories may have had as deep an effect on contemporary fiction as his poems have had on modern poetry. Denis Donoghue feels that "his stories will wear better than his poems, because the stories keep him rooted in the particular incident." [1] Many modern writers, ranging from Flannery O'Connor to Robert Creeley, share this view. The apparently effortless telling, the informal (and often unresolved) plot, the emphasis on character presented through salient details, and above all, the reliance on dialogue—these trademarks of a Williams' story occur repeatedly in contemporary writing. Yet mere copying of one stylistic device or another has never insured success, as many imitators of the supposed "Hemingway" style or "Faulkner" style have discovered. There are two primary difficulties in discussing Williams' short stories: first, the great variety of them; and second, the poet's insistence that a story is an amoral art form, that—as the most free of art forms—it has no responsibility to be anything other than a "formal" arrangement of words.[2] Because the tradition in the American short story is didactic (Hawthorne instructed, whereas Poe only bewildered), critics have attempted too often to find explicit messages in stories which Williams intended rather as "a good medium for nailing down a single conviction. Emotionally." [3] As he explained in 1950,

> What shall the short story be written about? . . . . Something that interests the writer seriously, as a writer (not necessarily a man for in that case the interest would be moral and perhaps best NOT represented as a short story). He writes about the way his interests, as a writer, strike upon the material, of some event, graphically presented.
>
> The result is life, not morals. It is THE LIFE which comes alive in the telling. . . .[4]

Warren Tallman discusses the problem of reading contemporary fiction in his perceptive introduction to *New American Story,* an essay which begins with praise for Williams and Stein as two "battlers" for new American writing:

Change forces other changes, and as a direct result of these efforts to rediscover the sources of vitality the longtime ascendency over fiction of chronological continuity weakens as markedly as representational form had already weakened in painting. Obviously, you can't make it down to more primary levels of consciousness by walking in the same old ways down the same old streets. Consequently, the firm progress from a beginning to a middle to an end gives way to stream of consciousness, free association, improvisation. And this shift to a circling, side-winding, wandering progression opens out liberating possibilities for the man of words. However, the consternation among readers who couldn't stand to ride on a novel without a plot track was at least as great as had been the consternation among viewers who refused to look at a painting unless they could find a picture. Because this consternation was shared by readers and critics alike, a mistaken generation focused attention not upon the new energy and variety in the writing but upon unpuzzling in the old ways the new works that emerged. Works that should have been studied in light of their linguistic potential were studied instead in light of their semantic potential. The consequences go on to this day in the vast collection of explications and interpretations that have plowed through the masterworks of our century in attempts to turn up Truth, Wisdom, Reality and Morality. Patient and praiseworthy as the best of these attempts have been, the general effect has been to conceal the new art that has emerged by handing it over to the old Jehovahs.

But if the semantics of the works ("the science of meanings") carried the critics and the colleges, the syntax ("the ordering of word forms") carried the writers. For critics, stream of consciousness, free association and improvisation have been so many twists and turns that lead—once straightened out—straight home from at sea. But for writers these leaping, crisscross and erratic—because pathless—pacings open out new beauty, variety and power in the language. No man can ever go beyond that form of writing life which leads to words . . . .

The chief difference, then, between the older American writing and the new is that between writing considered as a means to an end, sentences used as corridors leading to further rooms, and writing considered as an end to itself. The latter will seem limited only to readers who fail to realize that books contain not persons, places and things but words . . . .[5]

Just as Williams had, throughout the 1920's, berated authors who considered writing as philosophy or theology instead of as literature, so he continued his attempts to do "something new with the words." [6] His admiration for the techniques of Stein and Joyce directed his fiction, his own work in their media. Yet Williams was honest enough to maintain his own discipline: art must never copy anything, even other successful art. He had to find his own way—a way likely more simple and direct than Joyce's [7] and yet richer and more humane than Stein's. The results of his experiments in writing short stories show that Williams was as apt in using organic form here as he was in poetry. They also show that, for Williams, "the life" that most often comes alive in the telling is of a person he understands, admires, or even loves. Although many of his stories were written during the 1930's, most of them are neither cynical nor dispirited. More of them reveal what the poet was to declare a decade later: "damned if I do not believe you find the greatest tenderness only among the most coarse." [8]

Early Fiction

Despite much talk of Williams' easy use of autobiographical elements in his fiction, his earliest stories are strained and self-conscious. The doctor-poet who appears frequently as narrator or participant is not the Williams we have come to expect. In later writing the doctor is comparatively unobtrusive; in contrast, the use Williams makes of that persona in his first published fiction, "Three Professional Studies" (1919), which opens with "The Doctor":

> I go in one house and out of another practicing my illicit trade of smelling, seeing, hearing, touching, tasting, weighing . . . . I am a young man, I am in perfect health, I am agile, good-looking. I do not smoke since it drugs the intelligence; I want all my reactions . . . .[9]

After declaring that he needs no "courage" to write and to practice medicine, Williams next describes two cases, two "everyday" problems of which he makes both literary use and medical (the "professional" of the title can well be ambivalent). "Mrs. M." and "Something" describe women who do show courage of a sort; yet that is not the connection Williams makes. His emphasis is on the doctor's reactions to these

women and their situations—and in 1919 his reaction is one of near
disgust:

> The children dig into the mush and chew it off the spoons. The largest
> boy age eight glances sidewise, sees mother is not looking, shovels out a
> spoonful from brother's dish. My God do they like it? Haven't they
> enough? Screams. Mother rushes at him, slaps his face. The children
> do not even know I am in the room.[10]

Perhaps a more pervasive impression is that of Williams' self-consciousness. Attention is on the doctor, not the patient, as the ending of the last
sketch indicates: "I walk out of the back door, I lift my nose. I smell
the wind." [11]

"Danse Pseudomacabre" (1920) followed a similar approach: two
brief anecdotes of death, connected only through the doctor's use of
them as material. The transitory paragraph between the two echoes a
passage from *Kora in Hell,* the idea of life as a dance, here subverted
to the deaths as "danse." The second vignette, much the stronger of the
two, concerns a baby dying from meningitis. Instead of focusing on the
doctor, this story ends with the ironic revelation of the probable cause
of the child's disease, its baptism. In its use of understatement and the
rhythms of actual speech, this closing paragraph foreshadows much of
Williams' later fiction:

> It is an infection?
> Yes.
> My wife is Catholic—not I. She had him for baptism. They pour water
> from a can on his head, so. It runs down in front of him, there where
> they baptize all kinds of babies, into his eye perhaps. It is a funny thing.[12]

In 1923 Williams published "Three Letters," another story with an
episodic structure, and "The Accident," which, although it begins with
a death, assumes as subject a much less weighty incident. The latter
is in many ways the beginning of Williams' concentration on unimpor-
tant but real happenings. As he was to write,

> a mere "thrilling" account of an occurrence from daily life, a transcrip-
> tion of a fact, is not of itself and for that reason a short story. You get
> the fact, it interests you for whatever reason; of that fact you make,
> using words, a story. A thing. A piece of writing.[13]

In "The Accident," the setting is spring. A child falls down. The sympathy evoked by his dirty face brings six factory workers into the story. But, again characteristic of Williams' avoidance of "moral," this sympathy in no way changes the child's world. Neither does it unite the observers. It simply exists, and the child recovers by himself.

In most of his earliest stories, Williams as doctor-poet is himself the narrator. But as he writes more fiction, he begins to use other points of view. His employment of a narrator other than the doctor becomes an important device: it allows him to avoid either a conventional moral judgment or a reaction consistent with the doctor's persona. It also gives him the chance to use various idioms, a means to display what he has learned from his years of "listening." Most important, the interplay between patient and doctor serves a valuable function in itself, that of supplying a wider social context for the story proper. One of Williams' primary concerns in his fiction is presenting a full story. Although he defines the story form as that which raises "one particular man or woman . . . to the distinction of being an individual," [14] he criticizes Gertrude Stein's "Melanctha" (even while admiring it immensely) because it does not include a sense of the whole:

> "Melanctha" is a thrilling clinical record of the life of a colored woman in the present-day United States, told with directness and truth. It is without question one of the best bits of characterization produced in America. It is universally admired. This is where Stein began. But for Stein to tell a story of that sort, even with the utmost genius, was not enough *under the conditions in which we live,* since by the very nature of its composition such a story does violence to *the larger scene which should be portrayed.*[15]

In many of his stories, Williams succeeds in this wider purpose. Whether his sense of the times and conditions comes from his inclusive detail ("two large iron double beds standing there as if they had been two boats floating in a small docking space, no carpet, no other furniture"); from his rare understanding of people ("What you gonna do to my mother? the boy asked"); or from his constant use of seemingly real speech ("Oh, he makes me tired. He says it's all my fault"), Williams does quickly establish setting and cultural level. The narrator is not only a vehicle for getting a story told but an integral part of the circumstance which has produced the story. It is not surprising, then, that the story itself can often be told very briefly because Williams has already provided much background for the characters to come and for their behavior.

The Knife of the Times

That this collection of short stories was published in 1932 gives some explanation for its title. Williams' patients were particularly hard hit by the Depression; he is to write his most socially aware prose and poetry during this decade. "The plight of the poor in a rich country, I wrote it down as I saw it. The times—that was the knife that was killing them." [16] In Williams' 1949 lectures on the short story, he describes in detail his own impetus toward writing stories on more than an accidental basis. In 1932, he recalls, the story form seemed viable because of "the heterogeneous character of the people":

> I lived among these people. I know them and saw the essential qualities (not stereotype), the courage, the humor (an accident), the deformity, the basic tragedy of their lives—and the *importance* of it. You can't write about something unimportant to yourself. I was involved.
>
> That wasn't all. I saw how they were maligned by their institutions of church and state—and "betters." I saw how all that was acceptable to the ear about them maligned them. I saw how stereotype falsified them.
>
> Nobody was writing about them, anywhere, as they ought to be written about. There was no chance of writing anything acceptable, certainly not salable, about them.
>
> It was my duty to raise the level of consciousness, not to say discussion, of them to a higher level, a higher plane. Really to tell.
>
> Why the short story? Not for a sales article but as I had conceived them. The briefness of their chronicles, its brokenness and heterogeneity —isolation, color. A novel was unthinkable.
>
> And so to the very style of the stories themselves.[17]

"My duty," "involved," "maligned," "falsified"—Williams leaves no question about his motives for writing these stories. Feeling so deeply as he does about many of his subjects, the amazing thing is his ability to avoid the maudlin or proletarian literature which permeated the 1930's. Williams' devices for objectifying the story (a variety of narrators, the seemingly tough doctor and tougher milieu, the sharp focus and usually brief narration) and his preference for the *telling* episode over the merely exciting help him avoid most of the common traps. But it is interesting that, of Williams' three story collections, *The Knife of the Times* is the most slanted toward evoking a reader's sympathy for the situation of its characters.

The title story, for example, describes a Lesbian relationship. As lead-off story, such an episode will receive disproportionate emphasis and falsely leads critics such as J. E. Slate to conclude that "many Williams stories deal[ing] with sexual perversion," [18] when very few do. The title implies that circumstances affected Ethel and Maura's behavior; yet such inference is false. They have sufficient money; in fact, they meet as Ethel comes to New York to join her sister, who has been abroad. Told in third person, the story is less immediate than most of those in the collection. Williams recalls the impetus for this story: "to find a woman telling me about her experience intrigued me. She was not shocked, just amazed." [19] Similar weaknesses plague "The Sailor's Son," the story of homosexuals. Again told to the doctor by a woman, the tale of Manuel is also fragmentary. Perhaps the best of these sexually oriented stories is "A Descendant of Kings," the somewhat ironic account of beachboy Stewie, who has been reared by his fierce grandmother to be a stud. "There was damn little for him to do," never having finished the eighth grade, being used by numerous women until his sexual prowess ended. Williams uses an omniscient point of view here, to make the boy more understandable. In many respects Stewie is a victim of "the knife of the times."

More typical of Williams' later stories, and more compatible blendings of technique and theme, are "Mind and Body," "A Visit to the Fair," and "Pink and Blue." In the monologue and dialogue of the first story Williams characterizes Ingrid, the Norwegian woman whose identity comes to us through the physical symptoms of her illness as well as through her speech. Her reminiscence and philosophy show a complex woman, seemingly at great variance to her deformed husband. Much like Corydon of *Paterson* IV, the woman has few appealing qualities. Because her depiction is important to Williams (he refers to a similar character in the *Autobiography* and also in *Paterson* V), she presents an interesting artistic problem. How to draw an unsympathetic person so that she attains dignity? As he did so often in other writings, Williams relied on Ingrid's speech: "I have found," she says with surprising gentleness, "that we must live for others, that we are not alone in the world" (48).

In the friendship of Bess and Mr. Tibbet lies an illustration of this same need. "A Visit to the Fair" is one of Williams' strongest arguments for people to enjoy life, to be treated as though they have value. Again, the camouflage of woman as narrator; again, the possibly objectionable situation, one man escorting another man's wife; again, the sense of the poverty of the 1930's.

"Pink and Blue" continues the depiction of the times, here with brides like Belle Tompkins whose simple depravity leads her from husband to husband in search of social approval. Again using an observer-narrator, Williams manages to depict lonely people in their misdirected search for love (Cupid's Clubs, violence, sex). The poverty here is personal, spiritual, as well as financial.

The best story of this first collection, perhaps Williams' "Melanctha," is the longer "Old Doc Rivers." [20] For one of the first times in this period of his fiction, Williams narrates the story himself. He knew Doc Rivers and in him saw much to admire—dope, junkie, drunk that he became. As Williams presents him, "confident, a little disdainful, but not unfriendly. He knew them all," Doc Rivers' life was his work. He would go "anywhere, anytime, for anybody." Yet something was missing, and Rivers became the victim of the culture he was ostensibly saving. In a description much like his view of Poe, Williams summarizes:

> He was far and away by natural endowment the ablest individual of our environment, a serious indictment against all the evangelism of American life which I most hated—at the same time a man trying to fill his place among those lacking the power to grasp his innate capabilities . . . .
>
> Intelligence he had and force—but he also had nerves, a refinement of the sensibilities that made him, though able, the victim of the very things he best served (89–90).

A fitting conclusion to the collection in that Rivers represents the best of men cut down by the times, this story is also Williams' attempt to portray that life with which he too was involved. In his various methods of characterizing the older doctor, he is able to include the operations they shared, patients they had in common, and the social milieu which surrounded them both. Understanding Rivers is easy for Williams because he too can feel the waste, the impact of city life ("we have lost touch with ourselves"), and "the awful fever of overwork" (102).

Williams tries hard to create sympathy for Rivers. He draws from actual medical records, conversations with other doctors and patients, and his own knowledge, always creating scenes painstakingly to give us the rough yet kindly doctor. "He was one of the few that ever in these parts knew the meaning of all, to give himself completely" (103). And yet the story is in no sense a paean. For, once well into his dope habit, Rivers is a real danger to his patients. It is then that his society deifies him, reacting to the legends and the wild charisma rather than to his formerly valuable qualities ("always the wrong reasons," as Williams said about Poe's acceptance).

A "pure product of America" like Elsie of the 1923 poem, Doc Rivers went "crazy" in his own way, and Williams closes the long narrative with an image reminiscent of the ending of "To Elsie." [21] The story of Rivers has begun with the one-word sentence, "Horses." Williams emphasizes then the satisfaction a man received from his dependence on the horse and how quickly changed was that simplicity with the coming of the car. The story ends, ironically, with Rivers being driven out in his car, holding one of his wife's Blue poms on his lap, "for in those days he himself never sat at the wheel" (105). Rivers was a man, yes, but a man out of control.

Life Along the Passaic River

Williams' strongest collection of stories is the second, published in 1938 after *Blast* had used many of the stories in 1934 and 1935.[22] Using an episodic narrative structure much like that of "The Colored Girls of Passenack—Old and New," Williams relishes the anecdotes and details of that life both in the opening title story and in "World's End," the closing piece. Most of the other stories—"Jean Beicke," "The Girl with a Pimply Face," "A Face of Stone"—treat individually the same kinds of character in the doctor-oriented narratives that are Williams' forte. It is as if only the size and shape of the story determined its structure, whether it fitted into the longer sequences as an episode or stood on its own as a full story. As Williams wrote, "The short story consists of one single flight of the imagination, complete: up and down." [23]

The tone of these stories, and of the collection as a whole, differs radically from that of *The Knife of the Times*. "Colored Girls" is one of the few stories in the earlier collection that do not berate the culture of the 1930's. *Life Along the Passaic River,* for the most part, uses understanding rather than vindication as its dominant tone. The role of the title story is to establish the kind of life in question; the subsequent stories illustrate the bravery or humor or solidarity of that life; and the closing story summarizes it all, with a tweak of the nose for the traditional source of strength in a culture like this, its religion.

Like the scenario for a movie, "Life Along the Passaic River" zooms in on "a spot of a canoe filled by the small boy who no doubt made it . . . west of the new Third Street Bridge, midstream" (109). Williams is at home here, in the details of the town bordering the river, the description of the young boy and others like him. He moves to the men lined up, waiting for work; and then picks out a few and gives us dialogue from the hitchhiker and the tough six-footer. Next he swings to describe the young suicide at the morgue, five months pregnant with twins. "If you can make sense out of that, go to it. It's all right to be wise, but you got to watch that too. There's no way to learn it easy" (113).

Williams' compassion colors the portraits of this life that he knows so well. He has dropped the device of having someone other than the doctor narrate the story, perhaps because he is following the same pattern he has taken in poetry: maturity and command of techniques enable him to use "I" effectively, with no hedges, no subterfuge. This is truly the doctor's view of his people. The tone is lightly ironic, almost sardonic. [24] "Further downstream at the County Bridge," the story progresses, and Williams remarks none too slyly, "It's an eye opener what you have time for these days." Each character we meet is out of work, lost, involved in crime because there's nothing else; yet in the mass of these men, Williams finds those of nobility and honor.

The persona's language is an apt cover for his reactions to the characters. "Swell looking muscles. What for?" "All you gotta do is rake in the old coin. Is that so?" The question undercutting the initial assumption, the reliance on vernacular (but rarely on slang), the short statement—all contribute to the terse idiom that seems to characterize the narrator. Such an idiom is, of course, highly effective when broken.

"A Night in June" illustrates a turn from the brusque to the gentle. The tired doctor, delivering a child to a woman he hasn't even remembered as a former patient, is brought through a long night to this realization:

> With my left hand steering the child's head, I used my ungloved right hand outside her bare abdomen to press upon the fundus. The woman and I then got to work. Her two hands grabbed me at first a little timidly about the right wrist and forearm. Go ahead, I said. Pull hard. I welcomed the feel of her hands and the strong pull. It quieted me in the way the whole house had quieted me all night.
>
> This woman in her present condition would have seemed repulsive to me ten years ago—now, poor soul, I see her to be as clean as a cow that calves. The flesh of my arm lay against the flesh of her knee gratefully. It was I who was being comforted and soothed (142).

After this profession of love for the experience, Williams again avoids the sentimental by returning quickly to the business at hand, putting drops in the baby's eyes, burying the afterbirth, taking count of the other children. The closing scene similarly rests on that objective detail which draws attention away from the doctor:

> How many is that? I asked the other woman. Five boys and three girls, she said. I've forgotten how to fix a baby, she went on. What shall I do? Put a little boric acid powder on the belly button to help dry it up? (143)

This particular story, one of the most direct recountings of Williams' experiences as a doctor, cannot help but suggest the 1919 "Something" (see p. 106). We are struck with the difference in Williams' attitude toward the suffering women. The woman of the earlier story he described as if she were a block of wood, a "thing" as the title suggests: "Oh. Agh. Ah—Hold this. Hold her head. She subsides into bovine passivity. Trembles a little like a cow about to be slaughtered. . . . What is this woman?"[25] No later story except "A Face of Stone" approaches this tone; but since it is a study of the doctor's gradual initiation into understanding, there are more differences than similarities.

"Four Bottles of Beer" is another central story, important thematically and technically.[26] Much in keeping with the doctor's attitude in "A Night in June," the narrator-doctor admires the woman whose child is ill. Like the later Clara in *Many Loves,* this mother questions the doctor about his personal life ("Does she cook for you?/ Yes./ And you eat it?/ Why yes./ I couldn't eat nigger cooking"). Williams likes the openness of the young Polish woman. He leaves after his call with the four bottles of home brew and the accomplishment of having used only dialogue throughout the story. Even the opening is the woman's greeting, "He's asleep." Stories such as this give credence to Williams' description of his stories as being "written in the form of a conversation which I was partaking in."[27]

Several other stories from this second collection are entirely dialogue. Often, these are the particularly short accounts, similar in effect to the group of short poems collectively titled "Detail." Long interested in the language as spoken, Williams creates a variety of effects by changing narrators—his mother, an ex-serviceman, the many patients. True to his belief that a man's language is a way into his character, Williams shapes some stories around the conversation: the story opens with "Hello" and closes with "Goodbye." Structurally, Williams can do little more to stress the importance of the characters' effects on one another.

For Williams, fiction was a way to re-create a genuine existence, perhaps his own as well as that of the other characters in his stories. As he reminisced about the 1938 collection, "The subject matter is the same as that of the earlier stories but I had matured as a writer. I was much freer. I could say what I had to say."[28] And what Williams "had to say" was about his "townspeople." He no longer considered himself an oracle to his patients; he too had learned humility. As he wrote in his *Autobiography:*

> They had no knowledge and no skill at all. They flunked out, got jailed, got "Mamie" with child, and fell away, if they survived, from their perfections.
>
> There again, a word: their perfections. They were perfect, they seem to have been born perfect, to need nothing else. They were there, living before me . . . (288).

Jack O'Brien in "Under the Greenwood Tree" is a good illustration of Williams' admiration. A handyman, usually down and out, O'Brien wins the doctor's respect because he "lives uncomplaining. Self respecting. . . . It's the way he rides evenly over the times. The way he takes the weather" (231). O'Brien's story is one of the few Williams prefaces with explanation, a paragraph interesting for its statement about both Williams and O'Brien:

> The chief cultural influence in a community is not always self apparent. If, as Keyserling says: localism alone can lead to culture (and this I give my life willingly to experience and to prove) Jack O'Brien is to me one of the princes of the world that I know (225).

Time and time again Williams' stories praise the characters who swim against the current. The "savage brat" of "The Use of Force," Belle Tomkins in "Pink and Blue," Margaret and Helen from "The Farmers' Daughters," "Jean Beicke," "The Girl with a Pimply Face," and many others share the quality Williams once described as "Toughminded. Tough. To be able to take it," with a quick qualification that the best way to take it is to be "soft enough, yielding enough." [29]

Technically, emphasizing character tends to strip much material from the episode. In Williams' stories there is seldom any preliminary description: a patient enters, the phone rings, the doctor enters a house. The conflict is identified early, that the labor is difficult or the patient, hostile. Description of even the central character is minimized; in one case we hear about "ugly bunches of varicose veins" rather than about a face. Most stories move quickly to the end because Williams focuses on single episodes (a "brush stroke" rather than a picture).[30] Often, endings are incomplete. They answer the central conflict rather than including all the implied points.

Mona Van Duyn takes her cue from the title Williams first gave his collected stories, *Make Light of It*. She relates the title to his prose technique, "The actual direction of the stories is almost always 'made light of' and this off-hand effect is accomplished through . . . the casual dropping of the crucial insight along the way, while the story hurries on to end in non-symbolic detail." She also points out Williams' "cutting across the main line of the story with both seemingly and genuinely extraneous detail." [31]

Later Stories

Beer and Cold Cuts, the third group of stories Williams included in his 1950 collection, contains several major pieces and a number of fragmentary glimpses of the people he loved. "Ancient Gentility" describes the old Italian migrant sharing his innate dignity with his snuff. "Comedy Entombed" refers to another spirited woman, this one undergoing a miscarriage. Several of the stories are as much "Exercises in the Variable Foot" as his late sequence of poems: "Above the River," "In Northern Waters," "Frankie," "The Final Embarrassment," "The Good Old Days," and particularly "Verbal Transcription—6 A.M." The latter story is a one-page masterpiece of a wife's monologue after her husband has suffered a heart attack. Another impressive story is "The Red Head." "I'm going to have a baby!" the twelve-year-old girl repeats. "And then she'd sob and blow her nose and they'd walk on and on, round and round the block . . . the two girls in front and the two boys a few paces back of them" (283–284). The terror in the scene is framed by society's view, "They're so cute," and underlined by the doctor's concern. "Where can they turn for advice if we cut them off?" In two pages Williams evokes a convincing picture of the trapped adolescents—and their unresponsive culture.

That some of Williams' late short stories do not reach the quality of those written in the 1930's suggests, more than any technical deficiency, his change of emphasis. After 1938, short fiction is less interesting to him because most of his energy is going into the Stecher novels, the plays, and *Paterson.* Just as Williams' short poems were try pieces for his late longer work, so the short story led him to the more inclusive shapes to come: as he saw Joyce's progress, *"Dubliners to Stephen Hero to Ulysses to Finnegans Wake.* I say that it took off from the short story. It makes a delightful Field of Mars—for exercises in the Manual of Arms. I think that's its chief value." [32] Yet the techniques of these stories were to serve Williams well in his later work, largely because his rationale for fiction was so expansive.

In 1949 he defined the objectives of the short story: "The art would be, by the style, to wed the subject to its own time and have it live there and then. Have it live." [33] Reminiscent of Henry James's concept of freedom in the novel, this suggestion is detailed by correspondingly free corollary principles. Speaking of Kipling, O. Henry, Kafka, Poe, and Hemingway, Williams asks, "What is the common quality in all these changing styles?" In answer, he refutes the usual assumption of "plot" ("not a stereotyped snaring of the interest, a filling in of necessary documentary details and a smash finish") and goes on to list two particulars of the structure he admires: (1) "They all have a frame—like a picture" and (2) "There is a punch, if you like. But . . . maybe today we'll shift the emphasis and get a punch from having no punch. Maybe the buildup and the documentation will be merely hinted" (299). The object of the form of a story is to be "natural," Williams contends.

In these remarks, Williams emphasizes action rather than description: "It is not to place adjectives, it is to learn to employ the verbs . . . so that the pieces move naturally—and watch, often breathlessly, what they do" (302). As illustration Williams recalls Thomas Mann's "Death in Venice," a story more passive in its apparent plot structure than most; "to take decay, despair and elevate the details to an action, to greatness"—that act had Williams' admiration.

"Try all sorts of effects," advises Williams the craftsman. "You can try various modes of writing—more freely. . . . The short story is a wonderful medium for prose experimentation." Once again coming to the heart of his approach to literature, Williams suggests that the writer "try to follow the action of some characters you can *imagine.* . . . Crawl into the man's head and how get inside a woman's head, being a man? That is the work of the imagination" (305). Actual dialogue is important in re-creating the character, as is a thorough knowledge of the subjects. But as for any preconception about what kind of characters should be the subject for fiction, Williams only questions, "The hero? Who is a hero? The peasantry? There is none. Men and women faithful to a belief? What belief?" (302). Williams was also concerned with the writer's tendency to oversimplify character. In several of his later stories he experimented to show the complexities of characters who could have been one-dimensional. Helen and Margaret, "The Farmers' Daughters"; the hitchhiker in "Around the World Fliers"; the unnamed woman in "Inquest." Of the latter story Williams noted,

> Most of us are not individuals any more but parts of something. We
> are no one of us "all" of anything . . . . So why not write of three
> people as one? That's what my story tried to do, make itself more than
> one, three in one. Imagine a woman looking at herself three ways (302).

The woman waiting for the bus prompts three characterizations, one
of a factory worker, another of an instructor in philosophy (a little
drunk), a third of a dancer—all women somewhat less than virtuous.
The last two pages present the woman's relationship with "good old
Doc" who advises her to "quit it" but does what he can to help her
out of her promiscuity.

"The Burden of Loveliness" dwells on the same need, of a woman
to give her sex freely. These stories of the 1940's point increasingly
toward Williams' concern with the virgin-whore distinction of *Paterson* V. What constitutes virtue, the giving or the withdrawing?
M. L. Rosenthal describes this recurring theme as Williams'

> special interest in women—what they are really like, how they grow
> into their maturity, their sources of strength and weakness, their real
> relationship to the oversimplified visions of male sexuality . . . . It is
> at once a matter of the normal erotic range of interest and of curiosity
> and of something else, a romantic sense of mystery pursued through the
> unorthodox methods of the realist.[34]

Striking evidence of this interest, I think, is the fact that "The
Knife of the Times" and "The Farmers' Daughters," those stories
which open and close the collected stories, are much the same. Two
women, incapable of being understood by the men who love them,
find solace in each other. That the lesbian relationship in the earlier
story has given way to a limitless friendship in the later suggests
Williams' move away from the sensational elements in his culture. In
"The Farmers' Daughters," Helen's love for Margaret is in no way
selfish. Helen gains nothing but sorrow for her affection. Both the
doctor and Helen admire the whore, for, as the doctor tells her, "in
many ways you are the best of us, the most direct, the most honest—
yes, and in the end, the most virtuous" (371). Murdered finally by
her young husband of four months, Margaret was Williams' last
short-story character. He had worked fifteen years on the long story,
retitling his collected stories after the final version. In it, he seemed

to have unified many single impressions of the shorter sketches through the years. In the stories of Helen and Margaret—first written separately, and then in several different versions of the final—we surely find the evidences of "the knife of the times"—a times that Williams found, to his sorrow, went beyond the physical poverty of the Depression and into the spiritual poverty of the prosperity to come. In what kind of culture, the story asks, can a man shoot his wife in the back and have the death be labeled "accidental"? And, more important, in what kind of culture can a man shoot his wife in the back?

"No one came to the funeral but her family and me," Helen tells the doctor after it is all over. "They didn't open the casket. There were no flowers beside the bunch of red roses I'd sent her" (373).

A letter from Margaret has stated earlier, phrased with Williams' sad irony, that "New Orleans was beautiful, so much better than New York to live in" (372). This suggestion of the betrayal of place, one of Williams' principal tenets, brings to mind his early praise of Kenneth Burke's stories. They were effective, Williams thought, because Burke was writing from his own knowledge, his own location: "From the shapes of men's lives imparted by the places where they have experience, good writing springs." [35] Or, as Faulkner, another writer Williams admired, once phrased it: "Art is simpler than people think because there is so little to write about. All the moving things are eternal in man's history. . . . " [36]

CHAPTER NINE

Canvas I: Longer Fiction

THERE is little question that the 1930's were years of transition for Williams. In retrospect several changes become apparent: (1) his turn to prose with the same control, the same idiomatic ease, that he had shown in his poems nearly twenty years before; (2) his deepening awareness of people and their problems; (3) his search for his life's meaning through relationships with people rather than through investigations of American history, as in his writing of the 1920's; (4) his increasing dissatisfaction with the shorter forms of literature (short poems, one-act plays, stories), leading him to novels, full-length plays, and longer poems like "Two Pendants for the Ears" and, of course, *Paterson;* (5) his insistence that, particularly in troubled times, art is the only means to truth. In a 1941 essay, he directed the artist, "Write to correct lies." And he defined *truth* for the artist as "that which permits all questions to be answered freely in the unrestricted terms of his art." [1] Williams' poems show his "unrestricted terms": long lines, short lines; staggered stanza patterns, mobile arrangements. The poems of the late 1930's are varied and sometimes ragged. But despite their various shapes they evince Williams' basic concern with mankind. His elegy for D. H. Lawrence shows Williams' grief for all mankind as well as the poet:

> Poor Lawrence
> Worn with a fury of sad labor
> to create summer from
> spring's decay. English
> women. Men driven not to love
> but to the ends of the earth.
>
> (*CEP,* 361)

His poems to "Adam," his father, and "Eve," his mother, continue the questioning of men's lives, all foreshadowing the "divorce" themes to come into full play in *Paterson*. In "Adam" he pictures the stoic Englishman growing up in the tropics,

> Naked on a raft
> he could see the barracudas
> waiting to castrate him
> so the saying went—
> Circumstances take longer—

The poem is filled with images of cold and darkness, love used for "a purpose cold as ice," men waiting for their "inevitable end," knowing that "never,/ never, never would/ peace come" (372).

Working through this bitterness is to be one of the processes of *Paterson* and the shorter poems of the 1940's. As Williams recalled in 1958, "We spoke earlier about learning about poetry. In this phase I was learning about life." [2] Yet, as always, Williams the artist was riding herd over Williams the humanitarian. How to feel, and still to control? As he wrote in the opening issue of *Contact*, 1932:

> There is no sense in slobbering at the mouth over humanity and writing that way. We die every day, cheated—and with written promises of great good in our hands. To plead a social cause, to split a theory, to cry out at an evil which we all partake of—gladly; that's not writing. The words themselves must stand and fall as men. A writer has no use for theories or propaganda, he has use for but one thing, the word that is possessing him at the moment he writes . . . . [3]

That Williams the craftsman could label *Finnegans Wake* "incomprehensible" gives some indication of his technical direction at this time.[4] Clear in style, quick in pace, Williams' writings during the 1930's contain few discussions of "how to write," few aesthetic themes. Whereas *Kora in Hell, Spring and All,* and *The Great American Novel* reflect an apparent disdain for a wide audience, Williams tried earnestly now to make himself understood, but at no sacrifice of art. With the *avant-garde* magazines dominated by political writing, much of it inferior in quality, Williams remained adamant about the level of his production. One of the most interesting products of this concern with life, times, and art is his 1937 novel *White Mule*. An effective mixture of old themes and new, the book is much closer to Williams' short stories than to his earlier novels, *TGAN* and *A Voyage to Pagany*.

White Mule

    This story of Flossie Herman and her family had its genesis too during the fruitful 1927 winter.* Williams' drafts of the Pischak story include not only the birth scene already quoted (see p. 91) but the description of a mother very much like Gurlie Stecher in *White Mule*. What made Williams change his focus from the Pischak-Fairfield matrix to that of his own wife's family may have been his separation from her during the year of these beginnings. One is reminded of his statement to Kenneth Burke in 1933, "I have gradually made enough notes, here and there, to keep me busy clearing them up and developing them for a long time after I retire—if ever. I should dread an old age divorced from the thoughts and actions of my more vigorous years." [5]

Once begun, the novel grew by chapters because Richard Johns was publishing it serially in *Pagany* (from 1930 to 1932). In fact, Williams gave Johns credit for keeping him at the book in the press of his other work. (The reciprocal encouragement between Johns for *White Mule* and Williams for the magazine *Pagany* is touchingly described in the recent *A Return to Pagany*.) Williams reminisced that he was like Dickens, "always just up to the publication deadline." [6] The chapter organization—each section complete in itself—suggests this kind of pressure; yet there is no question about the unity of the book. What is more important than the chapter deadlines in Williams' comment about the novel is his mention of Dickens. For *White Mule* is in many ways reminiscent of a *David Copperfield* (and *In the Money* of a *Bleak House*). Williams in his own way is much concerned with the workings of society, the abuses of it, and consequently the story is as much that of Joe Stecher, the migrant printer, as it is of his daughter Flossie.

We must also consider that one of Williams' most endearing traits was his receptiveness. Consistently ready to listen, he was usually humble before articulate men. His correspondence with the New

---

*Parts of it may have been written earlier. Williams suggests that some drafts were made in 1923 (*A Return to Pagany*, p. 127).

Jersey schoolteacher David Lyle; his deference to Pound, Louis Zukofsky, Robert Lowell; his gratefulness at being sent poems by young writers—Williams' "search" only broadened with the years to include all of his culture.[7] His fascination with the Joe Stecher story in the *White Mule* trilogy is symptomatic of that quest to understand. Business was foreign to Williams. Interested throughout his life in strikes, unions, and the more sociological ramifications of industry, he grew increasingly aware of the economic and political aspects during the Depression. Pound was sending him Social Credit literature; David Lyle was discoursing on economics;[8] he was himself writing for proletarian magazines, and one assumes that he read at least the issues that his own stories and poems appeared in. His poems during the 1930's also suggest his absorption in economics and business, though usually from a personal point of view. Given Williams' growing interest in economics, the emphasis the trilogy comes to take—consistently away from the baby Flossie and toward the ideology of her mother, Gurlie, and father, Joe—seems hardly accidental.

With his customary awareness of what character is on stage when, Williams gives nearly one-third of *White Mule's* twenty-two chapters to Joe and his business dealings. In the other chapters, which focus ostensibly on Flossie the baby, Joe stands as the major character in relation to her. On the opening page, the scene of Flossie's birth, it is Joe who says, "Don't you think you'd better cover it up so it won't catch cold?" Gurlie, the disappointed mother, had just made one of her blunt if honest remarks, "Take it away. I don't want it. All this trouble for another girl."[9]

From this initial characterization of the parents, *White Mule* moves predictably. Gurlie, the acquisitive, proud Scandinavian, demands that Joe make more money. Joe, the stoic and equally proud German, does. In the daring of Joe's business venture lies the thread of plot for both *White Mule* and *In the Money*. Trying to win the government printing contract away from his present employer, Joe confronts black lists, sabotage, possible murder. His danger parallels that of the baby who is delicate from birth, yet is cared for only by the inept schoolgirls her mother employs. The suspense—and there is suspense—is real, if understated. Williams recounts some events in retrospect; others are depicted as they happen but without emotion, often in Joe's laconic speech.

Just as Joe is struggling to succeed economically, Flossie is struggling to stay alive. She lives through infection, whooping cough, general weakness; and then she faces summer in New York. Luckily Gurlie takes the baby and her older sister Lottie to Vermont, so Flossie lives. (Gurlie's most endearing quality is her love of the outdoors. The chance to leave New York, for whatever reason, is readily taken.) It is during their absence from Joe that his own struggle comes to a head, and here Williams' artistry in his straight, direct prose is evident. By separating Joe from the family, he makes both appear more vulnerable. Joe is alone during the tense months of leaving his job and readying his own printing shop, waiting for the bids to be opened. Similarly, Flossie and Lottie exist without Joe. By alternating between Joe's scenes and those of the children surviving as best they can in Vermont, Williams keeps the attention clearly on Joe.

The story is Joe's also, by default (reviewers agreed that Gurlie is a hateful woman [10]). Although there is some rationale for Gurlie's selfishness and although Williams himself liked the woman's prototype,[11] his methods of characterizing her allow us little sympathy. Our view is external; we see Gurlie laughing too loudly, talking bluntly, scolding her "little Dutchie." In contrast, we know Joe's thoughts. Williams devotes several chapters to Joe's introspection, once just after Flossie's birth, again after he has made his business move. In each case, Joe fits the mold of Williams' traditional hero: questioning, intuitive rather than logical, stubborn. After Flossie's birth, Joe muses about American economics:

> America, he thought as he sauntered, the United States of America—money. Without money, nothing. Money. Men who work should have enough money. In Berlin men worked. Here they had strikes—to get more money. A few worked. That's not the way. Everybody should work. Everybody should work the best that he knows how . . . . men should work—hard, well, honestly. And they should be paid for it, well paid (13).

As immigrant, Joe questions the ideals of his chosen country, but his reproof is tinged with sorrow. Like the men of Williams' *Grain* essays, Joe dreams about America's promises, admiring most man's right to fulfill himself in work: "do it well, to see it perfect, to have it come out best, to enjoy the work for that" (15). Unfortunately

America in the 1930's no longer offered men the right to work. Day after day Williams faced destitute patients, people eager to work, too proud to take charity, failed—so Williams saw it—by their country. And yet those who did have work were striking. Better economists than Williams were stumped. Joe Stecher's quandary—although in a story set nearly thirty years earlier—is in some respects typical: held down by his present employers, disillusioned by the greediness of the unions, Joe feels he has no recourse but to go into business for himself. In becoming a capitalist, Joe seemingly denies the years he has worked actively in the printers' union. And while he criticizes men who live from the stock market, he deviates strangely from company loyalty when he starts his own firm, with a somewhat atypical $50,000 backing. Yet the impression Williams gives, despite the "facts" of the business deal, is that Joe is "the pure artisan, the man who has not yet been alienated from the product of his labor and who thinks of money as the reward of labor and nothing else." [12]

Earlier in the book Joe has seen his fate. Caught between Gurlie's ambition and his own, he describes his life as "a battle for something without value at the cost of all that he knew of that was worth while" (20). After all his machinations, Joe's final recognition of his pride comes during a ball game. Here Williams used his most contrived juxtaposition, with Joe's thoughts triggered by the detailed descriptions of the game:

> Looks good, said Joe's neighbor. Thought he might put in a pinch hitter that time but I guess it worked out all right at that.
> Better take out some more insurance, thought Joe, while I have the chance. You never can tell (278).

Williams employs Joe's wry humor to good advantage as he thinks about possible sabotage, even attempts on his own life, in the midst of more routine business details. A line like "It was smart baseball, just the stuff Joe delighted to see" is followed by evidence of Joe's own "smartness," and the passage as a whole reinforces the earlier images of Stecher as a "smart Dutchie." The ball-game scene, Joe's last in the novel, builds to its climax with Joe walking toward the pitcher's mound after the game is over. The position of control, raised above the rest of the field, prompts him to think, "Nothing finer. But is it worth it?" His admiration is colored with uneasiness, for his close look has revealed things he had not noticed before. The tone is mildly ominous, and *In the Money* only intensifies the sense of foreboding.

The fact that *White Mule* ends with the chapter titled "The Ferry Children," showing Flossie and Lottie at their happiest as they play with the impoverished mountain children, is more substantiation for the tone of Williams' treatment of Joe's enterprise. Economic security means nothing to the Vermont farmers; yet their children thrive in their natural surroundings. Again the device of juxtaposition saves Williams from making any oversimplified generalizations.

Because the novel does begin and end with the children, and because Williams writes so convincingly about them, critics reacted largely to them. Only a few stressed Joe's part in the story, either as businessman or father. Perhaps it is this overemphasis of the baby's role that led readers to see *In the Money* (1940) as less satisfactory and *The Build Up* (1952) as a weak novel. Yet Williams had planned that the story would move toward Joe: "The third volume will end without the baby as a principal character. It has to. The social theories of yesterday finally become arthritic and Joe dies among their rigidities." [13]

It is interesting that in 1937 Williams was himself acting as critic to A. J. Cronin's *The Citadel,* another novel about doctors and ethics and love:

> What Dr. Cronin doesn't see is that, as Ezra Pound would say, it's money and its misappropriation and artificial scarcity that are at the back of our troubles, and that unless you see the thing through to its source you can see nothing.[14]

There is no question that Williams was troubled about economic philosophies during the 1930's. Pound was writing pamphlets for the Social Credit cause; Earle Davis, in his recent study of Pound and economics, lists Williams among the followers of Social Credit along with Gorham Munson, Archibald MacLeish, James Laughlin IV, and other writers.[15] *New Democracy* and the *New English Weekly,* Social Credit journals, contained essays by Pound and essays, poems, stories, and letters by Williams. The best-known evidence of Williams' agreement with Pound that the financial aristocracy ("usurers") must not control society [16] comes in *Paterson* with his accounts of SUM, Hamilton's plan to industrialize New Jersey. Yet, themes of selfish gain and waste occur throughout Williams' writings. He writes in 1934 of America's banks which had, by the time of Andrew Jackson, "succeeded in diverting every nickel of the government funds into their private coffers." About the practices of banks in his own century, Williams summarizes:

> Dizzily they conceded credits to allied corporate interests, at the same time calling small loans in order to pinch out the individual borrower, thus intrenching themselves in the monopoly and impoverishing the little man more and more until he should leave the field or take less and less in wages.[17]

Yet Williams the critic is always the optimist: "Usury is *not* inherent in Capitalism. . . . Neither Fascism nor Communism is necessary for the understanding and putting into practice of social justice in America *if* the brains of the country can be marshalled to face the problems involved."[18] This common motif in Williams' writings of the 1930's centers always on his complaint *"not* against government but against usurpation of government by a class, a group . . . which would subvert the freedom of the individual."[19]

Whether the economic pressure which exists is great or small, man dies just as quickly, Williams thinks, in "the living hell-stink of today." In *White Mule,* he is admittedly less concerned with banks and credit than with the Paul Herman–Joe Stecher story, but the culture as he presents it reflects what he was to call "the economic imbecilities of the age."[20]

In the Money

Williams' view of the novel was that it must be as free to find its shape as a story or a poem. Nevertheless, *White Mule* is structurally a more conventional novel than either of the books to follow. Attention focuses alternately on Joe's business and the baby's life, with only the visit from Uncle Oswald and the two Carmody scenes being in any way extraneous. With Oswald, as well as with the drunk Carmody and his patient wife, Williams attempts none-too-subtle contrasts for both Joe and Gurlie. But in the second novel, there are several characters worked in mostly because Williams wants to use the material, not because they are integral to the Stecher story. Old Dr. Mabbot who vaccinates Lottie and Flossie, the women behind the museum with their wonderfully mundane conversations, the young girls telling each other good night, the little girl in the red skating cap (an excerpt from the 1927 manuscript), Dan McColum the New York politician—as Williams says, "Some of the conversation was put down verbatim from things said to me by patients. . . . Bits here and there date back thirty years." [21]

The more leisurely development of the Joe Stecher plot here derives from this pattern of unhurried inclusion. Much less attention is given Flossie, partly because the old doctor's description in his pamphlet on the two-year-old is true: "A larval year," Dr. Mabbot terms it; "largely hidden from our view, it gives the mind its enduring form." [22] Williams focuses on Flossie only when her behavior is upsetting, indicating her changing attitudes toward her life. One of the most interesting scenes is the baby's fear of the dark in a strange room. This highly effective chapter comes just after Joe has met angrily with his former employers and just before the attempt on his life is made. Flossie's inarticulate cry of what Williams called the "unending misery of an unalterable world" (225) parallels Joe's own feeling as he confronts dishonesty and hostility as deep as the darkness of Flossie's room. Then, with his usual sense of proportion, Williams alleviates the tone by bringing in carefree Oswald, arms laden for the joyful Christmas.

Because the story in this second, longer book is primarily Joe's, and because it is close to being one of the Horatio Alger tales Williams considered too "pat," he makes greater use of the characters of Uncle Oswald and the various aunts to illustrate the charms of the "unsuccessful" people. When Joe is compared with Oswald, he falls short in many ways. Oswald, the loving giver, fills the house with beauty; the girls adore him. The easy life style of Aunts Olga and Hilda is also a decided contrast to that of the busy Gurlie, who can deposit her daughters for the summer and write not one letter during the months' absence. Although Williams is evidently trying to broaden his canvas (his 1937 "Visit with Tchelitchew" praises the wider view [23]), emphasis stays with Joe. Again through interior monologue as well as dialogue, Joe gives us the central conflict: single man in the hands of an uncaring society:

My policy! What else? My policy! Nothing works efficiently any more because of that idea. Church, government—the only thing that works is one man that pays attention to what he is doing and knows what to do about it . . . . Anybody could solve the troubles of the world in fifteen minutes—if people had good will—and somebody wasn't preventing it, for a profit. And for the satisfaction of establishing "my policies" (180–181).

For Joe, the support of his employees is the impetus that gives him confidence to continue—ironically so, since he has in one sense betrayed his own employer initially. When his press order is taken from him and his printing site condemned, he still goes on, knowing that he can deliver the product, once his people come to work for him. Joe's love of those people, illustrated by the scene with the all-too-human Miss Gregg, keeps him from the impersonality of the Wynnewood-Crossman executives. It is also the best explanation for the closing scene of the novel, Joe's tying plums on the new plum tree, to the delight of his daughters. Here Joe is only a loving and understanding father, trying to welcome children after their months in the country and knowing that the new house in the suburbs is less charming than it is strange. This is again Joe Stecher at his considerate best. Being "in the money" has not changed him.[24]

The Build Up and *The Autobiography*

Between the second book of the Stecher trilogy and the last came a dozen years of war, illness, and terrific production. The four books of *Paterson* were finally written and published, as were Williams' last short stories and the major plays. Williams was writing frantically, dashing off the autobiography in a winter, readying himself for his final great period of poetry. It is not surprising, therefore, that *The Build Up* is a somewhat different kind of novel, one with a broader scope, with some of the previous unhurried details telescoped into shorter episodes. Thomas Whitaker compares it to Williams' *Autobiography;* in fact, the two were written within a year of each other, covering many of the same events: "narrative blocks are shorter; tone is more anecdotal; there is more explicit commentary; and the pace is much more rapid."[25] While this comparison may apply to the last third of the novel, in which Williams summarizes the years 1907 to 1917, most of *The Build Up* continues in the pattern already established. Such scenes as young Lottie preening before a mirror in a locked bathroom, the Stechers' first musicale, the malicious Valentine, the rain-soaked pies—these well-defined episodes, interesting and amusing in themselves, fit together for a calculated composite effect.

Williams' procedure in this novel seems similar to his approach in his earlier books. As he had written in 1937 of *White Mule,* "Of course the story's invented. The principal characters in it are taken more or less from life and the incidents are, in the main, accounts I have heard of past happenings, but all the detail is my own." [26] For the writer to use "true" happenings and yet "invent" his own story places great emphasis on his method of that re-creation, his knowledge and use of "detail." Akin to what Williams saw as Shakespeare's greatness, he praises Ford Madox Ford's abilities in *Parade's End:* "In his very perception and love for the well-observed detail lies Ford's narrative strength . . . . his understanding of the particular." [27] So we have Oswald's painstaking work with the Christmas chains described as thoroughly as Joe's search for high-quality ink. The passion for detail stems from a greater impetus, Williams continues, that the novelist know his people: "The true test is his affection for them, top to bottom, a moral, not a literary attribute, his love of them, his wanting to be their Moses." [28] And as he concludes in a 1937 essay, "Without faith in humanity . . . there's no faith in art." [29]

Williams' emphasis on accurate detail is not, he contends, a way toward naturalism or even realism. He admires Djuna Barnes, Joyce, Cocteau, but criticizes "the 'plain' novel style—Anderson, Hecht, Bodenheim" because

> they are unobservant and thoughtless (too intent on the people and places and close stench) . . . . They are false, false as newspapers which lose everything among the news . . . .
>
> You've got to know—not as a journalist but as an understanding. The journalists see too much unrelated material. The understanding, sight, imagination creates the character and *sees* the material in relation to that . . . . the actual realism which we are used to and need . . . is important but accessory.[30]

The writer, then, employs the telling detail, ordered somehow under his own understanding to best express the life of the characters involved. Williams' concern with characterization dominated his theories of the novel, as well as of other forms of writing. In his 1936 libretto for the Washington opera, he established his "nonsequential" approach toward finding "the character center" (see p. 138).[31] One assumes Williams would have agreed with T. S. Eliot, who, in his Introduction to Barnes's *Nightwood,* defined the novel as "a book in which living characters are created and shown in significant relationships."[32] Plot, action, even scene, proceed from well-defined characters. As Williams had said a few years earlier, "Plot is like God: the less we formulate it the closer we are to the truth."[33]

For Williams in the early Stecher novels, the character of Joe Stecher is his "center." Although he sees Joe's ideology as obsolete, Williams still greatly admires him. His kindliness and consideration are described in the *Autobiography* as well as the novels; and his accidental death in 1930 brings to a close the life of a man who was, for Flossie, "her lifelong god and protector."[34] In the first two novels, Joe is at the height of his career; it is evident that Williams admires his daring. The third book, however, has finally to deal with the tragedies of Joe's life: the death of his only son; the scandal of Lottie's lover; greatest of all, Joe's pro-German sympathies during World War I and subsequent ostracism for those sympathies. As Williams wrote in the *Autobiography,* "It is incredible how much can happen in a few years—from happiness to disaster" (155). The understatement and irony of *White Mule* and *In the Money* are no longer adequate modes for expressing Joe's state of mind; Williams' problem is the technical one of either using Joe as central consciousness, varying his customary tones, or turning to other central figures. Williams chooses the latter: *The Build Up* has many foci.

Every member of the Stecher family becomes important, Lottie most of all. As the developing young woman, she gives Williams the chance to display his great understanding of how a woman thinks, behaves, loves. His portraits of Lottie in adolescence are as vivid and accurate as his depictions of Flossie as baby.

Gurlie, too, appears to better advantage in this novel than ever before. Given the means to establish her position in Riverdale, she becomes a positive force instead of a shrew. Flossie as the gentlest and youngest woman in the family gets less attention, serving as a reminder of Joe as well as a woman in her own right. While the other characters have been more fully developed, Joe's character has been inexplicably changed. He has lost much of his forcefulness, and bitterness marks his outlook. Williams scarcely mentions his business; he views him always in social and domestic situations. The introspection earlier used in characterizing Joe has given way to exterior observation and, in some passages, direct explication. Paul, the third child and first son, is the last member of the family. His birth scene is as memorable as Flossie's, though subsequent views of him are hurried.

Partly because of this diffuse focus, *The Build Up* is more a comedy of manners than the other novels are. Factually, of course, the Stechers' life takes them into wider circles than their own family. Then, too, Williams' attention, by 1952, had shifted from questions of economic philosophy to those of social interaction. As the poems of the 1950's show, his main interest lay in how a man existed with his fellow human beings, not what injustices a banking system perpetrated.

The real difficulty in writing *The Build Up*, I think, stemmed from Williams' own part in the Stecher story. First as a suitor for Lottie's hand, in unfortunate competition with his own brother; then as Flossie's fiancé and husband, "Charlie Bishop" usurps too many scenes in which his importance to the Stecher theme is questionable. The self-consciousness implicit in this situation is expressed later when Williams explains, "I had trouble. I found much of what I was writing was too personal. I had to change names, fictionalize situations, so that living persons would be protected." [35]

Whatever the last section of *The Build Up* accomplishes, Williams' *Autobiography* may do it better. Told in the seemingly casual anecdotal style, Williams' account of his life emphasizes experiences that have been central to his writing: early prowess in school, the sabbatical years and trips abroad, friendships with writers and artists, summaries of his first reading and teaching tours. The plethora of his experiences as a doctor is swept into only a few chapters—one beautiful description of the reciprocity Williams found between his medicine and poetry—so that the man who emerges is more poet than physician. Sherman Paul, in his perceptive study of Williams' late writing, speculates that such an emphasis might be, either consciously or subconsciously, Williams' vindication of his role as writer after years of detractors had classified him as primarily doctor.[36] Williams himself admitted about the writing of the autobiography, "It was good therapy for me." [37]

Although reviews were generally favorable, people close to Williams expressed disappointment with the book: there were inaccuracies, chronological errors, omissions of both persons and episodes that should probably have been included. Nearly one-fifth of the book dealt with the 1924 trip to Europe, an experience important to Williams but not one which comprised 20 percent of his life. Mrs. Williams herself suggested that the book was too hastily done. Yet perhaps all these objections are also indices for the success of the writing. The *Autobiography* is genuinely idiomatically Williams. When was he ever *not* hurried? When had a logical proportion shaped the events of his daily life? As Alfred Kazin said recently about the genre of autobiography, "Each person writes the autobiography he was meant to write," and further,

> The important thing is that the honesty one strives for is the honesty of a form. It can never be the honesty of details alone. One can never be entirely sure; one can never be entirely accurate; but the fact remains that every person who tells a story owes himself one responsibility —to tell it in such a way that what he remembers will compose a certain meaning.[38]

For Williams, with his determination to work from a "character center," conveying a sense of himself and the events important to the growth of that self may well have been as much as a single book could do. As he wrote to Norman Macleod,

> I told it in the only way I could tell it, in a series of incidents as I lived them. I didn't say much of the lives of others except as they briefly knocked against mine. Thus many names have been left out. It isn't a story of the times during which I lived. It is as though I were a trout living in the water of my own stream, shut away in its waters, only rarely breaking the surface.[39]

In structure, true to Williams' description above, there are countless "concrete" episodes, usually juxtaposed much as are the sections of *Paterson*. Yet there are also very succinct philosophical passages, more explicit than most of Williams' writing before 1950 and often related to the themes he is to be working with in *The Desert Music*, *Journey to Love*, and *Paterson* V. One example is this description of the way in which the doctor is privy to the essential language of his patients. The discussion, however, becomes more than a treatise on the idiom, as Williams moves into the humane implications of that idiomatic speech.

> The physician enjoys a wonderful opportunity actually to witness the words being born. Their actual colors and shapes are laid before him carrying their tiny burdens which he is privileged to take into his care with their unspoiled newness. He may see the difficulty with which they have been born and what they are destined to do . . . .
>
> But after we have run the gamut of the simple meanings that come to one over the years, a change gradually occurs. We have grown used to the range of communication which is likely to reach us. The girl who comes to me breathless, staggering into my office, in her underwear a still breathing infant, asking me to lock her mother out of the room; the man whose mind is gone—all of them finally say the same thing. And then a new meaning begins to intervene. For under that language to which we have been listening all our lives a new, a more profound language, underlying all the dialectics, offers itself. It is what they call poetry. That is the final phase (361).

Statements like this reveal, with greater force than his writing in the occasional essays, the most important insights of Williams' long and somewhat hesitant life. For him, reminiscing too was a tactile process, dependent on sorting through and organizing the "things" of his life. As Robert Creeley pointed out, *"The Autobiography* more than any of his other books, now, is the place where the materials of his work are given—not done, but there to be found and related . . . to their forms in his art." [40]

Published in 1951, the book closes with the chapter on *Paterson*, the fullest expression to that date of Williams' primary concerns for his world and his art. Yet that chapter too is a good illustration of the Williams' prose mode, for after a discussion of the poem and its purpose, he breaks abruptly into the conversation among his young grandson Paul, a guest John Husband, and himself as they visit the city of Paterson. Paul "wanted to know how fast the car would go. Eighty I said. Then do it. Hmmm" (392). Young Paul's remarks, colored with his fierce search for danger, counterpoint the rest of the scene which closes the book—poemlike in its indirection, yet leaving us somehow with the sense of Williams, the daring and restless poet, a man who through the life of writing described here had been brought to what he termed "long-range contentment."

> Nine-tenths of our lives is well forgotten in the living. Of the part that is remembered, the most had better not be told: it would interest no one, or at least would not contribute to the story of what we ourselves have been . . . .
> I can't tell more than I know. I have lived, somehow, from day to day; and so I describe it, from day to day, as I have struggled to get a meaning from my failures and successes. Not that my conclusions have been profound. But even the most trivial happenings may carry a certain weight (xi).

As this introduction to his *Autobiography* suggests, through the Stecher novels and his own story Williams was approaching the wise self-knowledge of the late poems. The longer prose seems to have provided new and viable channels for this most important of his explorations.

CHAPTER TEN

Canvas II: The Plays

IN 1937 Williams linked his *American Grain* essays, the novel *White Mule,* and his libretto *The First President* because all expressed "the idealism of America . . . the great themes of American life and aspiration in the past." [1] With his usual tendency to overlook distinctions of genre, Williams identified his first major drama as an integral part of his writing. So it is. But to Williams the drama as form was also very special, capable of relying on speech stripped to its essentials for a great part of its effect. The dialogue that pervades Williams' poems and essays, and dominates his fiction, could become in drama the entire *modus operandi.* That Williams early recognized these possibilities is evident in that he wrote many short plays, several of them in verse, before 1915.

"I was so anxious to succeed in the theater," Williams recalled. "My first interest was the theater." [2] From 1903 to approximately 1915, Williams was active in amateur theatrical groups in both New Jersey and New York. Throughout his life he followed the theater, but his interest in writing for it resumed late in the 1930's when he was searching for the broader view, writing the Stecher novels and planning *Paterson.* In fact, he was never so enthusiastic about the novels as he was about the plays written during the same period: *The First President,* 1937; *Many Loves,* 1940; *A Dream of Love,* 1948; *Tituba's Children,* 1950. Of these, only *Many Loves* has been produced by professional groups (one year in the Living Theater repertory, 1959). *A Dream of Love* has had short productions, largely amateur. *The First President,* libretto for opera and ballet, has yet to be produced, although Theodore Harris has written a score for it. To my knowledge, *Tituba's Children,* in many ways Williams' best play, has never been produced.

Letters from theatrical agents who refused the plays when Williams offered them indicate that they found little "dramatic conflict" or "plot." [3] Much as Peter, the disappointed angel in *Many Loves* says to the playwright, "Here, in / the third act, when the business should be/ coming to a head . . . . No heat, no lifting of the scene,/ no tension." [4] Once again Williams was at variance with current concepts of art, with his insistence on a form suitable to the play itself, an organic shape dependent for the most part on major characterizations. It is interesting that in his notes for a play about his mother, Williams speaks in some detail about the characters and themes, but says only briefly about plot, "What happens at the end, if anything, God only knows." [5]

One of Williams' best statements of his rationale for theater occurs in his Introduction to *The First President* where he defends the non-sequential order of the scenes in the libretto. Freed from "plodding fact—the mere historicity of events—an audience will be liberated to follow something else." [6] He had written in 1935 that "the effect of today is not and can no longer be linear. It is simultaneous, expansive." [7] Williams' old objections to history, aired so thoroughly in his writing of the 1920's, are here renewed. To him, the sense of a man is not chronological; that Washington's character did not vary was its strength. Pushed only by the "purest motives," Washington fought throughout his life those people who would ruin America, usually "for private ends." As Williams wrote, "The character of Washington itself, in this case, forms the libretto."

Yet the dramatist must wonder, what does such an assertion demand, technically, structurally? For Williams, each play was a different problem; each had "its own distinctive mode of experimentation." [8] Here, Williams chooses several scenes to show Washington's concern with the larger good, juxtaposing them to highlight the contrast between his motives and those of other men. In one scene the cheering inauguration crowd becomes the angry mob of the Citizen Genêt affair (multiple-scene action with a soft Mount Vernon idyl heightens the anger of the primary scene). Again, the play moves abruptly from the dignified Snow ballet, which closes with a soldier dying for the President, to the scene of Washington and his men at Valley Forge, stranded there because of a few men's avarice. Williams' plays share the themes of his fiction and poetry as well as their techniques of juxtaposition, concentration, and characterization through dialogue. The opera presents Washington not as a brilliant leader but as a humble, defeated man who never achieved his greatest dream. Washington's thwarted love for Sally Fairfax does not come into the play; yet it is from that love, Williams believes, that Washington derives his greatness. Williams sees the essence of his character as love, great love, transferred to "the mob, to the common, to the people" (317). As in much of his other writing, it is often the defeated man who wins; the descent that gives up the true wealth.

> The wealthiest man in the colonies, the most successful, most important and the most richly deserving, Washington had been all his life used to defeat—so that it never surprised him and out of it he built his genius (319).

For a writer so reliant on a character's language, it is interesting that Williams gives Washington few lines to speak in the libretto, that in fact Washington sings only one song (in places the music is intended to drown out Washington's voice). Williams sees him as a stolid, inarticulate man, usually bested by the glib and the eloquent (Hamilton, Arnold, Lee, the young townsmen), winning out over them by strength of character alone. Williams realizes the difficulty of presenting Washington as a hero ("No life as great as his had as little of the eternally dramatic about it" [307]). Limited by language, he turns to music to be the answer. He thinks wistfully of verse drama, but realizes its impracticality ("there is no poetic drama today" [304]) and turns back to music.

The Short Plays and *Many Loves*

Part of Williams' difficulty as a budding dramatist was that he gave no attention to the length of his plays. The one-acts are very short; the longer plays are closer to two-acts than full-length plays. While such considerations in 1970 are less important, several agents in the 1940's did complain about his unorthodox playing times. Remembering his definition of a short story as "a single flight of the imagination, up and down," [9] one can see how similar was his approach to drama. In 1927 he defined a play as being "primary realization coming up to intensity and then fading (futilely) in self. This *is* the technique, . . . the natural drama." [10]

Williams' early short plays nearly all seem to be these "natural" treatments of history; yet the underlying theme in each has more to do with the values of a man's life than it does with the historical event he is caught up in. The 1909 *Betty Putnam* is one of Williams' strongest indictments of avarice. Set during the Salem witch trials, the play concerns Rev. Nicholas Noyes's plot to get the land adjoining his own. He threatens to accuse his nephew and Betty Putnam as witches if their lands are not signed over to him. Tersely done, the dialogue is effective, with Betty emerging as the first of Williams' strong and impetuous women. The Revolutionary War playlet *A September Afternoon* sets the death of young Barney Lane at the hands of the Redcoats in the quiet countryside. One cannot but question his concept of honor as Barney dies in his sister's arms. *No Love* or *The Fifth Star* is a fragment describing Benedict Arnold, a man Williams seemed fascinated by in many of his writings.

As Walter Scott Peterson suggests in his book on *Paterson,* much of Williams' writing can be described as dealing with either "acquisitive" or "non-acquisitive" love.[11] With figures like Arnold and Washington, Williams sometimes presents them in romantic situations, seeming to use their marital relationships as indices of character. Another early play, *Sauerkraut to the Cultured,* is a comedy of courtship, the lovers (one English and one Dutch) contesting for Lena Bach. In Amsterdam of 1680, with Lena's father dominating the play, honesty and genuine love win the day. Williams' notes for *Under the Stars* suggest a related theme, as Washington probes his own anger following Lee's cowardly withdrawal from battle. Is his own pride too strong? Is he angry with Lee because he loves him or because he wants to belittle him? *The Battle of Brooklyn* also centers on Washington, again the figure of self-abnegation, and his relation to the common people of his day. With the exception of *The Comic Life of Elia Brobitza,* a 1919 play about an old woman mystically rejuvenated through love, Williams' early efforts show him reaching into the "truths" of history for the ostensible plots of his plays, a practice probably suggested by his veneration for Shakespeare as well as his interest in American history. It is no accident that he presents the British—or attitudes related to the British—as inferior to American, or otherwise native, counterparts. It is ironic, however, that Williams' vigorous championing of America was not better served in the language of these early plays. Dialogue is frequently stilted, and phrasing, particularly of the lower-class characters' speech, seems inappropriately genteel. Williams' insistence on "common language" is only to develop later, once he has learned to listen.

The "Detail" poems of language transcribed "hot" and the dialogue used in *The Great American Novel* and "The Descent of Winter" suggest that Williams' ear is growing more acute. One set of undated pages, presumably later, titled simply "The Play," contains nothing but fragments of a doctor's conversation with patients, most of them women. The distinctive voice in each episode (and the humor) make these notes some of Williams' best dialogue; each paragraph is a "Verbal Transcription: 6 A.M." in miniature. The notes for *Women Are Such Fools* indicate the same approach, that Williams is beginning with the language rather than the plot of the play. As early as 1927, he had included in his work sheets for "The Descent of Winter" this page, demanding for the drama a freedom not only in language but also in subject matter:

> Suppose nowadays you can see a woman's bare ass when she leans over scrubbing the front porch, what of it? . . .
> From the center of the heap of cobble stones grew a tuft of rank grass. Interpret it as you will.
> Talk about walking around with labor pains, I was walking around with pains in my head.
> I work for eighteen women and they're not any different from men. (Things like this you'll never find in a play).[12]

Elsewhere in this 1927 outpouring of prose and poetry, Williams comes frequently to the concept of drama as workable form. What is needed, he writes, is "a simplification, a brushing aside of scaffolding. . . . *This* is what should be taught a dramatist: Loosen."[13] Referring again to Shakespeare's anonymity, Williams stresses that a dramatist understands all men: "It is out *through* the bottom of all personality" that the dramatist writes.

> Why must I be myself when I say, God damn women who entrench themselves behind children and then razz hell out of the man who is slaving the shit out of himself for them . . . . Write it: it is so. Put it in his mouth—with all fire in it and there's the beginning.[14]

The three playlets of *Many Loves* (1940) are evidence that Williams took his own advice. Fragmentary, "common," with the language of early versions toned down for publication, the playlets within the play deal with several variations of Williams' pervasive theme of love. The first playlet, *Serafina,* portrays man's search for a woman who can satisfy him, with the woman's need for love equally (if inarticulately) emphasized. *The Funnies* shows conflict among three generations, with the youngest, Anne, being driven into first hasty romance and then a possible lesbian relationship because of dissension at home. The third playlet, *Talk,* comes back to the woman-doctor bond, emphasizing the young mother's need for outlets: wine, talk with her friends, perhaps more. Clara, a continuation of the Polish mother in "Four Bottles of Beer," is the best-drawn character of the play. Her motives are clear, depicted without rationalization: "I'm trying to do my job as a sweet mother and it's killing me. I'm telling you—killing me. If I quit the whole mess of this having children and sent it to hell and gone out of my sight, I'd be a better woman—and that's the truth" (76–77). But she is wise too, as the quasi-romantic doctor feigns impatience: "Talk, talk, talk! Everything runs out finally into talk" and she answers calmly, "Doesn't it though —and isn't it restful" (85).

Written separately, the three playlets seemed to fit together when Williams was asked to do a play for a local production (he had recently seen Noel Coward's set of three short plays). Unfortunately, the connecting dialogue which serves as frame seems weak when contrasted with that of the playlets. Reminiscent of his first short stories that deal with aberrant sex, the scenes between playwright Hubert and Peter, the homosexual backer, present only the surface conflict. Hubert comes across as a romantic fop who lacks the courage to tell Peter he loves Alise, his leading lady. His primary concern is not Alise; it is not even the play he is directing at the time; it is rather his verse drama to come, not yet written. While we identify somewhat with Hubert's love of the theater and his aspirations for it, we cannot accept his reactions to Peter's obvious suggestions. Alise is driven to enough anger by the end of the play that she carries a gun; Hubert scarcely recognizes what is happening around him. After Peter arranges a bizarre wedding on stage (for Hubert and Alise), he calmly proposes to Hubert,

> Don't sulk, Hubert. Look—this is my
> last evening. I claim it. After
> the ceremony is over we'll take Alise
> and pack her into her little bed—
> so she can get her beauty rest
> against tomorrow evening.
>   She'll
> agree, and you and I shall steal
> away . . . It is my privilege! (99–100)

Ironically, Williams' belief that a character must be known through his speech, evident in so much of his writing, seems to fail him here. Hubert's dialogue, like Peter's, is far from convincing.

Perhaps Williams was more interested in creating a regular verse than he was in characterizing Hubert and Peter. Perhaps, too, having included much about his dramatic beliefs in *The First President,* he wanted to continue that rather self-conscious discussion of poetics. Whatever the circumstances, some critics did not greet *Many Loves* (subtitled *Trial Horse No. 1*) with enthusiasm. Several complained that it was too busy, with four separate stories in process. Others felt that the action was unresolved. Donald Malcolm, writing in the *New Yorker,* best explains Williams' efforts toward unity: each of the three playlets he finds

> essentially undramatic, in that each fails to arrive at a natural and effective climax. Part of the function of the patron, then, is to compensate for this deficiency. It is his relation to the scene, rather than the conclusion of the scene itself, that is the crux of the action. In the balance between Peter and Hubert lies the real struggle, with attention focused in each play on Alise, the woman who will take Hubert from Peter.[15]

Malcolm's explanation gives importance to Williams' direction that the actress who played Alise was to take the female lead in each of the three playlets. In effect, the vignettes of love are related more closely because of the central, stable character. And there is ample evidence in the repartee between Alise and Peter, the antagonist, that the play focuses on man's relationship to women. As Peter says to the stagehands just before the wedding, "There is/ something in this

man—as in/ any man—not to be benefited by a marriage" (101). And
to Alise:

> Do you think he loves you?
> Don't make me laugh. He doesn't even
> love himself. He is as specialized
> as a foxhound. He waits only to
> be loosed by his writing. That aside,
> he is a prisoner, dim-witted, furious,
> angry at his prison . . . (102).

The mystery and violence of an Alise, pregnant with Hubert's
child (as she matter-of-factly tells the minister) and ready to kill
for his affection, grows into the richer character of Myra Thurber
of *A Dream of Love*. And Myra's husband, Daniel, is in some ways a
synthesis of Hubert and the doctor of *Talk*. Williams' preoccupation
with women and men, and the lives they choose for themselves,
brought him from plays taken from history to contemporary themes;
from Washington to the most common of Americans; and from short,
plot-dominated plays to long character studies, plays as Hubert described them "to turn our minds a little to the light," projecting
"above the coarseness of the materials . . . tragic without vulgarity"
(92).

A Dream of Love, Tituba's Children, The Cure

Making use of the actual took Williams to the three playlets of *Many Loves,* but his disappointment with their somewhat limited effects led him to the device of dream or illusion in *A Dream of
Love*. The playwright who presents only what is superficially evident
has frequently missed his drama, Williams suggests. The lives of Doc
and Myra Thurber, for example, seem complacently happy. It takes
Dr. Thurber's scandalous death as he makes love in a New York hotel
room to bring that marriage out of its normality into—not disillusion,
but fulfillment. The ostensibly "common" must be elevated; only
Myra's love can erase the horror of her husband's betrayal. Again the
theme of love occupies Williams, doubly concerned here with its
definition as well as with its artistic portrayal. As he had written in

Many Loves, love today might best be presented "with a coalscuttle.
. . . by spitting in it" (92–93). The problem, as Williams saw it, was
that much writing about love "intruded too much upon our passion
and tended to make it seem artificial. . . . All love poetry close
enough to be tolerated must, today, be reticent—to penetrate."[16] In
language as well as in act, this dilemma is the Thurbers' drama, for
Myra's question is only "Did he love me?" It is the memory of their
life together she is determined to salvage.

Williams' staging suggests that the Myra-Daniel relationship is
his chief interest. Using the hotel room scene only as part of the dream
sequence, he emphasizes instead several preliminary episodes characterizing Myra and Daniel, and then focuses on Myra after her
husband's death, with the reaction to the scandal coming in as "chorus." Josephine the maid, Mr. Tennant the milkman, and even Dottie
Randall the mistress present the community reaction. In his notes for
the play, Williams made several references to the chorus, seeming to
rely on the oldest of methods to achieve that broader significance
which had been less evident in *Many Loves.*

Early drafts of *A Dream of Love* show that each character was to
have a "prologue speech," modeled after those in *Romeo and Juliet.*
In addition to identifying the characters, they were to serve as a
means of summarizing the action.[17] As the final version stands, however, this preliminary exposition occurs through dialogue. Doc and
Myra talk about their love; and the central Williams' poem, "A dream/
we dreamed/ each/ separately/ we two/ of love/ and of desire/ that
fused/ in the night" is introduced. That the dream is "more than
a little false" sets an ambivalent tone early. Is the blazing white light
of young love false? Or is the poet speaking of *any* dream of love?

Later, Thurber visits the Randalls, Dottie whom he loves and
Cliff, her businessman husband. We suspect that Williams has other
themes in mind than love for Cliff. A caricature of the man of action
("You've got to go after it. . . . You got to watch everything"[18]),
Cliff is impatient with talk—the talk which seems to be the basis for
Dottie's attraction to the doctor. Yet there are contradictions in Cliff's
presentation: he uses archaic diction at times and stands shamefaced
under Dottie's verbal attacks, even while he has crudely offered to let
her sleep with Thurber:

> Look, sweetheart—I'm not kicking. You want to meet him in the
> city? Meet him. Go ahead. And I tell you, if you'd only be a little
> decent to me . . . [He hesitates a moment.] . . . I wouldn't care if
> he took you to a hotel and you went to bed with him (140).

(Some indication that business had other overtones for Williams is
found in his notes for the play, referring vaguely to "Theme, the
present tragedy, the effectiveness copied from US. The perfect pattern
of Standard Oil.") Cliff as Williams presents him is far from plausible,
a parallel to that other strange businessman in the drama, the milkman. Within a week after Doc Thurber's death, Mr. Tennant wants
to marry Myra ("With you back of me I'm going to clean up" [19]),
primarily as an aid to his new business plans.

Accurate as he usually is with dialogue, Williams' inept characterizations of Cliff and Mr. Tennant seem inexplicable unless he was
trying to justify Thurber's infidelity by presenting him as the only
sensitive man in the play, a man who had pointedly *not* made money
from what could have been a lucrative profession. An alternative title
for the play was *Innocent Blackguard*.

This dichotomy of characterization in the men's roles is coupled
with the device of the building storm (Williams often spoke of his
admiration for *Lear*) to create for the play a climax which does not
proceed obviously from the action. The climax occurs after Thurber's
death, when he has returned in a dream-illusion to answer Myra's
questions. As he attempts to explain that his love for her is renewed
through other loves, her anger grows with the storm, to her renuncia-
tion of him,

> God damn you!
> There is a blinding flash of lightning, followed
> by thunder and wind. The lights on the stage go off (213).

The scene changes to the hotel room flashback for the conversation
between Dottie and Thurber, which ends with a military charge,
flags flying, complete with drums and artillery, to symbolize their in-
tercourse. Juxtaposed with this triumphant, black-humored scene is
Myra, waking from sleep, alone, in the quiet kitchen. The phone
rings and she answers it, "Hello. Yes. I'm sorry—the doctor died a
week ago. I'm sorry you haven't heard it but it's true" (223). Then

she walks casually out of the kitchen, for the first time since Thurber's death a week before. Myra's resumption of her normal life implies her acceptance of the doctor's philosophy about love; yet the focus of the play has been throughout more on Thurber than on Myra. Given what we know about her, we are not so sure she can be easily convinced of her husband's underlying devotion.

One agent did question the focus of the play.[20] Perhaps Williams intended the interest to lie with Thurber, as this early notation suggests:

> his, the M. D.'s respect, devotion to her is profound: for the first time in his life he sees the implications and the fact of monogamy (the whole man and the man whole).
> He SEES—and the light it casts through and through his life is brilliant—He stands in amazement before it . . . . before her, her life given; desperately assailed by the tragedy of her life . . .[21]

Yet the dramatic line of the play forces the attention away from Thurber to his wife. Even the epigraph Williams chooses, from Aeschylus' *Agamemnon,* describes the grief of Menelaus after Helen's absence. "He stands by in silence, dishonored, but without reproaches. . . . Yes, in his longing after her . . . a phantom will seem to rule his house" (107). Except for the reversal in roles, the action of Williams' play fits this synopsis closely.

Clinton Atkinson, who has produced *A Dream of Love,* is not bothered by the question of focus. He considers the play "a major American work" because of its thematic intensity:

> We may not associate great loves, the grandeur of emotion, with suburbia, but Williams demonstrates . . . that the meaningful, the great, and the tragic do indeed hide in the commonplace. The imagery is sparse and common; the plot line is redundant and flaccid. But this play in production . . . is unbearably vivid . . . . and the redundance of incident becomes the pattern of inevitable circumstances circling the treadmill of life.[22]

Atkinson has pointed out also that Williams had little help from either the professional or the academic stage.[23] Plays cannot be judged until they have been produced; yet most of Williams' plays were not seen until many years after they were written, if then. Williams' most exciting drama, *Tituba's Children* (1950), has never been produced. The play takes him again to the Salem witch trials, with Tituba the slave both instigator and victim of the hysteria. Some of the difficulties in staging this play are that it requires as yet unwritten music in several scenes (indeed, the "Giles Cory Ballad" is a sort of refrain); it alternates between Salem, 1692, and Washington, D.C., 1950; and it has no ostensible "hero." The modern protagonists are Mac McDee, a young official in the State Department, accused during the McCarthy investigations of being a Communist; and Stella Rajuputsky, tough yet kindly night-club hostess. Concerned with the Senate attitude toward supposed Reds, Stella and her Negro waitresses present a Halloween entertainment, a dramatization of the Salem witch trials. Williams uses the dual character device of *Many Loves*: Washington Senators double as Salem magistrates; Stella plays the roles of the innocent Elizabeth Procter and Sarah Good; Mac is John Procter. The strength of the play lies in the tight fusion of modern and seventeenth century, for not only does the scene alternate between the two but the modern happenings are similar to those taken from history. Toward the climax of the play, actors and actresses change on stage from Puritans to U.S. Senators, and the trial shifts from that of John Procter to Mac McDee. And the chorus asks, "Must this terror be repeated? Is this the horror of Giles Cory's doom come to destroy us?" [24]

The vacillation between present and past also gives Williams the opportunity to vary his speech in terms of both diction and cadence. The tone for the witch trials is set by narration taken directly from historical accounts of the proceedings. Another highly dramatic effect occurs when contemporary dialogue mimics that from the Salem trial, as when Senator Yokell asks Stella, during McDee's trial, whether she ever "signed the book." As the court accuses Stella of bedeviling Mac's wife, Mac defends her with lines directly from John Procter's defense of Elizabeth. Since each woman is innocent, the speech is immediately applicable.

The climax of *Tituba's Children* comes when McDee is allowed to speak for himself in response to the charges of the court. In a moving series of speeches in which Mac's explanation of his liberalism is juxtaposed with the chorus' sad foreshadowing, the play comes to its powerful end. Senator Yokell asks, "Have you finished, sir?" Mac replies, "I have." And then comes the tragic ending, "You will be indicted, Mr. McDee, for contempt and placed under arrest. This hearing is closed" (299). The "Giles Cory Ballad" is heard as epilogue, and Williams' first tragedy has ended.

As in every other mode of his writing, Williams' plays move from his interest in autobiographical and historical elements to more finished work that draws the best techniques from the earlier writing, fusing them into effective drama. Although *Tituba's Children* has been overshadowed by Arthur Miller's *The Crucible,* written three years later (perhaps when the country was more ready to accept censure), it is Williams' most compelling drama. The theme of personal love has broadened to include social responsibility, a selfless emotion from which the characters gain no personal satisfaction. As Katharine Worth describes the play,

> It [the situation] demands a style of tragic dignity to which modern prose idiom is notoriously inimical. Williams solves the problem by using speech and ballad from the Salem period to express the passions of a less articulate people . . . .
> Here is a poetic imagination working in dramatic terms. Williams seems to be fully extended dramatically when he attempts this kind of tension between verse and prose, writing at a lower level of intensity in verse alone, as in *The First President,* or in prose alone, in *The Cure.*[25]

As the last of Williams' full-length dramas, *The Cure* is more a thematic continuation than a technical one. Flat prose of an undistinguished nature is used throughout, but appropriately so, for there is nothing distinguished about Connie Mitchell, the young housewife turned nurse; Prospero, the rough convict who is secretly her patient; and George her husband, another man cut from Cliff Randall's mold. Williams' interest here is not dramaturgy so much as it is Connie's psychology. Why does she do what she does? Why does any woman respond? From Betty Putnam to Alise to Myra and Stella and Connie, Williams draws the same heroine: shrewd yet compassionate, rough but morally good. In *A Dream of Love,* Doc Thurber had discussed the dilemma a man faces in respect to woman:

> A man must protect his price, his integrity as a man, as best he is able, by whatever invention he can cook up out of his brains or his belly . . . . He must create a woman of some sort out of his imagination to prove himself . . . . just as a woman must produce out of her

female belly to complete herself—a son—so a man must produce a woman . . ." (200).

The nurse Phyllis of *Paterson* IV is a close parallel to Connie, and in reading the two characters' lines, one is reminded of Williams' note about the *Paterson* IV episode: "It is an auditory image here— a formal image—a compositional segment." [26] As he had written else- where in his drafts, "plays are to be heard more than seen." [27] One clear illustration of his belief in the auditory impact comes in *A Dream of Love* during the doctor's lovemaking with Dottie. Instead of endearments, Thurber quotes Greek to the little housewife, for the *sound* of it.

Repeatedly, Williams' emphasis on hearing, on language, accounts for his seeming indifference to the action line of a play. He includes all that is integral to the theme, no more, no less. He is also careless about his "heroes": Hubert, Dr. Thurber, Mac McDee, George Mitchell—these are hardly stereotypes of either tragic figures or nice guys. They are, as Williams predicted, commonplace. His indifference to a hero figure is indicated in his notes for the play about his mother: "The Old Woman puts much stock in the future life. Which is the hero—if there is one." [28] Perhaps the hero in a Williams play is, as H. Donohue suggests, Williams himself. [29]

The question remains, can a playwright omit the traditional quali- ties and characteristics of drama and still have drama? Williams, of course, would say Yes, so long as the play has unity in itself (given the changes in theater in the last fifteen years, critics would probably be more receptive to Williams' innovations today than they were twenty years ago). Williams the playwright is a hard figure to judge, how- ever, for even in the tradition of poet turned playwright—T. S. Eliot, Robert Lowell, Archibald MacLeish, Tennessee Williams—Williams is atypical. Most poets show their poetic inheritance by writing verse drama. As Katharine Worth points out, however, Williams, much as he spoke of it, did not write verse drama per se but rather "attempts to integrate verse into a prose texture for special effects of contrast and illumination." [30] His concept of prose and poetry as reciprocal parts of a whole serves him reasonably well in *Many Loves* and even better in *Tituba's Children*. Perhaps it operates at its best in his final drama of amalgamation, *Paterson*.

CHAPTER ELEVEN

Canvas III: *Paterson*

MANY recent studies of *Paterson* concentrate on the unity in its
five books. The poem is well worth such intensive explication; even
in full-length studies such as Walter Scott Peterson's and Joel Conarroe's, much goes unsaid. Numerous critics have considered *Paterson*
in the American tradition of *Walden, Song of Myself, The Bridge,*
and *The Cantos*.[1] Yet perhaps another essay on Williams' epic can
be justified if we see the poem as the culmination of Williams' years
of struggle to convey his world in total.[2] The importance of this aim
is increasingly evident in his notes and letters. In January of 1943
he writes to James Laughlin that he wants to compile a book of
many kinds of writing—poems, prose-poem "improvisations," drama,
prose—to serve as a showcase for "just what I have always been trying
to do."[3] (Such proposals as this evince again that Williams meant
it when he declared that writing was writing, regardless of genre.)
From his discussion of this suggested book, he moves to *Paterson,*
and we see its great significance to him as final "saying":

> "Paterson," I know, is crying to be written; the time demands it; it has
> to do with all the peace movements, the plans for international in-
> filtration into the dry mass of those principles of knowledge and cul-
> ture which the universities and their cripples have cloistered and made
> a cult. It is the debasing, the keg-cracking assault upon the cults and
> the kind of thought that destroyed Pound and made what it has made
> of Eliot. To let it into "the city," culture, the benefits of culture, into
> the mass as an "act," as a thing.

"Act," "thing," the poem as "a small (or large) machine made of
words"[4]—Williams viewed *Paterson* as the epitome of a vital art
form. He would probably not have welcomed comparisons between
it and earlier epics, for rather than write a traditional poem, he aimed
for a "keg-cracker." In fact, he did not intend to write an epic at all,

only a poem to encompass his world. Work sheets show many attempts: the dialogue between two doctors, other prose-poem matrices titled "Musings of a Midwife," short segments which grow incredibly, once incorporated into the poem. Fragments from early drafts suggest that he did not realize how long or how complex the poem would eventually become. These drafts, in addition to the many early poems of "The Descent of Winter" and the shorter poems ranging from "The Wanderer" to the variety of those titled "Paterson," indicate that writing *Paterson* was hardly an orderly experience. It is little wonder that Williams put it off as long as he could, although he was speaking about it as a long poem as early as 1928.[5]

Louis Martz suggests, "More and more, as the books of *Paterson* appeared, all Williams' writings began to look like by-products, preliminary steps, the results of 'practicing' . . . for the central work of his career."[6] During the 1930's Williams' short stories appear to have satisfied him in making more immediate use of his local, his experience; then the Stecher novels and the plays widened that coverage. None of this writing, however, was poetry, and Williams believed too strongly in the efficacy of the poem to avoid it forever. But poetry when he returned to it had to be not neat and impersonal, but loose in structure and committed in feeling. For Williams, the days of Objectivist poems were over. He spoke in 1943 of the world of art's being "a looser, wider world where 'order' is a servant not a master. Order is what is discovered after the fact, not a little piss pot for us all to urinate into—and call ourselves satisfied."[7] And as early as 1937 he had championed the involvement of the artist in human concerns. He considered Stevens' "The Men That Are Falling" the best poem in *The Man with the Blue Guitar* because in it "Stevens has shown himself the man, the artist in all the profundity of his aroused sensibilities, no longer fiddling around with thoughts but embodying thought in an adult thrust with all his mature weight behind it.[8]

Perhaps the true capability of the long poem had struck Williams in 1934 when he reviewed Pound's *Cantos*. He spoke then of poetry as a "daring thought toward a constructive understanding of human destiny." This greater purpose, to lift men "above the sordidness of a grabbing world," can be achieved only through the details of the actual. Yet details alone are inadequate, Williams wrote. The poet must digest "the mass of impediments" and then create a full picture of his culture. "Where but in poetry can all things be not only spoken of freely but dwelt upon to the enhancement of the intelligence . . . . Pound has *enlarged the scope of poetic opportunity*. He has the tact and the daring."[9] It is in this essay also that Williams praised Pound's use of the actual writing of Adams and Jefferson, with little if any modification. He admired this "flavor" and, more importantly, the flexible structure that allows its inclusion.

Impressed as he was with the *Cantos,* Williams knew too well that his own poem would be very different from Pound's chiefly because, as he wrote in 1941, Pound "has never had any love for or understanding of the people . . . . He lacked a knowledge of man, plain and simple."[10] In Williams' awareness of (and sorrow for) his culture he differs radically from Pound. How similar is *Paterson* technically to the points stressed in this review: expansive structure, a line based on time instead of accent, the use of original materials in their pristine forms. *Paterson* is clearly the growth of Williams' earlier enthusiasms.

From Plan to Poem

From its inception *Paterson* appears to have had four parts, partly because of its tie with the seasons, partly because of its progression along the course of the river: above the falls, the falls itself, the river below the falls, and the entrance to the sea.[11] Then, too, as Martz suggests, Williams may be slyly referring to Eliot's *Quartets,* since he waged a running if admiring battle with Pound and Eliot throughout his life (Williams' admiration for *Four Quartets* is, however, real; he calls them "studies in form, searches for new ways to verify . . . the deepest experiences of a man"[12]). His early dedications of the four parts reveal much about the genesis of the epic:

I. To H. G. [Horace Gregory] for his clear mind and gift for history.
II. To K. S. for the way, at ninety-six years her body has shrivelled symetrically from 168 pounds to 68, uniformly, without deformity.
III. To E. W. [Edgar Williams] for the talks we had together as young men. (Part I rather to F. W. [Florence Williams] for her clear mind and bitter arrow's flight at the peak of pointed speech.)
IV. To D. L. [David Lyle] for his studies of the tracks by which the various categories of knowledge are inter-related.[13]

Gregory's *A History of American Poetry, 1900–1940,* impressed Williams, as did his introduction to the reissue of *In the American Grain.* In 1944 and 1945, Williams' letters to him were particularly frank in their discussions of Eliot's influence, Americanism, art. Gregory to Williams represented the "learned" approach to poetry, but somehow, in his own hesitation about *Paterson,* Williams responded to what he had previously ignored: "you seem to offer me what I want." [14] Since Book I includes more history than the other books, the dedication seems appropriate.

With the mention of K. S., whose identity remains unknown, Williams reinforces his admiration for people, his awe at the mystery of the body, perfect still after such change as this. His expression of love here suggests his 1941 criticism of Pound's preoccupation with learning. Pound might know ancient literature, said Williams, but "Everything touching those great basic understandings upon which the century was turning, the newer comprehensions of physics, chemistry and especially biology in their relations to the mind of man were a closed book to him." [15] Williams' insistence that knowledge of the present does not proceed entirely from knowledge of the past is coupled in this dedication with his recurring wonder at man's will to survive. Many of Williams' best short poems are of such people as K. S., "To a Poor Old Woman," "Canthara," "The Widow's Lament in Springtime," "To Waken an Old Lady," "Old Men," and others. Of the four books, Book II with its park scenes and the emotional speech of Klaus Ehrens is in many ways the most sensual.

With his dedication to his brother Edgar, Williams suggests a theme which becomes more significant toward the end of *Paterson:* the place of memory in man's life. It is their "talks as young men" he recalls, and we remember his insistence in *The First President* that "the world of recollection is real." [16] Book III of *Paterson* again emphasizes past happenings, especially the climactic ones of fire, flood, and hurricane, all woven into the "Beautiful Thing" motif. As prize-winning architect, Edgar would perhaps sympathize with his brother's search for the satisfying shape. Perhaps there need be no essentially direct tie, since the influence of Williams' family and small town was great. As he recalled in the *Partisan Review* (1939):

> In retrospect my writing reveals plenty of allegiances—to the grammar school ideals of my public school bringing up . . . . I have never for-

gotten that thrilling world with all its magnificent hopes and determinations . . . . There were things I learned in my father's own Unitarian Sunday School to which I owe the staunchest allegiance today.[17]

His mention of Flossie here is revealing, for most of Williams' later writing is dedicated to her. As anyone who knew the couple remarked, Mrs. Williams was the rock, the stabilizer, the shrewd yet loving wife who brought Williams through his many storms, personal and artistic.

The dedication of Book IV to schoolteacher David Lyle shows again Williams' interest in a wide-ranging mind, in what he called an "encyclopedic consciousness." [18] Lyle's correspondence with Williams (beginning in 1938) was very influential in determining the scope of *Paterson*. Economics, cybernetics, social ills, the price of bread, the motives for murder—every subject was relevant in Lyle's picture of the world. Drafts of *Paterson* indicate that Williams felt somewhat remiss in knowing the facts and yet not correlating them meaningfully:

> You know about Dundee Dam, the sluices,
> the factories later on, and the Passaic
> strike twenty years back—the Irish, the
> Polack, the Wops . . . .
> You know all about
> these things: did you ever try to connect
> them up . . . . Or do you really
> care anything about writing? [19]

That Williams equates "connecting them up" with writing gives one important purpose of his poem. In one draft, he speaks directly to Lyle, "always the same thing, the language qua/ medium of exchange, David. To unlock it." [20] Masses of unused notes and drafts testify to the amount of material he was able to collect, even in the brief periods of working time available to him. Judging from the quantity of this material and the diversity of it, the surprising quality about the finished *Paterson* is its unity.

The Indians, the Dutch, the Negroes—many of the omitted segments fall into these categories. Garfield, the suburb east of Paterson on the Saddle River, had been an Indian center. Williams' drafts include several sets of notes on the Indian customs, particularly sun and fire worship (one from Bishop Ettwein's accounts; one in strange handwriting, perhaps that of Kenneth Burke). Other fragments include the text of a Lenape war song and an account of the Six Nations Treaty, which proposed an agreement to end war.

Williams' interest in the Negro ran throughout his writing, from the beauty of some Negro women to the foolhardy bravery of their men. As he had written in the *American Grain* essays, they are a united people, capable of sympathy and understanding. In the finished *Paterson,* of course, the "Beautiful Thing" is a Negro girl; but the notes suggest much heavier emphasis than this. "Narrative of a Colored Man: Noah Davis, 1859" is a five-page account of Davis' conversion. Williams mentions several letters from two Negro girls and also suggests that at least one minister in *Paterson* was to be a Negro: "The Colored section to be a unit: the second reading of the Minister's speech, the three letters, the colored bathers in the small lake." [21]

Williams' impressions of the Dutch settlers come not from reading or his own knowledge so much as from an old Dutchman with whom he talked. "I'm learning, without dog/ by the aid of a gentle old man," he wrote in one set of drafts; and in another, "A little story of Paterson as told by an old man." The man's reminiscence gives Williams the flavor of the early settlement ("the *Bible* on the icebox"), with its virtues of work, poverty, respect, love (this man may well be the narrator of Book IV, Section 3): "Never so far as I have known, with the exception of one disgrace—that of the Van Winkle murder —has the old town been disturbed in its Dutch quietness *until recent years.*" [22]

It is interesting, too, that Williams knows this gentle old man ("who takes off his hat to me a poet") because he contributed to a fund "for our beloved little church," as the Dutchman said. The themes of these separate groups of notes begin to appear: each culture respected something, gods or God or aged tribesmen. Each culture was impoverished (one excerpt from a Dutch will states "Item I give and bequeath my son Abraham ten shillings for his birthright"). Each had traditions and a language to carry them on (the Indians' songs; the Negroes' rhetoric and letters; the Dutchman's speech). Sadly, for Williams, these summaries are all phrased in past tense. "Until recent years" becomes a central phrase. As Williams wrote elsewhere in his notes for the poem, "There are no poor any more but the vulgar/

and the ignorant/ it is not as simple as you think to have money," and, again, "there is no modesty anymore/ the job is scanted/ no pride in it." [23] Williams' beloved migrant workers, their hungry yet flip children, had disappeared in prosperity. The easy money had helped to change them into what he described in these drafts as "its women/ brainless, its men moneymakers" [24] but more instrumental were the abuses of that money: "You know about the murderous price system—Tungsten, $450. a pound; the G. E. Krupp cartel and its defenders—." [25] As in the Stecher novels and his essays of the 1930's, Williams blames the financial system at least in part for the outcome of man. No one any longer values the well-done job; hence his theme of *shoddy* to come in Book V. People respond as they are asked to respond: to Alexander Hamilton, man was only a means to production. In his work sheets, Williams includes a detailed account of SUM and its role in developing *Paterson,* as well as many newspaper clippings about defective products and the inadequate money system. Had the poem, or Williams' realizations during the poem, led him further in this direction, he would have been prepared with many specific examples.

But Williams' primary concern was not with the fact that a loaf of bread cost 16 cents, but rather with the failure among human beings to love, to give. For his purposes, dividing men into Dutch, Negro, and Indian was meaningless, Williams came to realize. All men had lost virtue and pride:

> We leap awake and what we see
> tells us.
>
> Let terror twist the world! [26]

Economic necessity may have made them selfish, incapable of loving, but the postwar prosperity would seem to deny this explanation. So Williams turned to the theme of religion. One draft of *Paterson* IV opened with this chilling image:

> FORMER CHURCH PROPERTY
> FOR SALE
> IDEAL BUSINESS SITE
> a dry womb—in whose
> crevices: the weeds [27]

Unused, transformed from religion to business, the church which appears so importantly in Williams' descriptions of the Negro culture and the Dutch is here obsolete, unproductive. Like most of the females in *Paterson* (except for Mme Curie and the dogs), the church has ceased to give. Even its spokesman, the wild evangelist in the park, preaches (in the earlier drafts) a gospel of fear.

Other unused portions substantiate Williams' emphasis on the poverty of man's life. From his 1927 "The Descent of Winter" he quotes the story of his mother's friend Mestre and his help while another "friend" is cheating her of her estate. Another scene, of a baker and his family at supper, is accented with "old toothless Rose" and Philomena, the midwife (from "Musings of a Midwife"). Its gaiety is atypical: wine, joy at a child's birth ("iya, iya!"). Perhaps it was no oversight that Williams in his final version omitted the several passages about birth. The tone of *Paterson* is one of mourning, for the past. As he had written in 1939, when his plans for *Paterson* were beginning to form,

> More and more alone as time goes on, shut off from each other in spite of facile means of communication, we shrink within ourselves the more, the more others strike against our poverty.[28]

And, more tranquilly, in 1954,

> Our lives also have lost all that in the past we had to measure them by, except outmoded standards that are meaningless to us . . . . our social concepts, our schools, our very religious ideas . . . are greatly altered.[29]

The results of this change are documented in such shorter poems during the 1940's as the wise "Testament of Perpetual Change," with its lines of alternating idiom and its memorable, "Our stability is but balance, and wisdom lies/ in masterful administration of the unforeseen." [30]

Joel Conarroe has rightly remarked that Williams' work sheets for *Paterson* are sometimes more coherent than the finished poem.[31] It is as if Williams is writing more or less as he thinks, putting it all in, so that he can find his own way through the bewildering mass of material. Reworkings will omit lengthy transitions, build on refrain lines, and concentrate the total impression. Some passages which

were never included in the final poem are, however, too interesting
to be lost. This presumably early passage describes the purpose of
Paterson and illustrates Williams' more explicit mode:

> Sew the mind and body tight together Dr. Carel
> —together with catgut, maybe they will grow
> The city has been, among a few heads,
> the grinning tiger among his rocks. Knowledge
> is in marriage. It is difficult, it is—
> screaming at the top of his voice: We are starved
> for the knowledge of words, the words
> have fallen like leaves from the trees
> and lie under the tree waiting for a
> poetry that never comes to give them sap—
> while history and erudition gathered them up . . . .
> Divorce! divorce! Knowledge is divorced
> from its sources, and men like laboratory animals
> with their spinal cords severed
> celebrate the new era— [32]

The role of both poet and poem occupied Williams perhaps more
than most poets, for he felt that his method of writing was consistently at odds with the "accepted" practices of Eliot, Pound, and the
"philosophers." In this passage, his placing words at the mercy of
"history and erudition" suggests his mistrust of writing as anything
else *but* writing; the doctor's need to join mind and body recalls his
defense of both the sensual and the mental, the balanced man. The
poet as would-be repairer is hesitant, thinking only "maybe they
will grow."

Another kind of unity is marriage, one beginning for the understanding so desperately needed to withstand the frightening yet
majestic city. In his frustration, the poet resorts to ellipsis, then to
screaming; starved for the language, he comes finally to the pessimism
that colors Williams' writing of the 1940's: Divorce! Like the parts
of a dissected man, knowledge separate from its roots is useless ("we
know nothing, pure/ and simple, beyond/ our own complexities . . . .
In ignorance/ a certain knowledge," 11–12). Williams' concept of the
sources of knowledge is closely aligned with his notion of place.
Although he long championed the "local," the place a man intimately

knows, he subtitled *Paterson* "Any/ Every Place" and explained in 1938,

> In a work of art place is everything . . . . First we have to see, be taught to see. We have to be taught to see *here,* because here is every-where, related to everywhere else.
>
> Of only one thing, relative to a work of art, can we be sure: it was bred of a place. It comes from an application of the senses to that place, a music, and that place can be the middle of an African jungle, the Mexican plateau, a Parisian whorehouse . . . or a downhill street in a Pennsylvania small town. It is the particularization that is im-portant.[33]

While Williams insisted on the reciprocity between a man's local and himself, he had created no identity of city-man until fairly late in his thinking about *Paterson*. His usual attitude was that the city was "female" to the man (as in "Beautiful Thing" and "The Wanderer"), but that the man Carel-Williams-Paterson was a separate entity. As an early version of the opening to Book II phrased it, "Outside/ out-side myself/ there is a world/ female to my seduction . . . ."[34] An-other excerpt from this (probably) early version defines the poet-persona, much as Williams defined *Paterson* in his epigraph,

> He is a poet—who quotes
> from his own works, a woman—by proxy
> a high diver, an engineer, a cripple
> a hydrocephalic, an acromegalic
> interested in theology, a nigger wench
> with fine features, the rain
> and a pigeon: may his bones rest
> in peace [35]

We can recognize such figures as Sam Patch, the "Beautiful Thing," Klaus Ehrens perhaps, the rag-tag ends of humanity, a poet similar to Dr. Thurber who quotes his own poems in *A Dream of Love*. Others are meaningless: *Paterson* was in continual flux. In fact, Williams could never predict where he would be going in later books because he had no idea what would be used up in the present section. He found that materials kept expanding. One loveless man suggested others; contrast required that a few generous people be included; the textual changes demanded first prose, then poetry, and eventually drama. Chagrin marks Williams' letter to Horace Gregory in 1945: "I MUST BEGIN COMPOSING again. I thought all I had to do was to arrange the material but that's ridiculous. Much that I have collected is antique now. The old approach is outdated, and I shall have to work like a fiend to make myself new again." [36]

An early title page suggests how simple that "old approach" was to have been. Below the title one reads, "with the assistance of D. J. L. and M. N." The Lyle letters and those of Cress the distraught poetess were to be run into the poem proper at fairly regular intervals; the Lyle letters were even to have been published as an appendix. At that time also (1942) Williams suggested quoting in the introduction from his poems "Morning" and "Beautiful Thing" ["Paterson: Episode 17"]; he did not yet see how integral the latter poem would become in Book III. The outline for the proposed Book III, in fact, includes materials that are eventually placed in all four books: "an interpretation of the Falls . . . . Thinking over the sermon in the park . . . riddle in the Greek or Joycian sense . . . . The history of SUM— begin, also the history of the place. The Curie: radium lecture. Psychosomatic: the mind and body as it listens for the language . . . . First mention of the two murders" [37] and more; but no mention of the fire, flood, violence-gentleness theme which later accompanies the "Beautiful Thing" motif. It is not surprising that the last book in the original outline, Book IV, may lack some spontaneity (the material falls into much longer sections, for the most part), as Williams tries to "get it all said" after struggling with random notes throughout the first three books.

The Later Books

By the time Book IV came to be written, Williams had accomplished these things: he had

(1) defended his poetics as effectively as he had in *Spring and All;*
(2) created the mythic-actual Paterson and his many female counterparts;
(3) established a reciprocity between past and present, prose and poem;
(4) investigated man's relationships with nature, man, the city,

his occupations, the financial system, his loves, and his children;

(5) made us believe in the falls as language;

(6) convinced us that violence outweighed gentleness, that "There have always been more/ to burn down and destroy in the world/ than to build up the beauty of the world"; [38]

(7) proved to himself how naïve had been his opening outline:

    I. Giants (spring)

    II. Sunday in the Park (summer) "Pleasure. Happy, happy, happy!"

    III. Library (fall)

    IV. River (winter) "the conserver of life, solver—forgetfulness."

Just as the river was destined to be something other than a "conserver," Book II hardly reflected the pleasure and happiness suggested here. This was the book, as Williams told John Thirlwall, for which he had visited the park on Sundays, walked in it, "practically listened" to conversations around him. He could no longer pretend; his dissatisfaction with what he saw ("frank vulgarity") is clearly evident in that section.

Perhaps Williams realized what had happened to himself as he wrote about the direction Book IV was forced to take: "The river is getting old. It's been polluted by every sort of thing . . . it has gained experience." He had to follow the demands of his own experience; "people expect perhaps a triumphant development at the end which does not occur in life and does not occur in the poem." [39] While the term "triumphant" does not exactly fit Book IV, it is a much more optimistic book than either Book II or III. Full of sly affirmations of Williams' art, his belief in love, his cognizance of the intellect, Book IV strangely received much disappointed comment. As the "last" book, it was evidently supposed to provide essential answers for mankind—answers that came only ten years later for Williams. Reviewers were, in a way, conditioned for disappointment; no poem could have done all the things expected of this one.

Most objections seem to be directed toward the "Idyl: Phyllis and Corydon"; yet the dialogue here among the lesbian Corydon, Phyllis the young nurse, and Dr. Paterson is well done, though less complete than in earlier drafts. Giving much time to the episode makes the characters more memorable than the many fragmentary people of the earlier books, and such pictures of the "corrupt" city dwellers—particularly the effete Corydon—are necessary, too, as contrast for the depiction of Mme Curie, the real heroine of these first four books.

Williams had written of *Paterson,* "Everything I do or write is now, before all else directed, as extension, explanation to my two sons." [40] Part II of the last book opens with Dr. Paterson and his son attending a lecture on atomic fission. From pitchblende, beside the dullness of lead, the luminous stain—but only after "the hour, the day, the week . . . months of labor" (209). Juxtaposition of Columbus' discovering the "Beautiful Thing" makes Curie's discovery bear even more importance for Williams. From "dissonance," from defeat, comes discovery. In Book III he has foreshadowed this scene with his images of "stain," "radiance," used there to describe an "unfaltering" language. It is also one of the continuing themes of Book V.

The presence of the pregnant Mme Curie (as such, doubly creative) dominates most of this book. Unlike the physically exciting Phyllis and "Beautiful Thing," Curie excites because of her mind: "with ponderous belly, full/ of thought!" "Woman is the weaker vessel, but/ the mind is neutral . . . ." "And love, bitterly contesting, waits/ that the mind shall declare itself not/ alone in dreams." (209). As he wrote of her in his work sheets, "Curie: A different type of woman from the one just told/ The 'gist.'" And about contemporary women, Williams mourns, "Women have been for us unreal. We balk or turn away or trample them, our women are not the sea to us . . . . they are not knowledge." In contrast, he says, "Curie is woman and the sea to us." [41]

Instead of establishing this image of Curie as sea (not the image later in the poem, the sea of blood), why does William repeat that Curie is "a small Polish baby-nurse"? Because of his respect for the people of Guinea Hill? Because Book IV continues that pervasive argument with Pound: Curie, Phyllis, the nurses Williams has known —none is "cultured" in Old World traditions; all are "primitive." The long section in Book IV on credit ("Money: Joke") is the most obvious reference to Pound, but there are several other important related passages. The often-discussed artesian well passage (Book III) is directly involved here, with its concluding reproof that "water" may

be found here as well as in Europe. In Book IV Williams picks up
the motif,

> . just because they ain't no water fit to
> drink in that spot (or you ain't found none)
> don't mean there ain't no fresh water
> to be had NOWHERE . .
>
> (215)

His idiom here, as well as the original impetus for the well passage,
could easily have come from Pound's condescending letter to Williams
in 1941:

> I get very little American news, but shd/ welcome yr/ ideas as to
> what I dought to think about our native land and our rulers, naturally
> you object to thinking about its govt. and prefer to consider the
> anthropomorphology and composition of the humus and subsoil. . . .[42]

Williams draws the sections on credit and its abuses, the contro-
versies of art, and his image for discovery, "the radiant gist," together
at the end of Part II, as he asks Pound, "Will you consider/ . . .
LOCAL control of local purchasing power

> Difference between squalor of spreading slums
> and splendor of Renaissance cities.

> Credit makes solid
> is related directly to the effort,
> work: value created and received,
> "the radiant gist" against all that
> scants our lives.
>
> (218)

Williams' inclusion of letters from Allen Ginsberg, surely a local
product, involved in understanding his own place and time, also relates to this answer: as he has noted in an early draft,

> The lecture on uranium (Curie), the splitting of the atom (first time
> explained to *me*) has a literary meaning . . . in the splitting of the
> foot . . . (sprung meter of Hopkins) and consequently is connected

thereby to human life or death. . . . Three discoveries here: 1. radium.
2. poet's discovery of the modern idiom. 3. political scientist's discovery
of a cure for economic ills.[43]

With the opening of Book III, Part III, we are reminded of the
closing of the previous book, when Paterson declares, "I cannot stay
here/ to spend my life looking into the past:/ the future's no answer.
I must/ find my meaning and lay it, white, beside the sliding water"
(173). Unlike Eliot, who contended that past, present, and future
were one, Williams opts for the present as distinct in itself and introduces us to the two old yet vigorous people who determine much of
Part III's tone: Williams' English grandmother and the old Dutch
settler.

> Haven't you forgot your virgin purpose,
> the language?
>
> What language? "The past is for those who
> lived in the past," is all she told me.
>
> Shh! the old man's asleep
>
> —all but for the tides, there is no river,
> silent now, twists and turns
> in his dreams.
> (219)

Relying on that "virgin purpose, the language," Williams uses their
speech to give us the beloved old woman ("Virtue, she would
say . . . / is a stout old bird,/ unpredictable" [223]) and the Dutch
settler (226–232). Already the limited focus to shape *Paterson* V is
evident: these two, of all the people Williams had known, are chosen
to create the "last" of *Paterson*:

> You might think she had
>   a private ticket.
> I think she did; some
>   people, not many,
> make you feel that way.
>   It's in them
>   (223)

After his tribute to the indomitable woman (See "Dedication for a
Plot of Ground" and "The Last Words of My English Grandmother"), Paterson turns to the reminiscence of the Dutch settler,
"Stepping out of bed into a snow drift/ . . . then,/ after a porridge
breakfast, walk/ five miles to work. When I got there I/ did pound
the anvil for sartin', to keep/ up circulation" (230). His recollections are broken by the prose accounts of two senseless murders, the
killing of his baby daughter by Fred Goodell (a modern "$40-a-week
factory worker") and the 1850 hatchet and knife murders of the
John Van Winkles by their hired hand ("His object was doubtless
money [which, however, he seemed not to have obtained]" [232]).
The rhythms of Part III change noticeably as Williams includes a
Dutch nursery rhyme and then mimics its rhythm with his condem-
nation of man:

> You come today to see killed
> > > killed, killed
> as if it were a conclusion
> > > > —a conclusion!
> a convincing strewing of corpses
> —to move the mind
>
> > > > as tho' the mind
> can be moved, the mind, I said
> by an array of hacked corpses:
>
> > > > > War!
> a poverty of resource . .
> > > (233)

There can be no conclusion as such to Williams' long testament of
humanity, any more than there can be a conclusion to that humanity
itself. His mournful aside tells better than any vituperation the poet's
attitude:

> Oh that the rocks of the Areopagus had
> kept their sounds, the voices of the law!
> Or that the great theatre of Dionysius
> could be aroused by some modern magic
> > > > to release

what is bound in it, stones!
that music might be wakened from them to
melt our ears.
                (235)

No way to reach them; no way to govern them.

A mistaken "end" represented by the murders included here is the symbolic sea, a "sea of blood," "of indifferent man," [44] of death, as Williams describes it. Several pages of argument between the poet ("The sea is *not* our home") and his antagonist ("Yet you will come to it, come to it!") lead finally to the reappearance of man from the sea: "What's that?/ —a duck, a hell-diver? A swimming dog?" (236). The swimmer, accompanied by the dog of the earlier books, then slept on the sand, dressed in faded overalls, sampled some beach plums, and then "faced inland," like a Boone. Following this modern-day re-creation of the man Paterson, the last prose excerpt describes the hanging of the Van Winkles' murderer, "in full view of thousands who had gathered on Garrett Mountain and adjacent house tops to witness the spectacle." The poem closes almost in stasis, with ambivalent emphases on both a kind of justice and bloodthirsty human appetites. It is as if Williams is ready to admit that men are like this, many of them, drawn by the grotesque, the terror, the blood; but there are, too, those who respond best to beauty, to virtue. Williams intends to leave his readers with the notion of that one small seed of new life with which *Paterson* has begun (p. 12), floating in from the sea of blood, rather than the wide waste he has described in earlier books.[45] As Williams wrote in 1950 to José García Villa,

> The ocean of savage lusts in which the wounded shark
> gnashes at his own tail is not our home.
>   It is the seed that floats to shore, one word,
> one tiny, even microscopic word, is that which alone
> can save us.[46]

CHAPTER TWELVE

"Possessed by Many Poems"

IN many ways *Paterson* V represents a continuation of Williams' emphases not only in the first four books but in most of his last writing as well ("Asphodel" was titled *Paterson* in early drafts; several shorter poems were included as part of the epic). Although it was not published until 1958, Williams had been thinking of another volume as early as 1953 when he commented to John Thirlwall, "It's a possibility that there's something more to be said . . . . after all the violence . . . when all the stress has gone out of it . . . . you reverse the reel, let's say, and play it again and listen to its overtones."[1] The overtones of the first four books—the themes of art, virtue, woman's love, man's search for communication (and perhaps identity), the intellect—dominate Book V. Perhaps some confusion about the relationship between Book V and the rest of the epic arises from inaccurate definition of *theme* and *image:* themes are not necessarily images (the falls, the fire, the lame dog). It seems likely that a theme might continue even if one image or another has disappeared.

Paterson V

In Book III of *Paterson,* Williams has foreshadowed all his later writing: "What end but love, that stares death in the eye? A city, a marriage . . . The riddle of a man and a woman" (130). Then he moves immediately to art, as the only bulwark against death (in *Paterson* V he says it in capital letters, but no less clearly):

> Sing me a song to make death tolerable, a song
> of a man and a woman: the riddle of a man
> and a woman.
> > What language could allay our thirsts,
> what winds lift us, what floods bear us
> > > > past defeats
> but song but deathless song? (131)

Paterson as artist ("the voice!"), as lover of women, holds onto his vigor by staying close to the creative processes of both writing and birth. Yet often, as in Book IV, Williams' women do more than have children. We think of the truly productive Mme Curie, and also of the Abbess Hildegard who wrote her own funeral choral, to be sung by "all women." As Charles Tomlinson points out, the Abbess is also a European, not an American.[2] In searching for the deepest concerns of man, Williams is forced to transcend national boundaries.

As his poem to the Virgin Mary shows,[3] the feminine principle of gentle, giving love is hardly an American concept. Williams' focus in the 1950's has definitely shifted from searching for the American identity to reinforcing the universal traits and beliefs of all men. He speaks increasingly of the "classic," borrowing when and where he can: Theocritus, Sappho, J. A. Symonds' studies of Greek culture. By the end of *Paterson,* Williams has worked himself through his concern with nationality, a process made possible to some extent through the writing of that long poem. True to his belief that art begins with the local, *Paterson* I includes much early history. Book II, however, is concerned with people, presumably (but not necessarily) of Paterson; Book III, with the general written (and sometimes lying) accounts of the culture as found in libraries. The "factual" records are juxtaposed throughout this book with the living culture of love and violence, nature and human relationships. Then Book IV concentrates on the distillation of those general relationships by showing the traditions of family: Phyllis as *child* of drunken father; Williams and his *son* searching together; Marie Curie as both *mother* and discoverer, the best illustration yet of what "female principle" meant to Williams. So when we come to Book V, we are far beyond any limiting concerns with one man in one life. Man is free to draw on— indeed, must draw on—any resources to help find the answers, or perhaps to just keep his balance. Williams discusses art, the tapestries, other writers, but he never omits his local:

> WALK in the world
> (you can't see anything
> from a car window, still less
> from a plane, or from the moon!? Come
> off of it.)
> —a present, a "present"

world, across three states (Ben Shahn saw it
   among its rails and wires,
and noted it down) walked across three states
for it . .
         a secret world,
a sphere, a snake with its tail in
its mouth
            rolls backward into the past
                                                (249)

Man needs his resources—art, the real, the past, and the world of
private, even mythic, concerns. No one knows better than Williams
how tough it is to keep going. As he wrote in a 1934 "advice to a
young writer" column,

> If genius has anything to say in America it had better be strongwinded.
> . . . Life gets to be a battering down of the inessential. . . . I'd go so
> far as to say that everything a man can be taught in his youth has only
> this value, that unless he is a man it will kill him.[4]

Williams' preoccupation with *virtue* grows from his admiration for
women (when it relates to chastity; hence, the virgin-whore theme
of *Paterson*), but the term widens as the poem progresses to refer to
the way people—all people—live. Williams' sorrow over "value/
chipped away at an accelerated pace," the economic motif pointing
to a barrage of social ills, underlies perhaps the somewhat restricted
focus (and correspondingly gentle poise) of Book V. Williams has
preached and cajoled for forty years of writing—to what effect? His
final tactic is to withdraw, to concentrate on the people that he does
approve of ("our own are all that are real"[5]), and to write:

> all I can do (growing old) is to compose. It is the only recourse, the
> only intellectual recourse for an artist, to make, to make, to make and
> to go on making. . . . It is his *doing,* I mean, his only doing to com-
> pose: in a sort of night, in a sort of dumb philosophic stupor—except
> to himself where, within, there burns a fiery light, too fiery for logical
> statement.[6]

The themes of the last writing were those closest and dearest to him:
love, virtue, peace. In 1947 he had written to Louis Zukofsky that
men's self-seeking (and his own) irritated him: "Nobody sufficiently

writes to make us at least tolerate each other. But the good in poetry is a common good." [7]

Some of the admitted "changes" between Books IV and V occur because Williams had himself mellowed a bit; some, because any poem moves, any set of ideas develops. The eight years between these particular books had been agonizing ones for Williams: strokes, heart attacks, family disappointments, retirement, withdrawal of the Library of Congress appointment, cool critical reactions to Book IV of *Paterson* and *The Collected Later Poems.* Yet from it all had come a gravely tranquil poet. It seems no accident that after fulfilling his contract to Random House for *Make Light of It, The Autobiography,* and *The Build Up,* he turned almost exclusively to poetry (the one exception is the whimsical *Yes, Mrs. Williams,* in 1959, which may be in some respects another *Kora in Hell*). That prose throughout Williams' life had served as a laboratory for experimentation, but that in poetry he found jewels of a higher order, is evident in his concentration on poetry, once he knew that his writing years were limited.

> I have been ill, as you perhaps have heard. This is the second time I have been knocked out. But this time I seem to have come out of it with a clearer head. Perhaps it derived from a feeling that I might have died or, worse, have been left with a mind permanently incapacitated. That it has not happened is a piece of pure good fortune. As a result of the enforced idleness and opportunity for thought, it may be, I have brought hard down on the facts of a situation which can no longer be delayed in the bringing of it to a final summary. I must now, in other words, make myself clear. I must gather together the stray ends of what I have been thinking and make my full statement as to their meaning or quit.
>
> . . . .
>
> What will come of my "idleness," which has been forced on me by my illness, it is hard to say. Will I be able to maintain it? I should passionately like to use it for the further development of my reading and my thinking and my doing if I can. I don't want to go back to the practice of medicine. The opportunity to complete my task as poet has never seemed so hopeful and attractive as now. [8]

Williams' later poetry, that written from 1950 to 1962, is remarkable evidence of his steady technical accomplishment. More important, perhaps, even in these days of the carefully crafted poem, is the tone of

surety, of contentment, that colors these poems. The angry younger
man of the 1930's, who turned from poems to short stories in the
midst of his own personal depression, has come to realize that private
satisfactions are greater than public ones, that his own happiness (finding it when and where he could) is more important than the condition of the world surrounding him. Although Williams is at times
still displeased, still reproving, he has, however, found many things in
which to rejoice. Whether he muses with some sadness about the
neighbor he has never visited, or describes wryly the "young woman/
on whose belly I have never/ slept though others/ have," he is happy.
When he writes lovingly of his poetry—as he does in "The Desert
Music," "Asphodel," and *Paterson* V—or of his grandchildren—in
"Three Stances," "Suzy," and "Paul"—Williams is a man at peace
with himself.

   J. Hillis Miller has pointed out that many of Williams' late poems
deal with death. But even here, as a rule, there is tranquillity. Only
rarely does he rant; more often he affirms the power of love, as in
"The Rewaking" ("and so by/ your love the very sun/ itself is re-
vived") or in "Asphodel," where he declares of love that "Death/
is not the end of it." On occasion, he assumes the practical attitude
of the old goose described so well in "To Daphne and Virginia."

> there, penned in,
>   or he would eat the garden,
>   lives a pet goose who
> tilts his head
>   sidewise
>   and looks up at us,
> a very quiet old fellow
>   who writes no poems.
>   Fine mornings we sit there
> while birds come and go.
>   A pair of robins
> is building a nest
>   for the second time
>   this season. Men
> against their reason
>   speak of love, sometimes,
>   when they are old. It is

all they can do
　　　or watch a heavy goose
　　　　　who waddles, slopping
　　　　　noisily in the mud of
　　　　　his pool (78–79).

As Williams depicts it, one feels that old age is something to respect; that it brings wisdom and, with it, a slow coda of renewed, renewing love.

He seems newly aware not only of his wife and family, and of the place of death in his life, but also of man as admirable. Many of his late poems emphasize the good of mankind, perhaps partly because, as he writes in "The Gift," "All men by their nature give praise./ It is all they can do."

In the poems of *The Desert Music* (1954), *Journey to Love* (1955), *Paterson* V (1958), and *Pictures from Brueghel* (1962), Williams turns for inspiration to people he loves, and he loves them for somewhat different reasons than he had as a younger poet. The 1944 poem "To Ford Madox Ford in Heaven" praised Ford for his ability to "roust and love and dredge the belly full." In 1955 Williams praises his wife of "Asphodel" for her ability to embody love:

It was the love of love,
　　　the love that swallows up all else,
　　　　　a grateful love,
　　a love of nature, of people,
　　　animals,
　　　　　a love engendering
　　gentleness and goodness
　　　that moved me
　　　　　and *that* I saw in you (160).

He admires too those people who rely on feelings. He writes to Sister M. Bernetta Quinn,

In life (you show it by your tolerance of things which you feel no loss at not understanding) there is much that men exclude because they do not understand. The truly great heart *includes* what it does not at once grasp, just as the great artist includes things which go beyond him.[9]

To the arguments that Williams was a defeated man, that he had abandoned the principles of the local, the American idiom,[10] his poems are the best answer. The argument (that Williams had gone over to the other camp, as it were) runs that for forty years he taught that man's surroundings were the most valid source for his writing. The old woman munching on plums, the wind-blown brown paper, the sprig of Queen Anne's lace—all are segments of Williams' local. However, say these readers, Williams' last four books of poems are different. Not only is a whole sequence of poems based on graphic art, Brueghel's paintings, but there is frequent mention of music, drama, other poetry, other art objects. The green glass between hospital walls represented for them Williams' "real" local. These later poems are, they contend, making use of "traditional" references —literary, unreal, unlocal.

One could answer this assumption in several ways. To look upon Williams' interest in art as symptomatic of his impatience with the concrete world seems less defensible when one realizes that nearly every artist Williams admired is or was a devotee of the actual, the detailed depiction of life. It might also be considered that throughout his life Williams was deeply interested in the other arts. Few poets have been so willing to write introductions for plays (as well as plays themselves) or critiques for art exhibits. Having at one time played the violin, Williams felt that he knew music, and his admiration for dance also dated from early years. But it was to painting that he was most drawn, partly because his mother and many of his closest friends (Charles Demuth, Charles Sheeler, Marsden Hartley) were painters. We have seen that the technical ferment in graphic art intrigued and influenced him throughout his life.

Then, too, seeing the worn, white-covered collection of Brueghel's paintings lying prominently on Williams' desk forces one to appreciate that the prints of which he writes in "Pictures from Brueghel" are a part of his local—a local defined by him in this 1944 discussion of art:

> If, as I believe and keep always before my eyes, if art is a transference —for psychic relief—from the actual to the formal, and if this can only be achieved by invention, by rediscovery, by reassertion by the intelligence and the emotions in any and every age—and if the grand aspect of

this living drive is, when it occurs, a culture, then, I say, our chief occupation as artists, singly and jointly, should be the clarification of form, new alignments, in our own language and culture.

. . . .

I have maintained from the first that Eliot and Pound by virtue of their hypersensitivity (which is their greatness) were too quick to find a culture (the English continental) ready made for their assertions. They ran from something else, something cruder but, at the same time, newer, more dangerous but heavy with rewards for the sensibility that could reap them. They couldn't. Or didn't. But they both ended by avoiding not only the possibilities offered but, at the same time, the deeper implications intellectually which our nascent culture accented.[11]

There is promise in Williams' American local, but—perhaps greater—there is a responsibility to it that it be re-created in consonant, new forms. We notice too that Williams does not speak of the *objects* of a culture; he refers to the culture itself, an entity of great breadth and richness. As he had written early in *Paterson* V, "a place is made of memories as well as the world around it." For that reason, the poet Paterson is joyful as he remembers, the greatest of all human capabilities; and, as a result of this remembering, returns "to the old scenes/ to witness/ What has happened . . . ." In Book II of *Paterson* Williams has affirmed,

> Memory is a kind
> of accomplishment,
> a sort of renewal
> even
> an initiation.

Life, culture, is more than the objective real. The giant Paterson has been dreaming throughout the epic; dreams, too, must be given credence. Later in *Paterson,* Williams describes Audubon, who, in his Kentucky explorations, saw unicorn as well as buffalo. Even the most observant artist must be cognizant of the more-than-real.

Throughout his career, Williams championed the creation of new human life as one means of succeeding in the world, but he never forgot the necessity of artistic creation. In *I Wanted to Write a Poem,* he explained, "When you're through with sex, with ambition, what

can an old man create? Art, of course, a piece of art that will go beyond him into the lives of young people, the people who haven't had
time to create. The old man meets the young people and lives on." [12]
As Paterson the poet answers his own query in Book V, "What has
happened to Paris since that time?/ and to myself?/ A WORLD OF
ART/ THAT THROUGH THE YEARS HAS/ SURVIVED!"

The world of art mentioned here refers first to Soupault's *Last
Nights of Paris,* the novel Williams translated for publication in 1929.
He admired the prose of the book, but more important to him was
Soupault's concern with the mysterious Parisian whore—beautiful
woman? good spirit? voice of the night, of Paris? In the ambiguity
of this character may lie one source of Williams' later Paterson. At
any rate, his notice of the novel early in Book V introduces one of the
dominant themes of that section: ostensibly, the virgin-whore identity;
more subtly, the virtue of selfless giving. And on a wider base, the
definition of *virtue* itself.

Critics who read *Paterson* V as a paean to art are overlooking this
important cluster of themes. Admittedly, art to William is virtuous,
as is the true artist ("you cannot be/ an artist/ by mere ineptitude/
The dream is in pursuit!"). But so is the Portuguese mason who will
not be content with inferior material; the English grandmother who
loves well though unlawfully; all those men who have grace and
pity, who will struggle against "the age of shoddy." Virtue is doing
one's best, despite human frailties. The wise men in Brueghel's painting of the Nativity are virtuous, as is Brueghel, because "they had
eyes for visions/ in those days." So too is Joseph, husband of Mary,
because he believed the words of an angel speaking in his dream.
Were it not for Joseph's dream, who could have determined whether
Mary was virgin or whore? The pattern occurs again in Williams'
later writings: "The Farmers' Daughters" has as protagonist the
"virtuous" whore Margaret; *The Cure,* the housewife-nurse; "The
Desert Music," the Juarez whore. In an early version of the latter,
Williams describes "the virgin of her mind." [13] As he says firmly in
Paterson V: "no woman is virtuous/ who does not give herself to
her lover/ —forthwith."

Segments of these themes coalesce into one broad concern with
virtue; it is strange that some readers have found here instead an un-
reasonable emphasis on art. What seems to have been overlooked is that

Williams is using his art objects as a means of recapitulating, of drawing together, earlier themes. Just as the *Last Nights of Paris* introduced such motifs as personal identity, the wasting on of time, the
issue of chastity, so Williams' reliance on the Flemish tapestry *The
Hunt of the Unicorn* serves to interrelate many themes which have
appeared in all five books of *Paterson*. He does not need to summarize
didactically what he has already said. Neither does he leave the poem
to end with the concerns of Book V. Instead, he finds a concrete
object which embodies both the things of the culture he loves and the
personal qualities he has sought. Here is Nature—birds and flowers in
unimaginably vivid detail. Here is the young, mysteriously beautiful
woman. Here is the greater-than-real Unicorn, his horn breaking into
the high, white stars. Here is art, and of it Williams wrote joyously:
"They will not fade!/ Those flowers will not fade!" And the creation
of this masterpiece has been possible only because the artists were
"All together, working together" according to a *design*.

The tapestry is important not only as the culmination of many
separate themes but also as a way of perceiving Paterson the man.
Williams seldom presents art objects in isolation. The tapestry, for
example, appears as an integral part of Paterson's thoughts and experience, as in this passage:

> —every married man carries in his head
> the beloved and sacred image
> of a virgin
> whom he has whored
> but the living fiction
> a tapestry
> silk and wool shot with silver threads
> a milk-white one-horned beast
> I, Paterson, the King-self [14]
> (272)

Man's thoughts are a tapestry, a fiction: Paterson is in some ways the
Unicorn, the King-self. Williams' juxtaposition of phrases, often
without formal transition, effectively re-creates the suddenness, the
simultaneity, of human thought—in this case, of Paterson's thought.

It is a poet-Paterson of new resolution, of new decision, who
writes the poetry of the fifth book. In the earlier books, the poet

is a searching, ambivalent character, as susceptible at sixty-five to all impressions of his kaleidoscopic world as he was at thirty. Yet the many misreadings of the earlier books, singly and as a completed quartet, seem to have convinced Williams that the Objectivist approach had perhaps been wrong—or, if not wrong, at least too singular in its method to carry the weight of an entire long poem. Letting each fragment of image speak for itself was a precarious tactic, one incapable of guaranteeing uniform readings. Williams is now past the age of letting his readers find what they wanted in his poems. As he has written to Louis Martz, "I must now, in other words, make myself clear" (see p. 171). His attempt to make a "final summary" brings Williams to the newly explicit Book V of *Paterson,* as well as the poems of 1954, 1955, and 1962.

Paterson VI

The four pages of fragments or notes for a poem labeled *Paterson* VI serve to summarize Williams' late poems. The magnificent Lucy who "couldn't read or write," "vulgar/ but fiercely loyal to me," [15] might well have been another of his earthy heroines. Hamilton, with his nickname of "The Genius," had no need to create, only to "organize the country . . . stick together and make a little money," to exploit America much as had Cortez centuries before. In another fragment, Williams returns to Hamilton's term for the people, "A Great Beast," and reproves him: "he hated it/ of which he knew nothing and cared less/ and used it in his schemes." The description here sounds so much like Williams' usual criticism of Pound that we wonder whether the referent for *he* is intentionally obscure. Li Po, Sappho, Socrates, Aristotle—Williams mentions them all in opposition to Hamilton, but concludes the passage with praise for Washington, the inarticulate hero: "—Washington was a six foot four man with a weak voice and a slow mind which made it inconvenient for him to move fast—and so he stayed" (283). The theme, again, of American artists like Eliot and Pound leaving America while Williams remained, is more than suggested here, as Williams goes on to praise Washington's tenacity: "He had a will bred in the slow woods so that when he moved the world moved out of his way."

In Williams' later poems, it seems that the slow woods of America do produce the all-important "will." In "The Ivy Crown," only the force of the lovers' wills changes the cruelty of young love into something beautiful. In "Asphodel," man survives not because of any inherent quality, but because he decides to survive; and for a man like that—whether it be a Washington or a Jack O'Brien or a Williams—the world reserves some notice.

The will, the persistence, is evident too in these lines from the sixth book. Even here Williams manages to include a line of poetics: "Words are the burden of poems," and we are reminded of his declaration in 1954:

> I speak as if writing poetry were my sole concern and indeed it is finally so. For as far as I know all writing starts and ends with the poem. When I write a short story it might better have been a poem, and for an essay there is nothing so fine as a definition or defense of the art which deals with the poetic principle.[16]

There is also a passage on the now familiar dance, occurring in what is probably the most finished of these poems, "1/8/61," written about the poet's bedroom wallpaper. As if coming full circle, this poem also includes one of the precise images characteristic of Williams' earliest writing: that of "a frosty elm outlined in gayest/ of all pantomimes" (282).

Indomitable. A man close to death writing about gaiety, dance, birth. Williams' many self-portraits in this last decade (the sparrow, the pink locust, the King-self, the old poet) suggest that he was himself almost becoming a symbol for the endurance of all men. The poet as persona here parallels the hardy asphodel, growing in rock, without water, or the mysterious "red and yellow roses" he compares *Paterson* with in his notes for the poem:

> never a "garden" but bushes of roses,
> in a few square yards of soil,
> impossibly located at the foot of an outdoor
> stairway or under heavy trees, blossoming
> furiously—hard to explain.[17]

"Impossibly located" in Rutherford, Williams gained from his surroundings and went on "blossoming furiously." Louis Martz points out that although Williams' production in the 1940's and 1950's was tremendous, as it was through his fifty years of writing, "there is an order, a reason, a firm and central purpose to be discerned." [18] Much of that purpose has already been discussed in these last two chapters. Perhaps one of the most central of Williams' interests has yet to be described in relation to this later writing: his aim of fusing the usually distinct categories of prose and poetry. That all writing was, to Williams, writing is nowhere more evident than in the rhythms and structure of *Paterson* and in the rhythmic arrangement of the shorter poems of the 1950's. For one of the first times in his life, Williams was writing primarily poetry, but a poetry so based on essential prose rhythms that one could almost cite Pound's 1915 dictum,

> Poetry must be *as well written as prose*. Its language must be a fine language, departing in no way from speech save by a heightened intensity (i.e. simplicity). There must be no book words, no periphrases, no inversions. It must be as simple as De Maupassant's best prose, and as hard as Stendhal's.[19]

CHAPTER THIRTEEN

"The Necessity for Invention"

THROUGHOUT his life as writer, Williams was insistent on the new. Innovation was important partly because of his dissatisfaction with much of his own writing[1] and partly because of the direction which writing from 1920 to the mid-1930's had taken. Many writers were experimenting with prose-poetry mixtures; Surrealism, Dadaism, and Cubism gave precedent to all kinds of form (and formlessness). As Norman Holmes Pearson remarked recently, Williams' *TGAN* was not, in 1925, the fragmented account it might appear to be today, but rather a very "à la mode" piece of writing.[2] By the 1930's, however, Williams had determined the direction that much of his later experimentation was to continue: toward finding a new, more expansive line. As he wrote in 1931 of Pound's *Cantos:* "They [the lines] have a character that is parcel of the poem itself. (It is in the small make-up of the lines that the character of the poem definitely comes—and beyond which it cannot go.)"[3] Although Williams knew what he liked, he could not, at this time, give specific principles for that liking. In 1932 he made this plea for poetic tolerance of the widest sort: "The modern line must at least exclude no possibility of intelligent resource," with the conclusion, again, that Pound's line in his *Cantos* is "something *like* what we shall achieve."[4]

As we have seen, Williams turned to prose during the 1930's, his stalemate in poetry stemming partly from his interest in idiom. Fiction provided a means of letting the language of his characters shape not only their personae but also, in some cases, the stories being told.[5] With his own fiction writing, Williams could appreciate the strengths of a sharp, direct prose—and could realize, as Pound had twenty years earlier, the affinity between the best of both modes. As he stated in 1937, "To turn the writing of 'White Mule' from my usual interests in poetry meant no more to me than the carrying over of the same concerns for language into new conditions."[6] The "same concerns"—how to make language clear and vivid, real to both situation and persona—dominate his comments on prose writing; just as the very size of the "new conditions" (creating complete scenes and relationships rather than fragmentary or suggestive ones) forces him into even greater verbal precision.

After his own forays into fiction and drama, Williams returns to Pound's accomplishment in his epic, this time with an awareness of how easily Pound treats an "unpoetic" subject in the rhythms of poetry:

> It is impossible to praise Pound's line. The terms for such praise are lacking. There ain't none. You've got to read the line and feel first, then grasp through experience in its full significance HOW the language makes the verse live. It lives; even such unpromising cataloguing as his *Cantos* of the Chinese kings, princes and other rulers do live. . . .[7]

Here Williams is impressed with the variability of Pound's line. Ten years before, in 1931, he has praised his friend's inclusion of prose without disturbing the flow of the poem, the line being expansive enough to hold the prose. Yet it is to be another ten years (1951) before Williams comes to the "terms" as well as a possible structure for his own elusive line.[8] In 1951 he speaks somewhat tentatively about a "new measure"; by 1954, after writing many poems in the triadic line form, he explains to Richard Eberhart:

> By measure I mean musical pace. Now, with music in our ears the words need only be taught to keep as distinguished an order, as chosen a character, as regular, according to the music, as in the best of prose.[9]

Denis Donoghue echoes Williams' explanation in his praise of these later poems:

> This is verse at least as well written as distinguished prose. The measure is just sufficiently *there* to enforce discipline and to ensure that the writing (and the consciousness behind it) will be scrupulous, exact. . . . Williams is using a measure not to intensify but to control, to test the feeling as it meets the edge of the language.[10]

Coming as it does after nearly a half century of remarkably measureless verse, Williams' triadic line is notable for its regularity, its three-part structure of feet comparatively equal in time, if not in syllable count or accent occurrence. Such orderly arrangement helps the reader to experience the "repetition and expectancy" which have characterized meter through the ages. As I. A. Richards writes in his "Rhythm and Metre,"

> This texture of expectations, satisfactions, disappointments, surprisals, which the sequence of syllables brings about, is rhythm. And the sound of words comes to its full power only through rhythm. Evidently there can be no surprise and no disappointment unless there is expectation. . . .[11]

It is exactly this expectation of an order which underlay Williams' concept of the triadic line. Reminiscent of his enthusiasm for Poe's virtuosity with "sequences and intervals, his music,"[12] Williams insisted (1) that a measure of some kind was necessary, a means of giving the poem that regular, expected movement; and (2) that the measure be flexible, or, in his scientifically oriented terms, "relative."

The 1955 poem "A Negro Woman" illustrates well the general symmetry of the triadic line, with several important variations. The opening lines include two one-syllable segments, the first—*wrapped*—set apart because of both pronunciation difficulty and its grammatical place in the sentence; the second—*bareheaded*—separated for pictorial emphasis.

> A Negro Woman
> carrying a bunch of marigolds
>   wrapped
>   in an old newspaper:
> She carries them upright,
>   bareheaded,
>   the bulk
> of her thighs
>   causing her to waddle
>   as she walks. . . .

The leisurely, dignified pace is established. It is maintained throughout the short poem, lending strong emphasis to the metaphor which so surely places the woman in her proper, natural element:

> What is she
>   but an ambassador
>   from another world
> a world of pretty marigolds. . . .

The conclusion of the poem, expressed in a simile, reinforces the effect of the stronger metaphor. The woman walks on; and one wonders whether, in her innocent pace, there is not more characterization than in the two figures of speech combined.

> a world of pretty marigolds
>   of two shades
>   which she announces
> not knowing what she does
>   other
>   than walk the streets
> holding the flowers upright
>   as a torch
>   so early in the morning (*PB,* 123).

As Williams wrote, "Poetry has to do with pace and essence. It is the . . . key to linguistic character."[13]

The arrangement here is as effective visually as it is audibly. The three-line sequences give the impression of interweaving content, phrases independent yet closely related to the rest of the poem. Poems so arranged are usually wider than most of Williams' earlier writing, and the combination of space and print gives a leisurely effect. Audibly, such poems do move regularly: Williams' readings show that he gave each segment of line approximately the same duration in time. One line might contain three syllables; the next, twelve. The time value of each will be nearly the same, however, for various reasons of emphasis ("the use of pause, robbato, as characteristic of the speech").[14]

Arriving at the form of these late poems was no simple achievement. At least twenty years of experiments lay between the time Williams knew what he liked and the years when he found the means of obtaining that desired line himself; and much of that experimentation occurred within *Paterson.* We have discussed the thematic importance of his epic to Williams; the poem is perhaps of even greater significance as, in the poet's words, a field for working out the "problems of a new prosody."[15] The five books of *Paterson* provide much evidence of the various tactics Williams employed in trying to force a harmony between poetry and prose, before he realized that the harmony between the two was an inherent one, needing only to be used, not created.

Prose in *Paterson*

Williams' first attempts at enriching the poetic line of his epic were reminiscent of his practices in the *American Grain* essays: heavy quotation from original documents of history. He had spoken in the 1920's of the valuable "flavor" achieved by including such passages (indeed, his interest in their use seems to go beyond his affinity for speech as a means of characterization). Williams in 1935 justified Pound's use of "colonial matter" in the *Cantos* by explaining, "We cannot write well as man wrote well in the past . . . and have what we do hold the modern or the fullest content."[16] Williams thus recognized the validity of capturing the temper of the past, particularly when the relationship between present and past is important to the work being written.

In Book I of *Paterson,* the poet is intent on at least two emphases: depicting the myth and history of the city-man Paterson; and introducing the themes of wonder and fear, waste and usury, love and divorce, and poetics that will continue throughout the poem. Working, as he felt he must, from a montage of concrete episodes and images, he often combined both purposes when he relied on the prose excerpts from history. The savagery of the search for pearls at Notch Brook is vivid evidence of man's greed regardless of waste, with the prose itself lending noticeable rhythmic variety. The formally matter-of-fact narrative of the past is very different from Pound's later unrestrained cries of "waste":

> News of this sale created such excitement that search for the pearls was started throughout the country. The Unios (mussels) at Notch Brook and elsewhere were gathered by the millions and destroyed often with little or no result. A large round pearl, weighing 400 grains which would have been the finest pearl of modern times, was ruined by boiling open the shell (17).

Williams' inclusion of the passages on Jackson's Whites, Mrs. Cumming's death, and the foolishly noble Sam Patch ("some things can be done as well as others") also introduce important themes and simultaneously create the steady, nonemotional tone of the past narratives. The prose segments are usually quite well introduced (as the Cumming's episode illustrates a "false language" theme), fitting clearly into the mosaic of poetry.

Also in Book I, Williams shows a bit more daring as he relates three seemingly unconnected prose passages through thematic emphasis within the poetry (more commonly, the prose acts as a gloss for the poems). The line "They craved the miraculous" leads to the account of the human monster, a "natural curiosity" ranking in interest with the falls themselves. George Washington visited the deformed young man, the prose tells us. "A wonder! A wonder!" says the poem (reminiscent of the sea monster representing love), and the next prose excerpt describes the growth of Paterson, from ten houses to a city of 20,000 people. Then follows the capture of the 126-pound bass, another "monster" (19–20). By fitting the census report between these two descriptions of monsters, the horrifying aspects of the industrialized village are more than implied.

Several of the passages from the history of Paterson also relate to the theme of poetic theory that runs throughout the poem. Toward the end of Book I, Williams is working with the theme of "wealth"— wealth of poetic material and the questionable monetary wealth of modern society. The doctor who is more interested in tearing the label off a mayonnaise jar than in caring for either his patients or the young colored woman provides a good introduction to a culture represented by "In time of general privation/ a private herd, 20 quarts of milk/ to the main house and 8 of cream" (45). This 19-line enumeration is followed by the chattel inventory of one Cornelius Doremus, of total value, $419.58½. The contrast culminates in a long prose account of huge eels struggling in acres of fertile mud and the frenzy of men's catching them. A wonder, a plenty—but to be gathered only in the mud. "P. Your interest is in the bloody loam but what/ I'm after is the finished product" (50).* Much like the artesian well passage, Williams' "answer" to Pound's arguments is that one

* In Yale work sheets, the line from Pound follows the eel passage much more directly than in the final version.

must have roots in that mud, that bloody loam, to be productive. The running dialogue between the two poets seems to force Williams into the lower classes for illustration of his themes, as in his use of the Negro "Beautiful Thing" and the semiliterate letters of later books.

In Books I and II of *Paterson,* the poet is frequently to employ interesting bits of lore and gossip—some of them, one suspects, primarily for their interest; but as he moves farther into the poem, his prose passages come increasingly from modern contexts. These are of various kinds: news items direct from daily papers; prose restatements of themes presented more obliquely in poetry; passages apparently related to Margaret's murder in "The Farmer's Daughters"; excerpts from modern literature. But most of the contemporary prose excerpts come from actual letters—those written by the poetess Cress, Allen Ginsberg, Edward Dahlberg, Josie Herbst, and the letters in substandard English of T. and D.J.B.* While some of these appear at random, placed seemingly because of what they say rather than how they say it, the letters from Ginsberg and particularly Cress lend their respective sections much of the existing structure.

Cress's letters dominate Book II, the "people in the park" section (the first prose excerpt in Book I was also from one of her letters). Williams uses lines from her impassioned writing as the first and third prose selections in Book II, and also the eighth; and then, in rapid sequence, as the thirteenth, fifteenth, and eighteenth. What occurs between excerpts gives poignancy to each of the sections as it appears. The poet's sadness over (and disgust with) the people of Paterson as he walks among them makes his use of Hamilton's description of them, "a Great Beast," not entirely ironic. Cress is in some ways the voice of the common woman, in emotional need as well as financial, and yet articulate enough to try to get help from those who should be compassionate. Still, one irony of the modern culture is that even the "best" will not become involved and that the long torrent of words in the final letter, which closes Book II, goes unread by all but the most responsible reader.

Williams uses the second part of Book II for a masterful elaboration—indeed, a near explanation—of these working-class people, among whom "some sort of breakdown has occurred." He opens the

* These might be those referred to in Williams' notes at Yale as the letters from the colored girls that Kitty got for him.

section with prose passages questioning the traditional source of comfort, the church; and the equally traditional danger, the "Communists"; and then launches into a series of prose accounts of SUM, the theories of Hamilton, and the Federal Reserve System—only to return to Cress as one result of the entire program. Like Pound, Williams is placing some of the responsibility for the modern age (which he compares in this section to the "slow complaining of a door loose on its hinges") on economics. His sympathy with Cress in her position is evident from his closing for her letter,[17] as well as from his comments about the use of her letters to such an extent in *Paterson*. And the definite contrast between the textbook tone of the prose dealing with Hamilton and banking and the human rush of emotion in Cress's letters helps establish the basis for his sympathy.

Because so much of Book III deals by implication with the past history of Paterson (its accumulated culture, the fire, the tornado, the flood), most of its prose excerpts come again from the past, but only half of them are related to Paterson proper. These repeat the themes of wonder in the stories of the fire, the tightrope walkers, and the spectral cat; but each account now also includes violence or death and leads by association to the dominant series of prose passages in this book, those describing Indian and African ritual. Sacrifice, burial rites, the mourning period—these rites characterize cultures Williams considers "rooted" in such basic mores as brotherhood and respect for age and death, cultures different from (and stronger than) that of modern America. These customs become even more meaningful when we realize that often the avaricious white man caused the death in question. Leaving this emphasis on ritual and its unifying effects on a culture, Williams closes Book III with descriptions of an orgy at a modern bar, followed by one woman's lament for her murdered friend. The progression in the excerpts implies that frenzy, if not outright murder, is one ritual of contemporary society.

Book IV continues this emphasis on the degradation which exists even within possible promise. The travesty of fulfilling love in the "Idyl" among Phyllis, Corydon, and Dr. Paterson sets the tone for this concluding section: only in Phyllis' letters to her father is there any sense of love. The enthusiastic Ginsberg letters maintain this theme of virtue—the discussion which dominates Book IV—as the young poet shows both his respect for the older artist and his love for his native culture. Just as the tone of Book IV vacillates between composed certainty that men *will* live virtuously, *will* do their best, and sadness as Williams mourns the artificiality of some modern standards, so does the intent of the prose excerpts vary. Some are used to point up the desirable elements of the culture—Columbus' wonder at America's beauty, the restful quality of the hotel clerk's chance encounter. More, however, depict the negative: a political advertisement against "usury"; the 1779 murder of a neighbor, disguised to look like political revenge; the murders of the Van Winkles by their hired man. As the poetry of Book IV suggests, men's lives are motivated by their mistaken concepts of virtue: each murder described is for material gain, except for the most horrifying of all, that of the baby daughter by a man who was making a "good" living.

Man's inability to discriminate between what is valuable and what is not causes Williams to worry the definition of *virtue* through most of Books IV and V. "The virgin and the whore/ which most endures?" becomes the question, with a variety of personae used to illustrate Williams' answer. And as the thematic lines of all the books of *Paterson* converge, so too does Williams' use of prose become more various. The external patterns visible in Books I–III have given way to a less formal arrangement of elements: the poet is willing to move from poetry to prose whenever the need occurs, one medium being no more comfortable than the other to him. It is as if the fusion that he was insisting on in 1948 has finally occurred in fact:

> All the prose has primarily the purpose of giving a metrical continuity between all word use . . . . It *is* that prose and verse are both *writing,* both a matter of the words and an interrelation between words for the purpose of exposition, or other better defined purpose of *the art* . . . . prose and verse are to me the same thing, that verse (as in Chaucer's tales) belongs *with* prose, as the poet belongs with "Mine host," who says in so many words to Chaucer, "Namoor, all that rhyming is not worth a toord." Poetry does not *have* to be kept away from prose as Mr. Eliot might insist, it goes *along with* prose and, companionably, by itself, without aid or excuse or need for separation or bolstering, shows itself by *itself* for what it is.[18]

By the time of Books IV and particularly V, Williams has also reached the stage in his poetry that enables him to use it to clarify, explain, and summarize—purposes formerly left either to prose passages or to the technique of juxtaposition. The poet's use of a more subjective voice in his later poems permits more statement about the concrete objects and episodes which dominated early *Paterson,* and the looser poetic line in the later books (the two-part as well as the triadic) is appropriate to that new subjectivity.

> The moon was in its first quarter.
>   As we approached the hospital
>   the air above it, having taken up
>   the glow through the glass roof
>   seemed ablaze, rivalling night's queen (171).

Such easy rhythm, characteristic of the later poems like "To Daphne and Virginia" or "Asphodel," enables Williams to say a great deal: "As Carrie Nation/ to Artemis/ so is our life today" (180). Social comment can be made simply and succinctly, with few objective examples necessary for proof. The "voice" quality, too, that Williams was always aiming for was easier to maintain in this arrangement. But, as he has the persona of Mrs. Williams say within the poem, "(What I miss, said your mother, is the poetry, the pure poem of the first parts.)" (171). While it is true that early books of *Paterson* seem to be composed of groups of short, reasonably well-defined lyrics set among longer sections of loose poetic statement, and these both accented by the unquestionable prose passages,[19] the coherence of the later books derives not from any contrapuntal arrangement so much as from the unity within the many shapes of the writing. Whether lines are long or short, the poem continues its consistent pace.

What Williams has achieved in parts of *Paterson* IV and V, and in most of the triadic-line poems, is best described by Josephine Miles in her recent *Style and Proportion: The Language of Prose and Poetry.* Miss Miles contends that the modes of prose and poetry differ both in arrangement and in word choice. Poetry, in most cases, is recognized by its "design," but its words will more likely be monosyllabic or disyllabic, those most commonly spoken ("Prose, not poetry, is the specializer of language").[20] She concludes,

> most inventive in our day is the concept of American idiom, held by
> William Carlos Williams and others, which establishes the phrase as a

poetic unit and lets stress play across it by use of line structure . . . .
Williams keeps [the phrase] from prosaicness by the counterstress of
the line.[21]

There is tension, there is form; but most of all there is the seemingly
free voice speaking. The ardor of his fifteen years of writing *Paterson,*
as well as the earlier years of work in both poems and prose, has
brought Williams to his final speech—a speech as dependent on prose
rhythms as on poetic arrangement, but a satisfying and viable speech,
no matter which mode the reader prefers.

The Last Prose

Williams' last formal prose writing is far from "formal."
Yes, Mrs. Williams, his 1959 biography of his mother, draws from the
same beliefs about writing as did *Paterson* and the later poems. The
biography depends heavily on the speech of Hélène Williams herself.
In places it is little more than a sequence of her anecdotes (some of
them so short as to be told in a single sentence), with vertical space
rather than transitions used between them. Williams makes no
attempt to connect the fragments into any narrative pattern or
chronology. Since his mother lived with his family for nearly twenty-
five years, until her death at 102 in 1949, a sense of time is relatively
insignificant; the montage instead creates the impression of Hélène's
unchanging character.

So that he would have examples of his mother's speech, Williams
had through the years transcribed passages of her talk:

> All sorts of things would come out of her from time to time. I got into
> the habit of writing them down—on the back of an envelope, on any
> piece of scrap paper I could lay my hands on quickly—*so as to pre-
> serve the flavor and accurate detail.*[22]

These bits of her speech were originally "to be incorporated with
selections from her letters."[23] The finished biography includes few
letters, but Williams' insistence on them in this 1938 note foreshadows
his reliance on letters in *Paterson.* His aim in this long-planned
biography, as in so much of his writing, was to re-create the thing or
person so that he achieved "touch," the feeling of genuine immediacy.

If you make it a work of the imagination, she might have
said, it won't be me.

I'll fool you, old girl. I won't make it a work of
the imagination. I'll make it you.[24]

In his study of American poetry, Hyatt Waggoner terms Mrs.
Williams and Ezra Pound the two strongest influences on Williams
as poet.[25] While Williams had great admiration for his mother, he
admired her not for what she knew but for what she was: clairvoyant,
rash, foreign, and always womanly. She embodied the mystic, the
intuitive, those forces that Williams was drawn toward (if the world
was run by logic, there must be something better). Imperious and
whimsical, Mrs. Williams is dynamically presented in the long introduction to *The Dog and the Fever,* Quevedo's novella which they
translated together, as well as in the later biography.

Williams' rationale for prefacing the Quevedo book with the
profile of his mother may be as romantic as several of his attitudes
about her (he delighted to see her as frustrated painter, as mystic,
as the eternally feminine). In the late 1930's he wrote that the translating of the novella was "only the pretext: the real story is how all the
complexities finally come to play one tune, today—to me—what I find
good in my own life." [26] Seeing himself as her child, Williams finds
similarities between them: their love, their "vigor for living," [27] their
romanticism: "The truth and its pursuit was always at the front of
my mother's mind. It was a long time before I came to realize how
her romantic ideas had deceived her and me in the modern world"
(20).

The most important similarity between the poet and Hélène was
their appetite for life. Each had "partaken of many things, welcoming
them indiscriminately if they seemed to have a value—a color—a
sound to add still more to the intelligent, the colorful, the whole grasp
of feeling and knowledge in the world." [28] Hélène represented a
synthesis of both feeling and knowledge (as examples Williams gives
us accounts of her clairvoyant spells as well as her stirring recitation
in French of Racine's "Rome enfin que je hais!"). She was capable
of both stubbornness and sensitivity: "That old tree looks like an
animal" (132). But most important of all, to the poet, was her
encouragement, her force, for him in his life.

Men! men that accomplish great things are her ideal. She despised women and especially the modern emancipated woman. She would never understand her brazenness, her pretense of being equal with man and militantly asserting that equality. Look at what men can do! she would say. A woman can't do that.

By which she meant: My men can do that and let any woman try to equal it (141–142).

Living as closely to his mother as he did most of his life, Williams naturally wrote about her: the poems "Eve," "Two Pendants for the Ears," "The Horse Show," "An Eternity," and "The Painting"; notes for a play about her; the essay on tropical fruits; and the several versions of this biography. "Very seldom does a man get a chance to speak intimately of what has concerned him most in the past. . . . This is as good a way as any to pay her my respects and to reassure her that she has not been forgotten" (138).

That Williams was so insistent on writing this book about his mother—and that he himself plays the other major role in it—also gives the reader some important insights into his own character late in his life. The quixotic spirit that cannot be downed by reason— even in our own reasonable age—this Sam Patch-like identity, is one of Williams' proudest traits. And the persistence of his mother, who *would* wear her new shoes in the snow, is not unlike Williams' own unbelievable enthusiasms. Even the defiance, not to be subjected to the views of "betters," this too is assuredly Williams, who goes his own magnificently lonely way, creating theory when theory is out of fashion, to defend the practices he so consistently wrote from.

Tempted as the reader might be to ignore *Yes, Mrs. Williams* in a discussion of Williams' direction in prose, because of its incorrigible informality, this book too is further evidence of Williams' ability to change styles to meet the demands of his subject. The organic form of the biography nearly erases the voice of any imposed narrator, with all attention focusing on the subjects of the biography themselves. Much like Williams' own autobiography, this book places emphasis not on dates, transitions, or a large view, but on the intimate details and habits of speech which create Hélène Williams. In its fragmentary appearance, the book might suggest the earliest of Williams' prose, *Kora in Hell: Improvisations,* but there is no wandering here. Each bit of writing has been included for one purpose; the only free association has been within Hélène's mind in the legitimate throes of old age. The biography is more an extension of Williams' short-story technique, when everything except the essential dialogue and detail was omitted, and language was the important characterization device. In a sense, too, Williams had only a single purpose for the biography, just as he had for most of his better short stories.

Conclusions

In 1945 Williams wrote to Norman Macleod, "Whatever my life has been it has been single in purpose, simple in design and constantly directed to the one end of discovery, if possible, of some purpose in being alive . . . . Poetry, an art, is what answer I have." [29] No one can question Williams' dedication to his art: defined broadly, that of writing; more specifically, that of poetry. But as his quantity of writing in prose easily testifies, that other medium also intrigued him. In fact, Williams' progress in prose parallels the changes he made in his poetry.

Beginning with the subjective fragments of *Kora in Hell* and the more orderly but still extremely personal *TGAN,* Williams moved to distinguish poems from prose, and to speculate on the differences between the two, in *Spring and All.* His versatility in various tones and rhythms of prose became evident in the essays of *In the American Grain.* *A Voyage to Pagany* taught him to write clear, controlled prose, a prose which, even less cluttered and shortened, became the norm for the short stories and Stecher novels. Williams as persona is much involved in these stories, but never in the self-conscious, intruding manner of his earliest prose.

And then the return. After reaching the furthest point of objectivity in both prose and poetry, Williams began his own speaking again; he had never forgotten those "townspeople"; he had only struggled to control his didactic impulses. Now in the *Autobiography* and *Yes, Mrs. Williams,* by setting one anecdote against the next, he could achieve the meaning he had always intended. But first he had to work his way through *Paterson,* that gigantic attempt to correlate the clearest of prose with the most striking of poems. From that experiment, Williams' precise feeling for rhythms grew. The triadic line with its indefinable variable foot could only have sprung from the wealth of Williams' experimental writing, in poetry, prose, and combinations of both.

That Williams' career as writer ended as it began, with poetry, is no reason to feel that he found prose inferior. As Emily Wallace points out, "The prose cannot be dismissed, however, as merely self-discovery, self-therapy, experimentation, theorizing about art, though Williams did use the prose for those purposes . . . . Much is distinguished in its own particular forms." [30]

And what exists now of this distinguished prose? A collection of essays that are perhaps better known today than when first published in 1925; several plays which have been produced, one frequently; five novels, all of them now back in print; extant collections of essays and letters (with a second book of letters in process); a disarming autobiography; and, probably most important, numerous short stories which often appear in anthologies. For a man who wrote so quickly, and whose process of learning was a trial-and-error procedure, the results of these prose experiments should be especially gratifying. As Williams had himself directed, the only way to test a theory was to write: "to study what we have put down . . . and to take out of that what is useful and reject what is misleading." [31] One could only hope to endure the selection, the failure, the success (descent-ascent), so as to perhaps, finally, attain "the calm which true poetic achievement demands." [32]

By the last years of his life, "true poetic achievement" had come to mean writing that showed life, truth, and skill instead of quantity. The size of the canvas had ceased to matter, probably because he felt that he had made his full statement. (As Williams reminisced in 1958, "my two leading forces were trying to know life and trying to find a technique of verse." [33]) In praising Marsden Hartley's late paintings, Williams stated, "it has to do with the mind, the body and the spirit drawn gradually together into one life, and finally flowering, once." [34] Art as a process of fruition, gradual learning, and practice—Williams continued his writing year after year (or, more properly, minute after minute) because he firmly believed "in every man there must finally occur a fusion between his dream which he dreamed when he was young and the phenomenal world of his later years." [35] Williams had had that dream—love among all men—

and had pursued it throughout his career. As the young Willie had once said, in an early draft of *Paterson,* "I'm just a plugger. One idea, the only one I ever had in my life. But it's a tough one to lay . . . ." [36]

The late poems, the biography of his mother, *Paterson* V, "Asphodel": what more conclusive testament that Williams' theme became only what it had always been—man's need for love—a theme, however, expanded, deepened, focused away from himself toward those sharing life with him. "It is to assert love, not to win it, that the poem exists," [37] Williams wrote in 1951. That we might add "and prose" to his statement is only a small tribute to a man who knew that technique and knowledge were important, but not all-important; not unless he could define the writer first as a man who "believes in his world, he believes in his people, and that's the reason he's a poet . . . basic faith in the world." [38]

"It is a mark of genius when an accomplished man can go on continually developing," [39] Williams once wrote in praise of Wallace Stevens. That Williams did himself go on developing, ready to try any method, any measure, is certainly a tribute to both his dedication and his enthusiasm. But that he did succeed in so many of his attempts can only be a tribute to his genius with the language.

Notes

Introduction

1. Emily Mitchell Wallace, *A Bibliography of William Carlos Williams* (Middletown: Wesleyan University Press, 1968), xix–xx.

Chapter One

1. *I Wanted to Write a Poem,* ed. Edith Heal (Boston: Beacon, 1958), 64.

2. *The Selected Letters of William Carlos Williams,* ed. John Thirlwall (New York: McDowell, Obolensky, 1957), 265. Hereafter cited as *Letters.*

3. Microfilms of a 1947 address, Lockwood Memoral Library Poetry Collection, State University of New York at Buffalo. Hereafter cited as Buffalo Collection.

4. *Ibid.*

5. "Our Formal Heritage from Walt Whitman," p. 6, Buffalo Collection.

6. "Asphodel, That Greeny Flower," *Pictures from Brueghel* (Norfolk, Conn.: New Directions, 1962), 161–162. Hereafter cited as *PB.*

7. "Our Formal Heritage," p. 7, Buffalo Collection.

8. "The Work of Gertrude Stein," *The Selected Essays of William Carlos Williams* (New York: Random House, 1954), 118. Hereafter cited as *SE.*

9. "Our Formal Heritage," n.p., Buffalo Collection.

10. "11/28," *The Collected Earlier Poems* (Norfolk, Conn.: New Directions, 1951), 311. Hereafter cited as *CEP.*

11. "Briarcliff Junior College Talk," Buffalo Collection.

12. "Frankie the Newspaperman," *The Farmers' Daughters* (Norfolk, Conn.: New Directions, 1961), 271.

13. "Marianne Moore," *Essays,* 123.

14. *Paterson* (Norfolk, Conn.: New Directions, 1963), 66–67.

15. "*White Mule* versus Poetry," *Writer,* L, No. 8 (August 1937), 244–245.

16. Forrest Read, ed., *Pound/Joyce* (Norfolk, Conn.: New Directions, 1967), 239.

17. Fred Miller, "With a Kick to It," *New Republic,* XCI (July 7, 1937), 257.

18. "Notes for a 1941 Harvard Talk," Buffalo Collection.

19. Frederick J. Hoffman, *The Twenties,* revised (New York: Free Press, 1949, 1962), 212.

20. *"White Mule* versus Poetry," *Writer* (1937), 243.

21. "Comment," Buffalo Collection.

Chapter Two

1. "Tract," *CEP,* 129. For a complete discussion of Williams' poetry, please see my earlier book, *The Poems of William Carlos Williams: A Critical Study* (Middletown: Wesleyan University Press, 1964).

2. *The Autobiography of William Carlos Williams* (New York: Random House, 1951), 158.

3. Prologue to the 1957 edition of *Kora in Hell: Improvisations* (San Francisco: City Lights Books, 1957), 5.

4. As quoted by Constance Rourke in *Charles Sheeler, Artist in the American Tradition* (New York: Harcourt, Brace, 1938), 49.

5. Original Prologue to *Kora in Hell,* reprinted in *SE,* 5.

6. "The Descent," *PB,* 73.

7. *SE,* 14.

8. "Surrealism," in Richard Ellmann and Charles Feidelson, Jr., eds., *The Modern Tradition: Backgrounds of Modern Literature* (New York: Oxford University Press, 1965), 602.

9. René Taupin's premise in *L'Influence du Symbolisme Français sur la Poésie Américaine* (Paris: H. Champion, 1929), was that Williams owed a great debt to Rimbaud's *Illuminations* and to Duchamp, Gris, and others. In moderation, such a conviction must have merit, especially in regard to Williams' admiration for the painters.

10. *The Encyclopedia of Poetry and Poetics,* ed. Alex Preminger (Princeton: Princeton University Press, 1965), 664.

11. *I Wanted,* 15.

12. *SE,* 17.

13. "Bantams in Pine-Woods," *Poems by Wallace Stevens* (New York: Vintage, 1959), 25.

14. J. Gysbert Bouma, "A Study of the Prose Style of William Carlos Williams," unpublished dissertation, 1956, University of Pennsylvania.

Chapter Three

1. *Sour Grapes* (Boston: Four Seas Company, 1921), 40.

2. *Autobiography,* 146.

3. *I Wanted,* 30.

4. *The Letters of Ezra Pound, 1907–1941,* ed. D. D. Paige (New York: Harcourt, Brace, and World, 1950), 172–173.

5. "Comment," *Contact,* II (January 1921), n.p. Reprinted in *SE,* 27.

6. *Ibid.,* 28–29 passim.

7. "Yours, O Youth," *Contact,* III (n.d.), 14. Reprinted in *SE,* 34.

8. "Sample Critical Statement, Comment," *Contact,* IV (n.d.), 18.

9. *Spring and All* (Dijon, France: Contact Publishing Co., 1923), 1.

10. *Twenties* (1962), 209n.

11. "William Carlos Williams," Preface to *Collected Poems, 1921–1931,* as reprinted in J. Hillis Miller, ed., *William Carlos Williams: A Collection of Critical Essays* (Englewood Cliffs: Prentice-Hall, 1966), 63.

12. "Review of *Kora in Hell,*" *Contact,* IV (n.d.), 5, 7.

Chapter Four

1. "The Doctor" in "Three Professional Studies," in Margaret Anderson, ed., *The Little Review Anthology* (New York: Hermitage House, 1953), 242.

2. *Spring and All,* 44.

3. "Comment," *Contact,* II (January 1921), n.p. Reprinted in *SE,* 28.

4. A few years later, he praises Stein for her art with words, praise much like his for Joyce: "She has completely unlinked them [words] . . . from their former relationships in the sentence. . . . Each under the new arrangement has a quality of its own." "The Work of Gertrude Stein," *SE,* 118.

5. *Letters,* 62.

6. *Letters of Ezra Pound,* 184. Williams' deeper interest in Bird as a possible publisher for his poems is suggested in a February 9, 1923, letter from Pound: "if your *GT. Am. Nov.* sells 200 copies, I think he might do the poems (yours)" (*Letters,* 185).

7. *I Wanted,* 38–39.

8. *The Great American Novel* in R. P. Blackmur, ed., *American Short Novels* (New York: Thomas Y. Crowell, 1960), 309. Originally published by Three Mountains Press, Paris, 1923.

9. "The Work of Gertrude Stein," *SE.* 118.

10. This kind of phonetic play reminds one of Joyce in *Ulysses* and *Wake,* as well as in his comments about "plastic language." See Joyce's letter to Harriet Shaw Weaver in 1926, in Stuart Gilbert, ed., *Letters* (New York: Viking, 1955).

11. *I Wanted,* 39.

12. David Ferry, "The Diction of American Poetry," in Irvin Ehren-

preis, ed., *American Poetry*, Stratford-Upon-Avon Studies 7 (New York: St Martin's Press, 1965), 135.

13. Hugh Kenner, "A Note on *The Great American Novel*," *Perspective*, VI, No. 4 (Autumn–Winter 1953), 177–182.

14. Eli Siegel, "Williams' Poetry Looked At" (recording transcribed), as published by the Terrain Gallery, New York, 1964, p. 9.

15. Microfilms, Buffalo Collection.

16. Siegel, "Williams' Poetry Looked At," 9.

Chapter Five

1. "From: A Folded Skyscraper," *The American Caravan* (New York: Macaulay, 1927), 219.

2. *Autobiography*, 178.

3. *Letters*, 185.

4. *Ibid.*, 64.

5. *Caravan*, 219.

6. Nowhere in his writing does Williams mention any of Lawrence's essays, either in their earlier periodical publication or in book form. There is also scant similarity in the figures each man chose to write about (Williams considers only two of the twenty men in *IAG* as writers). Considering the fact that three of Williams' *Grain* essays were published before March of 1923 (Lawrence's book came out in 1923), and that two others followed rapidly, it seems that the impetus for this project must have occurred sometime before 1923. I realize that some critics are tempted to draw lines of influence from the *Seven Arts* group and Lawrence to Williams, but the fact that somewhat similar sentiments occur is hardly reason to claim direct descent. Somewhat less relevant but still significant is the fact that Pound considered *Seven Arts* "slop" (*Letters*, 122) and Lawrence a "bore" (*Letters*, 301).

7. In *Letters*, 187, Williams writes, "The book is as much a study in styles of writing as anything else. I tried to write each chapter in the style most germane to its sources or at least the style which seemed to me appropriate to the material. To this end, where possible, I copied and used the original writings, as in the Cotton Mather chapter, the Benjamin Franklin chapter and in the Paul Jones chapter, of which no word is my own. I did this with malice aforethought to prove the truth of the book, since the originals fitted into it without effort on my part, perfectly, leaving not a seam."

8. *The Great American Novel*, 320.

9. *In the American Grain* (Norfolk, Conn.: New Directions, 1956), 1.

10. Alan Holder, writing in "In the American Grain: William Carlos Williams on the American Past," criticizes Williams' biased presentation of

Indians throughout these essays. Williams' emphasis may not be balanced; it seems more to use the Indian as heart, as symbol of American originality. *American Quarterly*, XIX, No. 3 (Fall 1967), 499–515.

11. *PB*, 168.

12. *Letters*, 185.

13. Holder points out (*American Quarterly*, 509) that Williams' technique in this essay may have come from the practice in his text of the Indian chieftains' "speaking" to De Soto, one of them being a woman. See *The Narrative of the Expedition of Hernando De Soto by the Gentleman of Elvas in Spanish Explorers in the Southern U. S. 1528–1943* (New York: 1906).

Chapter Six

1. *I Wanted*, 47. Hugh Kenner's notes from *The Pound Era* ("Ghosts and Benedictions," *Poetry*, CXII, No. 2 [November 1968], 109–125) emphasize how great the influence of Henry James was on Pound and his friends. Pound read all of James from 1916 to 1918. Kenner sees such writing as *Prufrock, Hugh Selwyn Mauberly*, and Williams' "To Elsie" as outgrowths of James's prose.

2. *TGAN*, 327.

3. "The Three Letters," *Contact*, IV (n.d.), 10–13.

4. The Baroness seems to be modeled on the incidents described in the *Autobiography*, 164–165.

5. *A Voyage to Pagany* (New York: Macaulay, 1928), 11.

6. *Letters*, 104.

7. *Autobiography*, 219. This close reliance on actual people and events is not a weakening practice, as it turns out, but serves to emphasize Sherman Paul's point that Williams' visit to Europe was of great importance to him, that it was, in fact, "a test of allegiance to what he proposed to do as an American poet." *The Music of Survival* (Urbana: University of Illinois Press, 1968), 101.

8. "The Venus," *The Farmers' Daughters*, 214.

9. *Paterson*, 268.

10. *Last Nights of Paris* (New York: Macaulay, 1929), 17.

11. "Faiths for a Complex World," *American Scholar*, XXVI (Fall 1957), 453–457.

12. *Letters*, 104–105.

Chapter Seven

1. In his Buffalo work sheets, Williams wrote (and crossed out), "one of the springtimes/ of my life is likely to be lost/ because a crowd of

daffodils/ is springing from the ringing of/ those xxxxxx/ influenza, tonsilitis/ streptocuscuses never eat/ a meal in peace/ that host of/ dirty dripping// low down/ telephone bells."

2. "Talk is the most precious thing in the world . . . . but my interest in writing is so violent an acid that with the other work, I must pare my life to the point of silence . . . in order to get to the paper." "The Simplicity of Disorder," *SE*, 95.

3. See *Letters*, 75, 77.

4. *Ibid.*, 73.

5. In the first published version of "9/30" Williams writes of his being borne to land "but without you." *Exile*, IV (Autumn 1928), 32.

6. Because much of this original manuscript appears in "Notes in Diary Form," *SE*, and "The Descent of Winter," *CEP*, page numbers will refer to these in-print editions. Only when necessary will *Exile* page numbers be used. *SE*, 62.

7. *Exile*, 64.

8. Buffalo microfilms, entry dated October 29.

9. *Ibid.*

10. Williams is alluding here to Pound's categories of writers, at the top of which was inventors. As listed in Pound's *How to Read*.

11. *Exile*, 52.

12. *Ibid.*, 54.

13. Buffalo Collection of *Exile* version.

14. Buffalo Collection.

15. See *Letters*, 81.

16. "Excerpts from a Critical Sketch," *SE*, 107.

17. "A Note on the Recent Work of James Joyce," *SE*, 76.

18. "A Point for American Criticism," *SE*, 82.

19. "The Work of Gertrude Stein," *SE*, 116.

20. "Marianne Moore," *SE*, 122, 121.

21. Published by the Objectivist Press, the designation TO illustrates their belief in the efficacy of the single word "to." Titled *A Novelette and Other Prose (1921–1931)*, the volume also includes Williams' essays on Marianne Moore, Matisse, Joyce, Kay Boyle, Stein, Antheil, Kenneth Burke, and, in a somewhat different vein, the State of Virginia. It also contains two short stories, "The Venus" from *A Voyage to Pagany* and "The Accident"; the impressionistic "A Memory of Tropical Fruit" which appears again in *Yes, Mrs. Williams;* and a review of Clendening's *The Human Body*.

22. *Letters*, 100.

23. *Ibid.*, 105.

24. *PB*, 153.

25. *Letters*, 122.

Chapter Eight

1. Denis Donoghue, *Connoisseurs of Chaos: Ideas of Order in Modern American Poetry* (New York: Macmillan, 1965), 199.

2. "A Beginning on the Short Story (Notes)," *SE*, 296.

3. *Ibid.*, 295.

4. *A Beginning on the Short Story* (Yonkers: Alicat Bookshop Press, 1950), 21. This verson contains some notes not included in the *SE* version.

5. Warren Tallman, Introduction to Robert Creeley and Donald Allen, eds., *New American Story* (New York: Grove, 1965), 3–4.

6. "A Note on the Recent Work of James Joyce," *SE*, 76.

7. In 1919 Williams called Joyce's technique "childish—Victrola" (*The Little Review Anthology*, 241). In 1931 his reference is again to Joyce's devices: "It is not by a huge cracking up of language that you will build new work . . . (that is a confusion even when skillful)." "Excerpts from a Critical Sketch," *SE*, 110. See also *Letters*, 129.

8. Microfilm of "To All Gentleness" work sheets, Buffalo Collection.

9. "Three Professional Studies," *The Little Review Anthology*, 242, 241.

10. *Ibid.*, 246.

11. *Ibid.*, 247.

12. *The Farmers' Daughters*, 211. All references in text are to this edition of the collected stories.

13. "A Beginning on the Short Story," *SE*, 296.

14. "A Beginning on the Short Story," *SE*, 297.

15. *Ibid.*, 119. Italics mine.

16. *I Wanted*, 49.

17. *SE*, 300.

18. J. E. Slate, "William Carlos Williams and the Modern Short Story," *Southern Review*, IV, No. 3 (Summer 1968), 657.

19. *I Wanted*, 50.

20. Williams' own view of "Old Doc Rivers" was less complimentary. He wrote in 1930 to Richard Johns that he had been having fun writing extremely short stories, six of them, in contrast to his working on the Rivers story: "I was slaving away on that damned old Doc Rivers thing which nearly killed me. I can't work that way. It never got to be a unit, just wandered around trying to cover a big piece of ground." *A Return to Pagany*, eds. Stephen Halpert with Richard Johns (Boston: Beacon, 1969), 165.

21. "To Elsie" closes "No one/ to witness/ and adjust, no one to drive

the car," *CEP*, 272. Thomas Whitaker has included a good reading of this story in *William Carlos Williams* (New York: Twayne U.S. Authors Series. 1968), 98–100.

22. *I Wanted*, 63.

23. *A Beginning on the Short Story*, Alicat Version, 21.

24. J. E. Slate describes stories like this, in which Williams uses the doctor as narrator, as "stories in which the point of view is missing, formal structures in which the flaw functions as a part of the whole, giving it its meaning." While Slate seems to be redefining terms here, he goes on to stress that Williams' "closeness to the action of the story must appear as a deformity, a failure to invent, until the meaning of the story becomes radiantly clear." *Southern Review*, IV, No. 3 (Summer 1968), 660–661.

25. *The Little Review Anthology*, 243.

26. Originally published in 1930, "Four Bottles of Beer" could have been included in Williams' first collection of stories. Whether or not his omitting it was intentional, in tone and method it is more compatible with the 1938 stories.

27. "William Carlos Williams," interview by Stanley Koehler, *Writers at Work: The Paris Review Interviews*, Third Series (New York: Viking, 1967), 8.

28. *I Wanted*, 63.

29. *The Farmers' Daughters*, 317.

30. *SE*, 304.

31. Mona Van Duyn, "To 'Make Light of It' as Fictional Technique," *Perspective*, VI (Autumn–Winter 1953), 233.

32. *SE*, 305.

33. *SE*, 298.

34. Introduction to *The William Carlos Williams Readers*, ed. M. L. Rosenthal (Norfolk, Conn.: New Directions, 1966), xi.

35. "Kenneth Burke," *SE*, 132.

36. William Faulkner, *The Faulkner-Cowley File, 1944–1962*, ed. Malcolm Cowley (New York: Viking, 1966), 16.

Chapter Nine

1. "The Poet in Time of Confusion," *Columbia Review*, XXIII (Autumn 1941), 3.

2. *I Wanted*, 50.

3. "Comment," *Contact*, I, No. 1 (February 1932), 8.

4. Collection of Williams' manuscripts and letters, Yale University Library, New Haven, Connecticut. Hereafter cited as Yale Collection.

5. *Letters*, 137.

6. *I Wanted*, 61.

7. Despite many excellent sections in James Guimond's book *The Art of William Carlos Williams: A Discovery and Possession of America*, Guimond's insistence on seeing Williams' search in American history as constant throughout his life in very misleading (Urbana: University of Illinois Press, 1968).

8. The range of Lyle's correspondence must be sampled. I quote here from a letter of his dated December 1, 1938, expanded April 9, 1939 (Yale Collection):

He begins with the question, "what is your *real* substance" and uses to answer it Ulysses' speech about degree from Shakespeare's *Troilus*. He continues,

"The last being the D. H. Lawrence . . Everything is either a personal tussle or a money (symbol) tussle.

But . . with barter direct . . sidetracking money . . and with all the world's gold flowing into burial vaults . . such as Ft. Knox, which are complete with ditches, walls, flood waters . . etc . . .

with these things . . . you have to have a single substance law . . . . sources close to Whitehouse say because of direct barter etc . . . we will either have to go to Chinese wall, or . . long hours low pay and prodigious production to meet competition in world markets . . or . . prodigiously subsidize physical quantitative production for foreign giving away"

"all this slavery to develop" in a free country.

Keynes

"the world is being thrown into the wars and conquests pattern of Anabasis by a few men . . who are handling vast masses of living people as arbitrarily as a novelist handles his material."

9. *White Mule* (Norfolk, Conn.: New Directions, 1937), 1.

10. Fred T. Marsh, "William Carlos Williams' New Novel," *New York Times*, November 17, 1940, 7.

11. In *I Wanted*, Williams recalls that "the most interesting character in the story was based on my mother-in-law, a striking person, a Norwegian . . . . [she] had the dominating freshness of Eric the Red" (87).

12. Philip Rahv, "Torrents of Spring," *Nation*, CXLIV, No. 26 (June 26, 1937), 733.

13. "*White Mule* versus Poetry," *Writer*, L. No. 8 (August 1937), 244.

14. "A Good Doctor's Story," *Nation*, CXLV, No. 11 (September 11, 1937), 268.

15. Earle Davis, *Vision Fugitive, Ezra Pound and Economics* (Lawrence: University of Kansas Press, 1968), 107. See also Williams' comments in the *Writer* (1937), 244, and in "Pound's Eleven New 'Cantos,'" *SE*, 168–169.

16. Davis summarizes Pound's economic theses as follows:

1. The health, happiness, and prosperity of any nation or culture depend primarily upon the economic forces which control its production and distribution.

2. Good government encourages, arranges, or controls production and distribution so that the whole society has an opportunity to prosper.

3. The forces of special privilege or financial aristocracy must not be permitted to profit by manipulation of values or the means of production, particularly the money used by the nation. Alternate expansion or contraction of the currency eventually causes the decline of any nation.

4. The specific privilege of creating and controlling credit must be taken from banks of discount or usurers, the men who lend money not on capital or cash but from the presence of credit dependent upon deposits and book figures. The power of creating money "out of nothing" is the privilege of the government representing the whole of society. Abuse of the power of creating money contributes more than any other force to the decline of the nation.

5. Good governments make sure that the total money in circulation approximates the prices justly charged for necessary goods and services, this money being supplemented by national credit, not borrowed from private sources, if it is insufficient in amount to ensure distribution and prosperity.

6. The adoption of the Douglas Social Credit "dividend," the use of the Gesell stamp-scrip money, *or any other appropriate method of supplementing needed cash should be investigated and tried.*

7. History shows that the forces of special privilege are in vital conflict with the rest of society through the centuries. . . . Ignorance of the nature of money is the world's greatest sin . . . (116–117).

17. "The American Background," *SE*, 153.

18. "A Social Diagnosis for Surgery," *New Democracy*, VI (April 1936), 26–27.

19. "The Basis of Faith in Art," *SE*, 194.

20. "Pound's Eleven New 'Cantos,'" *SE*, 168, and "Against the Weather," *SE*, 214. As Richard Cordell wrote in "The Stechers Again," *Saturday Review of Literature*, XXIII (November 9, 1940), "It is written objectively: the novelist has no axe to grind, no economic, social, or political prejudices to dictate scene or character" (5).

21. *"White Mule* versus Poetry," *Writer* (1937), 245. Paul Rosenfeld noted that "The tension occasionally weakens: from chapter five to chapter thirteen the continuity approaches the loose one of a chronicle. The frequency with which the dramatic method of the bare dialogue is exploited also fatigues at times. . . . By and large, the well-varied scenes are cumulatively built up." "Williams the Conqueror," *Nation,* CLI (November 23, 1940), 508.

22. *In the Money* (Norfolk, Conn.: New Directions, 1940), 155.

23. Reprinted in *SE,* 250–254.

24. Accurate as many of Thomas Whitaker's observations are in his *William Carlos Williams,* I think he forces this scene and the closing chapter of *White Mule* into too symbolic an interpretation. Whitaker sees Joe's trick with the plums as a sign that "natural growth is yielding to engineered abundance" (109). Yet he had previously commented about Williams' "less portentous symbolic pressure" (108).

25. *Ibid.,* 110.

26. *"White Mule* versus Poetry," *Writer* (1937), 245.

27. " 'Parade's End,' " *SE,* 318–319.

28. *Ibid.,* 319.

29. "The Basis of Faith in Art," *SE,* 184.

30. Buffalo Collection.

31. Yale Collecton.

32. *Selected Works of Djuna Barnes* (New York: Farrar, Straus, and Cudahy, 1962), 228.

33. *Letters,* 146. To the Editor of *Twice A Year* Magazine in 1934. See also *Autobiography,* 368–369.

34. *Autobiography,* 274.

35. *I Wanted,* 87. Richard Eberhart shares this view, writing, "He belongs so much to the people he elucidates . . . he loves them so energetically . . . that he cannot get out of them. He would not offend the total historical situation." "Things as They Are," *New Republic,* CXXVII (November 10, 1952), 20.

36. Sherman Paul, *The Music of Survival* (Urbana: University of Illinois Press, 1968).

37. *I Wanted,* 86.

38. Elizabeth Janeway, ed., *The Writer's World* (New York: McGraw-Hill, 1969), 6, 7.

39. *Letters,* 300.

40. Robert Creeley, "A Character for Love," in J. Hillis Miller, ed., *Williams Carlos Williams, Twentieth Century Views* (Englewood Cliffs: Prentice-Hall, 1966), 161.

Chapter Ten

1. *"White Mule* versus Poetry," *Writer* (1937), 244.

2. *I Wanted,* 32. Perhaps Williams' interest in drama is much more important in the structure of his other writing than I have emphasized. The stories and scenes of novels that begin with "Hello" and end with "Goodbye," the heavy reliance on dialogue in many of the poems and stories, the trick of presenting a character and making it act before any description has been given—Williams the dramatist is at work in all forms of his writing. A poem like "Catastrophic Birth," probably the best statement of his violence-gentleness duality (the need for abrupt change as one way to new life), includes one stanza of monologue from the "big she-Wop": "Shut up! . . . Wait till you have six like a me./ Every year one. Come on! Push! Sure,/ you said it! . . . . Sweating like a volcano. It cleans you up,/ makes you feel good inside. Come on! Push!" *Collected Later Poems* (Norfolk, Conn.: New Directions, 1963), 8. Hereafter cited as *CLP.*

Similarly in the closing lines of "To All Gentleness" (*CLP,* 28–29) comes the picture of the "forewoman to a gang at the ship foundry," victim of three miscarriages ("Tough, huh?/ Never had a backache"). "The Controversy" is handled completely through dialogue; "A Cold Front" first describes the mother of eight, pivoting to her climactic single line of speech, "I won't have any more." Again and again Williams uses speech. As Kenneth Burke summarized his practice, "lyric utterance to him is essentially a flash of drama, a fragment of narrative." "William Carlos Williams, 1883-1963," *New York Review of Books* (Summer 1963), 46.

3. See letters from Audrey Wood and from a representative of the Rochester Philharmonic Orchestra, Yale Collection.

4. *Many Loves* in *Many Loves and Other Plays* (Norfolk, Conn.: New Directions, 1961), 88.

5. Yale Collection.

6. *The First President* in *Many Loves and Other Plays,* 308.

7. "New Direction in the Novel," *New Democracy,* V (November 1, 1935), 82.

8. Benjamin Spencer, *"Many Loves and Other Plays,"* *Modern Drama,* VI, No. 1 (May 1963), 97.

9. *A Beginning on the Short Story,* Alicat version, 21.

10. Buffalo Collection.

11. Walter Scott Peterson, *An Approach to Paterson* (New Haven: Yale University Press, 1967).

12. In addition to these, there were early plays titled *Plums, The Apple Tree, Frances for Freedom,* one described only as a precursor of Odets' *Golden Boy,* and possibly others.

13. Yale Collection.

14. Buffalo Collection.

15. Donald Malcolm, "Off Broadway," *New Yorker* (January 24, 1959), 74–76.

16. Buffalo Collection.

17. Yale Collection.

18. *Ibid.*

19. *Ibid.*

20. Letter from Audrey Wood, May 7, 1946, Yale Collection.

21. Yale Collection.

22. Clinton J. Atkinson, "In Search of Theatre," *Massachusetts Review* (Winter 1962), 335. As Katharine Worth describes this play, "An over-leisurely development of the preparatory action is perhaps Williams' most pronounced dramatic weakness." "The Poets in the American Theatre," *American Theatre,* Statford-Upon-Avon Studies 10 (New York: St Martin's Press, 1967), 101.

23. Atkinson, "In Search of Theatre," 331.

24. *Tituba's Children* in *Many Loves and Other Plays,* 289.

25. Worth, *American Theatre* (1967), 98–99.

26. Yale Collection.

27. *Ibid.*

28. *Ibid.*

29. H. E. F. Donohue, "An Occasion for Tremendous Music," *Massachusetts Review* (Winter 1962), 344.

30. Worth, *American Theatre* (1967), 97.

Chapter Eleven

1. Robert Lowell, "William Carlos Williams," *Hudson Review,* XIV (Winter 1961–1962); Joel Conarroe, "A Local Pride: The Poetry of *Paterson,*" *PMLA,* LXXXIV, No. 3 (May 1969); L. S. Dembo, *Conceptions of Reality in Modern American Poetry* (Berkeley: University of California Press, 1966); Sister M. Bernetta Quinn, *The Metamorphic Tradition in Modern Poetry* (New Brunswick: Rutgers University Press, 1955); M. L. Rosenthal, *The Modern Poets* (New York: Oxford University Press, 1960); Roy Harvey Pearce, *The Continuity of American Poetry* (Princeton: Princeton University Press, 1961); and J. Hillis Miller, *Poets of Reality* (Cambridge: Harvard University Press, 1965).

2. Among those who share this view are Denis Donoghue writing in

"The Long Poem," *New York Review of Books* (April 14, 1966); Louis L. Martz in *The Poem of the Mind* (New York: Oxford University Press, 1966); James Guimond in *The Art of William Carlos Williams, A Discovery and Possession of America* (Urbana: University of Illinois Press, 1968); Walter Scott Peterson, *An Approach to Paterson* (New Haven: Yale University Press, 1967); Emily Mitchell Wallace, *A Bibliography of William Carlos Williams* (Middletown: Wesleyan University Press, 1968); Sherman Paul, *The Music of Survival* (Urbana: University of Illinois Press, 1968); Thomas Whitaker, *William Carlos Williams* (New York: Twayne U.S. Authors Series, 1968); and John C. Thirlwall in "William Carlos Williams' *Paterson*," *New Directions 17* (1961). Williams himself in the Thirlwall essay admits to this view, p. 269.

3. *Letters*, 214.

4. "Author's Introduction to *The Wedge*," *SE*, 256.

5. See *Letters*, 216 and 290.

6. Louis L. Martz, "On the Road to *Paterson*" in *The Poem of the Mind*, 133.

7. *Letters*, 214.

8. *"The Man with the Blue Guitar*," *New Republic*, XCIII (November 17, 1937), 50.

9. "Pounds Eleven New 'Cantos,' " *SE*, 167–179 passim. Italics mine.

10. "Ezra Pound: Lord Ga-ga!" *Decision*, II (September 1941), 20.

11. As recorded by John Thirlwall in "William Carlos Williams' *Paterson*," *New Directions 17* (1961), 254.

12. Martz, *The Poem of the Mind*, 143. Also Yale Collection.

13. Buffalo Collection.

14. *Letters*, 236.

15. *Decision* (1941), 19.

16. *Many Loves and Other Plays*, 305.

17. "The Situation in American Writing," *Partisan Review*, IV, No. 4 (Summer 1939), 41–44.

18. "New Direction in the Novel," *New Democracy*, V (November 1, 1935), 81.

19. Yale Collection.

20. *Ibid.*

21. All materials from Yale Collection.

22. *Ibid.* Italics mine.

23. Buffalo Collection.

24. Yale Collection.

25. *Ibid.*

26. *Paterson*, 79. Hereafter cited in text.

27. Yale Collection.

28. "Introduction to *Charles Sheeler*," *SE*, 232.

29. "On Measure—Statement for Cid Corman," *SE*, 337.

30. *CLP*, 103.

31. Joel Conarroe, "The 'Preface' to *Paterson*," *Journal of Contemporary Literature*, X (Winter 1969), 39–53. See also my discussion of the techniques of *Paterson* in *The Poems of William Carlos Williams: A Critical Study*.

32. Buffalo Collection.

33. "Sermon with a Camera," *New Republic*, XCVI (October 12, 1938), 282–283.

34. Yale Collection.

35. Yale Collection.

36. *Letters*, 234–235.

37. Yale Collection.

38. *Ibid.*

39. *Ibid.*

40. *Ibid.*

41. *Ibid.*

42. Williams was so angry with Pound that he published this letter as a footnote to his devastating essay in *Decision* (1941), 24.

43. *New Directions 17*, 273.

44. *Ibid.*, 304.

45. That many readers responded more readily to the violence in *Paterson* than to its gentleness might be evidence of Nathaneal West's judgment: "In America, violence is idiomatic." *Contact*, Second Series (1932), 132.

46. *Letters*, 292.

Chapter Twelve

1. Yale Collection.

2. Charles Tomlinson, "Dr. Williams' Practice," *Encounter*, XXIX (November 1967), 68.

3. "To Eleanor and Bill Monahan," *PB*, 83–86: "The female principle of the world/ is my appeal/ in the extremity/ to which I have come./ O clemens! O pia! O dolcis!/ Maria!"

4. "The Element of Time," *Harvard Advocate*, CXX, No. 4 (February 1934), 10.

5. Yale Collection.

6. *Letters*, 239.

7. January 26, 1947; Yale Collection.

8. *Letters,* 298–300.

9. *Ibid.,* 309.

10. This appears to be the view of Richard Gustafson, who calls *Paterson* a "tragedy" in "William Carlos Williams' *Paterson:* Map and Opinion," *College English,* XXVI (April 1965), 532–539; of David Ignatow, writing in a personal letter to me as well as in the Introduction to the Beloit Williams *Chapbook;* and of Karl Shapiro, who in a letter speaks of *Paterson* as the "abandonment" of Williams' principles. Against these stands Sherman Paul, whose entire book discusses these later poems (*The Music of Survival*).

11. *Letters,* 226–227.

12. *I Wanted,* 22.

13. Yale Collection.

14. Another example of this interrelation is Williams' comment about Sappho in the Yale drafts of Book V, "Sappho was half a man anyhow—and she could WRITE—her tail in her mouth deny it who may: the virgin turned whore: an identity."

15. Included in *Paterson I–V* (1963), 284.

16. *SE,* xiv.

17. Yale Collection.

18. Martz, *The Poem of the Mind,* 126.

19. *Letters of Ezra Pound,* 48–49.

Chapter Thirteen

1. *Letters,* 264: "I look at what I have done, with *Paterson* for instance, and though at times I am impressed, at other times I find little to praise in my attempts."

2. Letter to the author, November 1969.

3. "Excerpts from a Critical Sketch," *SE,* 108.

4. *Letters,* 135.

5. Joe Gould's well-known but lost "oral history" of the 1930's is another example of the interest in idiom as the language of art during these years.

6. "*White Mule* versus Poetry," *Writer* L, No. 8 (August 1937), 243.

7. *Letters,* 191.

8. *Ibid.,* 299.

9. *Ibid.,* 326.

10. Denis Donoghue, "For a Redeeming Language," in J. Hillis Miller, ed., *William Carlos Williams,* 128.

11. I. A. Richards, "Rhythm and Metre," in Harvey Gross, ed., *The Structure of Verse* (Greenwich, Conn.: Fawcett Publications, 1966), 45.

12. Yale Collection.

13. *Ibid.*

14. *Ibid.*

15. *Letters,* 257.

16. "Pound's Eleven New 'Cantos,'" *SE,* 169.

17. See *Letters,* 233.

18. *Ibid.,* 263.

19. See Joel Conarroe's discussion in *PMLA* (May 1969), 552–555.

20. Josephine Miles, *Style and Proportion: The Language of Prose and Poetry* (Boston: Little, Brown, 1967), 98.

21. *Ibid.,* 119.

22. Don Francisco de Quevedo, *The Dog and the Fever,* trans. William Carlos Williams and Raquel Hélène Williams (Hamden, Conn.: Shoe String Press, 1954), 16. Italics mine.

23. *Ibid.,* 15.

24. *Yes, Mrs. Williams* (New York: McDowell, Obolensky, 1959), 34.

25. Hyatt Waggoner, *American Poets from the Puritans to the Present* (Boston: Houghton Mifflin, 1968), 373.

26. *Dog and Fever,* 19.

27. *Yes,* 33.

28. *Dog and Fever,* 22.

29. *Letters,* 238.

30. Emily Wallace, *A Bibliography of William Carlos Williams,* xiv–xv.

31. "Federico Garcia Lorca," *SE,* 230.

32. *Letters,* 250.

33. *I Wanted,* 82–83.

34. Yale Collection.

35. "The Tortuous Straightness of Chas. Henri Ford," *SE,* 236.

36. Yale Collection.

37. "In a Mood of Tragedy: 'The Mills of the Kavanaughs,'" *SE,* 325.

38. Statement of the poet, taken from "Symposium on Writing," *Golden Goose,* Series III, No. 2 (Autumn 1951), 90–91.

39. Yale Collection.

Selected Bibliography

Works of William Carlos Williams

Williams, William Carlos. "America, Whitman and the Art of Poetry," *Poetry Journal,* VIII (1917), 30–31.

"The American Idiom," *New Directions* 17 (1961), 250–251.

"An American Poet," *New Masses* (November 23, 1937), 17–18.

"An Approach to the Poem," *English Institute Essays, 1947.* New York: Columbia University Press, 1948, pp. 50–76.

"The Art" (poem), *Hudson Review,* XVI (Winter 1963–1964), 515.

The Autobiography of William Carlos Williams. New York: Random House, 1951.

Introduction to Ronald Bayes's *Dust and Desire.* Devon, England: Arthur L. Stockwell, 1960.

A Beginning on the Short Story. Yonkers: Alicat Bookshop Press, 1950.

The Build Up. New York: Random House, 1952.

"Cézanne" (poem), *Nation,* CXCII (May 13, 1961), 416.

The Collected Earlier Poems of William Carlos Williams. Norfolk, Conn.: New Directions, 1951.

The Collected Later Poems of William Carlos Williams. Norfolk, Conn.: New Directions, 1963.

Contact, I–V, eds. William Carlos Williams and Robert McAlmon. 1920–1923.

Contact, I–III, eds. William Carlos Williams and Nathaneal West. 1932.

"The Descent of Winter," *Exile,* IV (Autumn 1928).

The Desert Music. New York: Random House, 1954.

"The Element of Time," *Harvard Advocate,* CXX, No. 4 (February 1934), 10.

"Ezra Pound: Lord Ga-ga!" *Decision,* II (September 1941), 16–24.

"Faiths for a Complex World," *American Scholar,* XXVI (Fall 1957), 453–457.

The Farmers' Daughters. Norfolk, Conn.: New Directions, 1961. Introduction by Van Wyck Brooks.

"Free Verse," *Encyclopedia of Poetry and Poetics,* ed. Alex Preminger. Princeton: Princeton University Press, 1965, pp. 288–300.

"From: A Folded Skyscraper," in Alfred Kreymborg *et al.,* eds., *The American Caravan.* New York: Macaulay, 1927.

"The Future of the Creative Arts," *University of Buffalo Studies,* XIX, No. 4 (February 1952), 10–12.

Introduction to Allen Ginsberg's *Empty Mirror.* New York: Totem Press, 1961.

Introduction to Allen Ginsberg's *Howl and Other Poems.* San Francisco: City Lights Books, 1956.

"A Good Doctor's Story," *Nation,* CXLV, No. 11 (September 11, 1937), 268.

The Great American Novel in R. P. Blackmur, ed., *American Short Novels.* New York: Thomas Y. Crowell, 1960, pp. 307–344. Originally published by Three Mountains Press, Paris, 1923.

"Greeting for Old Age" (poem), *Hudson Review,* XVI (Winter 1963–1964), 515.

"Hart Crane," *Contempo,* II, No. 4 (July 5, 1932), 1, 4.

"Homage to Ford Madox Ford," *New Directions 7* (1942), 490–491.

"How To Write," *New Directions 1936.* Norfolk, Conn.: New Directions, 1936.

"How Verse Forms Create Something New," *New Republic,* CXXXIII (October 31, 1955), 16–17.

I Wanted to Write a Poem, ed. Edith Heal. Boston: Beacon, 1958.

Imaginations, ed. Webster Schott. Norfolk, Conn.: New Directions, 1970.

In the American Grain. Norfolk, Conn.: New Directions, 1956. Originally published by Albert and Charles Boni, New York, 1925.

In the Money. Norfolk, Conn.: New Directions, 1940.

"Jefferson and/or Mussolini," *New Democracy,* IV (October 15, 1935), 61–62.

Journey to Love. New York: Random House, 1955.

Kora in Hell: Improvisations. San Francisco: City Lights Books, 1957. Originally published by Four Seas Co., Boston, 1920.

"A Note on Layton," introduction to Irving Layton's *The Improved Binoculars.* Highlands, Jonathan Williams, 1956.

"Letter on Pound," *Quarterly Review of Literature,* V, No. 3 (1950), 301.

"Letter to an Australian Editor," *Briarcliff Quarterly,* III (October 1946), 205–209.

"The Letters of William Carlos Williams," *Golden Goose,* No. 7 (April 1954), 124–132.

"The Man with the Blue Guitar," New Republic, XCIII (November 17, 1937), 50.

Many Loves and Other Plays. Norfolk, Conn.: New Directions, 1961.

"Men . . . Have No Tenderness," *New Directions* 7 (1942), 429–436.

Microfilms of Dr. Williams' Manuscripts, Lockwood Memorial Library, Poetry Room, State University of New York at Buffalo, Buffalo, New York.

"New Direction in the Novel," *New Democracy,* V (November 1, 1935), 81–83.

"The New Poetical Economy," *Poetry,* XLIV (July 1934), 220–225.

"Notes from a Talk on Poetry," *Poetry,* XIV (July 1919), 211–216.

A Novelette and Other Prose, 1921–1931. Toulon, France: Imprimerie F. Cabasson, 1932.

"Objectivism," *Encyclopedia of Poetry and Poetics,* 582.

Paterson. Norfolk, Conn.: New Directions, 1963. Originally published in single volumes by New Directions, 1946, 1948, 1949, 1951, and 1958.

Picasso the Figure. New York: Louis Carré Gallery, 1950.

Pictures from Brueghel and Other Poems. Norfolk, Conn.: New Directions, 1962. Includes *The Desert Music* and *Journey to Love.*

Poems. Rutherford, N.J.: Reid Howell (privately printed), 1909.

"The Poet in Time of Confusion," *Columbia Review,* XXIII (Autumn 1941), 3.

The Selected Essays of William Carlos Williams. New York: Random House, 1954.

The Selected Letters of William Carlos Williams, ed. John C. Thirlwall. New York: McDowell, Obolensky, 1957.

The Selected Poems of William Carlos Williams. Norfolk, Conn.: New Directions, 1963 (expanded, 1968). Introduction by Randall Jarrell.

"Sermon with a Camera," *New Republic,* XCVI (October 12, 1938), 282–283.

"Seventy Years Deep," *Holiday,* XVI (November 1954), 54–55.

Introduction to *Charles Sheeler, Paintings, Drawings, Photographs.* New York: Museum of Modern Art, 1939.

"The Situation in American Writing," *Partisan Review,* IV, No. 4 (Summer 1939), 41–44.

"A Social Diagnosis for Surgery," *New Democracy,* VI (April 1936), 26–27.

"Sordid? Good God!" *Contempo,* III, No. 2 (July 25, 1933), 5, 8.

Spring and All. Dijon, France: Contact Publishing Co., 1923.

"Still Lifes" (poem), *Hudson Review* (Winter 1963–1964), 516.

"Stormy" (poem), *Poetry,* CI, Nos. 1–2 (October–November 1962), 141.

"Symposium on Writing," *Golden Goose,* Series III, No. 2 (Autumn 1951), 89–96.

Taped recordings of Dr. Williams reading from his poems, Yale Collection.

"The Three Letters," *Contact,* IV (n.d.), 10–13.

"Three Professional Studies," in Margaret Anderson, ed., *The Little Review Anthology.* New York: Hermitage House, 1953.

"To Write American Poetry," *Fantasy,* V, No. 1 (Summer 1935), 12–14.

A Voyage to Pagany. New York: Macaulay, 1928.

White Mule. Norfolk, Conn.: New Directions, 1937.

"White Mule versus Poetry," *Writer,* L, No. 8 (August 1937), 243–245.

The William Carlos Williams Reader, ed. M. L. Rosenthal. Norfolk, Conn.: New Directions, 1966.

"William Carlos Williams Reads His Poetry" (recording). New York: Caedmon Publishers, 1958.

"William Carlos Williams: Two Letters," *Golden Goose,* IV, No. 5 (October 1952), 29–32.

William Carlos Williams' manuscripts and letters. Collection of American Literature, Yale University Library, New Haven, Conn.

Yes, Mrs. Williams. New York: McDowell, Obolensky, 1959.

Closing Note to Louis Zukofsky's *"A" 1–12.* Ashland, Mass.: Origin Press, 1959.

Other Sources

Aiken, Conrad P. *A Reviewer's ABC.* New York: Meridian, 1958.

Angoff, Charles. "3 Towering Figures," *Literary Review,* VI, No. 4 (Summer 1963), 423–429.

———. "A Williams Memoir," *Prairie Schooner,* XXXVIII, No. 4 (Winter 1964–1965), 299–305.

Arnheim, Rudolf, W. H. Auden, Karl Shapiro, and Donald A. Stauffer. *Poets at Work.* New York: Harcourt, Brace, 1948.

Atkinson, Clinton J. "In Search of Theatre," *Massachusetts Review* (Winter 1962), 331–336.

Barnes, Djuna. *Selected Works of Djuna Barnes.* New York: Farrar, Straus, and Cudahy, 1962.

Bennett, Joseph. "The Lyre and the Sledgehammer," *Hudson Review,* V, No. 2 (Summer 1952), 295–307.

Beum, Robert Lawrence. "The Baby Glove of a Pharoah," *Perspective,* VI, No. 4 (Autumn 1953), 217–223. Issue devoted to articles on Dr. Williams.

———. "The Neglect of Williams," *Poetry,* LXXX (August 1952), 291–293.

Blackmur, R. P. *Language as Gesture*. New York: Harcourt, Brace, 1952.

Bouma, J. Gysbert. "A Study of the Prose Style of William Carlos Williams," unpublished dissertation, 1956, University of Pennsylvania.

Breslin, James E. "Whitman and the Early Development of William Carlos Williams," *PMLA*, LXXXII (December 1967), 613–621.

Brinnin, John Malcolm. *William Carlos Williams*. University of Minnesota Pamphlets on American Writers Series, No. 24. Minneapolis: University of Minnesota Press, 1963.

Burke, Kenneth. "Heaven's First Law," *Dial*, LXXII (February 1922), 197–200.

———. "The Methods of William Carlos Williams," *Dial*, LXXXII (February 1927), 94–98.

———. "William Carlos Williams, 1883–1963," *New York Review of Books* (Spring–Summer 1963), 45–47.

Butler, Gerald. "The Measure of American," *things,* No. 1 (Fall 1964), 38–46.

Calhoun, Richard J. "No Ideas but in Things: William Carlos Williams in the Twenties," in Richard E. Langford and William E. Taylor, eds., *The Twenties: Poetry and Prose*. De Land, Fla.: Everett Edwards Press. 1966.

Cambon, Glauco. *The Inclusive Flame: Studies in American Poetry*. Bloomington: Indiana University Press, 1963.

Carruth, Hayden. "Dr. Williams' *Paterson*," *Nation,* CLXX (April 8, 1950), 331–333.

———. "William Carlos Williams as One of Us," *New Republic,* CXLVIII (April 13, 1963), 30–32.

Ciardi, John. "The Epic of a Place," *Saturday Review,* XLI (October 11, 1958), 37–39.

———. "Thing Is the Form," *Nation,* CLXXVIII (April 24, 1954), 368–369.

———. "William Carlos Williams," *Saturday Review* (March 23, 1963), 18–20.

Coffman, Stanley K., Jr. *Imagism: A Chapter for the History of Modern Poetry*. Norman: University of Oklahoma Press, 1951.

Conarroe, Joel. "A Local Pride: The Poetry of *Paterson*," *PMLA,* LXXXIV, No. 3 (May 1969), 547–558.

———. "The 'Preface' to *Paterson*," *Journal of Contemporary Literature,* X (Winter 1969), 39–53.

———. " 'You Can't Steal Credit': The Economic Motif in *Paterson*," *Journal of American Studies,* II (1968), 105–115.

Cook, Albert. *Prisms*. Bloomington: Indiana University Press, 1967.

Cordell, Richard. "The Stechers Again," *Saturday Review of Literature*, XXIII (November 9, 1940), 5.

Corman, Cid. *"The Farmers' Daughters:* A True Story about People," *Massachusetts Review*, III, No. 2 (Winter 1962), 319–324.

Creeley, Robert. "The Fact of His Life," *Nation*, CXCV (October 13, 1962), 224.

Creeley, Robert, and Donald Allen, eds. *New American Story*. Introduction by Warren Tallman. New York: Grove, 1965.

Dahlberg, Edward. *Alms for Oblivion*. Minneapolis: University of Minnesota Press, 1964.

———. *Epitaphs of Our Times, the Letters of Edward Dahlberg*. New York: George Braziller, 1967.

Davenport, Guy. "The Nuclear Venus: Dr. Williams' Attack Upon Usura," *Perspective*, VI, No. 4 (Autumn–Winter 1953), 183–190.

Davis, Earle. *Vision Fugitive, Ezra Pound and Economics*. Lawrence: University of Kansas Press, 1968.

Dembo, L. S. *Conceptions of Reality in Modern American Poetry*. Berkeley: University of California Press, 1966.

Dijkstra, Bram. *The Hieroglyphics of a New Speech*. Princeton: Princeton University Press, 1969.

Donoghue, Denis. *Connoisseurs of Chaos: Ideas of Order in Modern American Poetry*. New York: Macmillan, 1965.

———. "For a Redeeming Language," *Twentieth Century*, CLXIII (June 1958), 532–542.

———. *The Ordinary Universe: Soundings in Modern Literature*. New York: Macmillan, 1968.

———. "Poetry and the Behavior of Speech," *Hudson Review*, XIV (Winter 1961–1962), 537–549.

Donohue, H. E. F. "An Occasion for Tremendous Music," *Massachusetts Review* (Winter 1962), 338–344.

Duffey, Bernard I. "Williams' *Paterson* and the Measure of Art," in Clarence Gohdes, ed., *Essays on American Literature in Honor of Jay B. Hubbell*. Durham: Duke University Press, 1967.

Durst, Martin. "William Carlos Williams: A Bibliography, I," *West Coast Review*, I, No. 2 (Fall 1966), 49–54. Part II, *ibid.*, I, No. 3 (Winter 1967), 44–49.

Eberhart, Richard. "Prose, Poetry and the Love of Life," *Saturday Review*, CXXXVII (November 20, 1954), 20.

———. "Things as They Are," *New Republic*, CXXVII (November 10, 1952), 20.

Eckman, Frederick. *Cobras and Cockle Shells: Modes in Recent Poetry.* Flushing, N.Y.: Sparrow Press, 1958.

———. "In Memoriam: William Carlos Williams," *Chicago Literary Times,* II (April 1963), 1.

Ellmann, Richard. "From Reneshaw to *Paterson,*" *Yale Review,* XXXIX (Spring 1950), 544–545.

———. "William Carlos Williams: The Doctor in Search of Himself," *Kenyon Review,* XIV (Summer 1952), 510–512.

——— and Charles Feidelson, Jr., eds. *The Modern Tradition: Backgrounds of Modern Literature.* New York: Oxford University Press, 1965.

Faulkner, William. *The Faulkner-Cowley File, 1944–1962,* ed. Malcolm Cowley. New York: Viking, 1966.

Ferry, David. "The Diction of American Poetry," in Irvin Ehrenpreis, ed., *American Poetry,* Stratford-Upon-Avon Studies 7. New York: St Martin's Press, 1965.

Fiedler, Leslie. "Some Uses and Failures of Feeling," *Partisan Review,* XV, No. 2 (August 1948), 924–931.

Fitzgerald, Robert. "Bejeweled, the Great Sun," *New Republic,* CXX (April 25, 1949), 22–23.

Flint, R. W. " 'I Will Teach You My Townspeople,' " *Kenyon Review,* XII (Autumn 1950), 537–543.

Foster, John Lawrence. "The Modern American Long Poem," unpublished dissertation, 1961, University of Michigan.

Franklyn, A. Fredric. "The Truth and the Poem," *Trace,* XII, No. 48 (Spring 1963), 32, 79–83.

Furbank, P. N. "New Poetry," *Listener,* LXXI, No. 1829 (April 16, 1964), 645.

Goll, Yvan. *Landless John: Jean Sans Terre,* trans. Lionel Able, Clark Mills, William Carlos Williams, and John Gould Fletcher. San Francisco: Grabhorn, 1944.

Goodman, Paul. "Between Flash and Thunderstroke," *Poetry,* LXXXVII (March 1956), 366–370.

Goodwin, K. L. *The Influence of Ezra Pound.* New York: Oxford University Press, 1967.

Gregory, Horace. *The Shield of Achilles.* New York: Harcourt, Brace, 1944.

Gregory, Horace, and Marya Zaturenska. *A History of American Poetry: 1900–1940.* New York: Harcourt, Brace, 1946.

Grigson, Geoffrey. "That Greeny Flower," *New Statesman,* LXVII, No. 1729 (May 1, 1964), 691.

Guimond, James. *The Art of William Carlos Williams: A Discovery and Possession of America.* Urbana: University of Illinois Press, 1968.

Gunn, Thom. "Things, Voices, Minds," *Yale Review* (Autumn 1962), 129–130.

———. "William Carlos Williams," *Encounter,* XXV, No. 1 (July 1965), 67–74.

Halpert, Stephen, with Richard Johns. *A Return to Pagany.* Boston: Beacon, 1969.

Harrison, Keith. "Places and People," *Spectator,* No. 7092 (May 29, 1964), 731.

Hawes, Henry. "Head-Shaking and Shakespeare," *Saturday Review of Literature,* XLII (January 31, 1959), 24.

Heal, Edith. "A Poet's Integrity: Letters from William Carlos Williams," *Literary Review,* IX (Autumn 1965), 115–119.

Hirschman, Jack. "William Carlos Williams," *Shenandoah,* XIV, No. 4 (Summer 1963), 3–10.

Hoffman, Frederick J. *The Twenties* (revised). New York: Free Press, 1949, 1962.

———. "Williams and His Muse," *Poetry,* LXXXIV (April 1954), 23–27.

Holder, Alan. "In the American Grain: William Carlos Williams on the American Past," *American Quarterly,* XIX, No. 3 (Fall 1967), 499–515.

Honig, Edward. "City of Man," *Poetry,* LXIX (February 1947), 277–284.

———. "The *Paterson* Impasse," *Poetry,* LXXIV (April 1949), 37–41.

Ignatow, David. Introduction to *William Carlos Williams: A Memorial Chapbook, Beloit Poetry Journal,* XIV, No. 1 (Fall 1963), 1–2.

———. "Williams' Influence: Some Social Aspects," *Chelsea,* XIV (January 1964), 154–161.

Jacobsen, Josephine. "Legacy of Three Poets," *Commonweal,* LXXVIII (May 10, 1963), 189–192.

Janeway, Elizabeth, ed. *The Writer's World.* New York: McGraw-Hill, 1969.

Jarrell, Randall. "The Poet and His Public," *Partisan Review,* XIII (September–October 1946), 488–500.

———. *Poetry and the Age.* New York: Knopf, 1953.

Kay, Arthur M. "*The Farmers' Daughters,*" *Arizona Quarterly,* XVIII (Winter 1962), 368–370.

Kennedy, Raymond A. " 'Let's to Music, Hubert!': An Impertinent Piece," *Massachusetts Review* (Winter 1962), 336–338.

Kenner, Hugh. "Columbus Log-Book," *Poetry,* XCII (June 1958), 174–178.

————. "The Drama of Utterance," *Massachusetts Review,* III, No. 2 (Winter 1962), 328–330.

————. "Ghosts and Benedictions," *Poetry,* LXII, No. 2 (November 1968), 109–125.

————. *Gnomon.* New York: McDowell, Obolensky, 1958.

————. "William Carlos Williams: In Memoriam," *National Review* (March 26, 1963), 237.

Koch, Vivienne. "The Man and the Poet," *Kenyon Review,* XIV (Summer 1952), 502–510.

————. *William Carlos Williams.* Norfolk, Conn.: New Directions, 1950.

————. "Williams: The Social Mask," *Poetry,* LXXX (May 1954), 89–95.

Koehler, Stanley. "The Art of Poetry VI: William Carlos Williams," *Paris Review,* VIII, No. 32 (Summer–Fall 1964), 110–151.

Kreymborg, Alfred. *A History of American Poetry: Our Singing Strength.* New York: Tudor, 1934.

Kunitz, Stanley. "Frost, Williams, and Company," *Harpers,* CCXXV (October 1962), 100–103.

Lamott, Kenneth. "Pilgrimage to Rutherford," *Contact* (July 1963), 41–43.

Lechlitner, Ruth. "The Poetry of William Carlos Williams," *Poetry,* LIV (September 1939), 326–335.

The Letters of Ezra Pound, 1907–1941, ed. D. D. Paige. New York: Harcourt, Brace, and World, 1950.

Letters of Wallace Stevens, ed. Holly Stevens. New York: Knopf, 1966.

Levertov, Denise. "William Carlos Williams," *Nation,* CXCVI (March 16, 1963), 230.

Lowell, Robert. *"Paterson II,"* *Nation,* CLXVI (June 19, 1948), 692–694.

————. "Thomas, Bishop and Williams," *Sewanee Review,* LV (Summer 1947), 493–504.

————. "William Carlos Williams," *Hudson Review,* XIV (Winter 1961–1962), 530–536.

————. "William Carlos Williams," in "Writers" (poem), *Notebook, 1967–68.* New York: Farrar, Straus, and Giroux, 1969.

Malcolm, Donald. "Off Broadway," *New Yorker* (January 24, 1959), 74–76.

Marsh, Fred T. "William Carlos Williams' New Novel," *New York Times,* November 17, 1940, 7.

Martz, Louis L. *The Poem of the Mind.* New York: Oxford University Press, 1966.

————. "The Unicorn in *Paterson:* William Carlos Williams," *Thought,* XXXV (Winter 1960), 537–554.

Massie, Lillian. "Narrative and Symbol in *Paterson*," unpublished dissertation, University of Arkansas, 1955.

Matthiessen, F. O. *The Responsibilities of the Critic.* New York: Oxford University Press, 1952.

Miles, Josephine. *The Primary Language of Poetry in the 1940's.* Berkeley: University of California Press, 1951.

———. *Style and Proportion: The Language of Prose and Poetry.* Boston: Little, Brown, 1967.

Miller, Fred. "With a Kick to It." *New Republic,* XCI (July 7, 1937), 257.

Miller, J. Hillis. *Poets of Reality.* Cambridge: Harvard University Press, 1965.

———, ed. *William Carlos Williams: A Collection of Critical Essays.* Englewood Cliffs: Prentice-Hall, 1966.

Milton, John R. "In Memoriam: William Carlos Williams," *Kansas Magazine,* No. 4 (1963), 54–56.

Mottram, Eric. "The Making of *Paterson*," *Stand,* 7, No. 3 (Fall 1965), 17–34.

Myers, Neil. "Sentamentalism in the Early Poetry of William Carlos Williams," *American Literature,* XXXVII (January 1966), 458–470.

———. "William Carlos Williams' *Spring and All*," *Modern Language Quarterly,* XXVI (June 1965), 285–301.

Nash, Ralph. "The Use of Prose in *Paterson*," *Perspective,* VI, No. 4 (Autumn–Winter 1953), 191–199.

Neussendorfer, Sister Macaria. "William Carlos Williams' Idea of a City," *Thought,* XL, No. 157 (Summer 1965), 242–274.

Noland, Richard. "A Failure of Contact: William Carlos Williams on America," *Emory University Quarterly,* XX, No. 4 (Winter 1964), 248–260.

Olson, Charles. *Projective Verse.* Brooklyn: Totem Press, 1959.

Ostrom, Alan B. *The Poetic World of William Carlos Williams.* Carbondale: Southern Illinois University Press, 1966.

Paul, Sherman. *The Music of Survival.* Urbana: University of Illinois Press, 1968.

Pearce, Roy Harvey. *The Continuity of American Poetry.* Princeton: Princeton University Press, 1961.

———. "The Poet as Person," *Yale Review,* XLI (March 1952), 421–440.

Pearson, Norman Holmes. "*The Farmers' Daughters* and *Many Loves*," *Yale Review,* LI (Winter 1962), 329–332.

———. "Williams, New Jersey," *Literary Review,* I (Autumn 1957), 29–36. (Special Williams issue.)

Peterson, Walter Scott. *An Approach to Paterson.* New Haven: Yale University Press, 1967.

Quevedo, Don Francisco de. *The Dog and the Fever,* trans. William Carlos Williams and Raquel Hélène Williams. Hamden, Conn.: Shoe String Press, 1954.

Quinn, Sister M. Bernetta. *The Metamorphic Tradition in Modern Poetry.* New Brunswick: Rutgers University Press, 1955.

Rahv, Philip. "Torrents of Spring," *Nation,* CXLIV, No. 26 (June 26, 1937), 733.

Raiziss, Sonia. *La Poésie Américaine "Moderniste," 1910–1940.* Paris: Mercure de France, 1948.

Rakosi, Carl. "William Carlos Williams," *Symposium* (October 1933), 332–334.

Read, Forrest, ed. *Pound/Joyce.* Norfolk, Conn.: New Directions, 1967.

Rexroth, Kenneth. "The Influence of French Poetry on American" and "A Public Letter for William Carlos Williams' Seventy-fifth Birthday," in *Assays.* Norfolk, Conn.: New Directions, 1961, pp. 143–174, 202–205.

———. "Master of Those Who Know," *New Leader,* XLIV, No. 39 (December 11, 1961), 29–30.

———. "A Poet Sums Up," *New York Times Book Review,* March 28, 1954, p. 5.

Rosenfeld, Isaac. "The Poetry and Wisdom of *Paterson,*" *Nation,* CLXIII (August 24, 1946), 216–217.

Rosenfeld, Paul. *Port of New York.* New York: Harcourt, Brace, 1924.

———. "Williams the Conqueror," *Nation,* CLI (November 23, 1940), 508.

Rosenthal, M. L. *The Modern Poets: A Critical Introduction.* New York: Oxford University Press, 1960.

———. "Salvo for William Carlos Williams," *Nation,* CLXXXVI (May 31, 1958), 497.

———. "William Carlos Williams," *New York Times Book Review,* August 29, 1965, pp. 2, 30.

———. "William Carlos Williams and Some Young Germans," *Massachusetts Review,* IV (Winter 1963), 337–341.

Seamon, Roger. "The Bottle in the Fire: Resistance as Creation in William Carlos Williams' *Paterson,*" *Twentieth Century Literature,* XI (April 1965), 16–24.

Sereni, Vittorio, trans. by Sonia Raiziss. "William Carlos Williams: An Italian View," *Prairie Schooner,* XXXVIII, No. 4 (Winter 1964–1965), 307–316.

Shapiro, Karl. *In Defense of Ignorance.* New York: Random House, 1952.

———. "Is Poetry an American Art?" *College English,* XXV, No. 6 (March 1964), 395–405.

———. *To Abolish Children and Other Essays.* Chicago: Quadrangle, 1968.

———. "You Call These Poems?" (poem), *Antioch Review* (Summer 1962), 162.

Siegel, Eli. "T. S. Eliot and William Carlos Williams: A Distinction," *University of Kansas City Review,* XXII (October 1955), 41–43.

———. "Williams' Poetry Looked At" (recording transcribed). New York: Terrain Gallery, 1964.

Slate, Joseph Evans. "William Carlos Williams and the Modern Short Story," *Southern Review,* IV, No. 3 (Summer 1968), 647–664.

———. "William Carlos Williams, Hart Crane, and 'The Virtue of History,'" *Texas Studies in Literature and Language,* VI (Winter 1965), 486–511.

Smith, Barbara H. *Poetic Closure: A Study of How Poems End.* Chicago: University of Chicago Press, 1968.

Solt, Mary Ellen. "William Carlos Williams: Idiom and Structure," *Massachusetts Review,* III, No. 2 (Winter 1962), 304–318.

———. "William Carlos Williams: Poems in the American Idiom," *Folio,* XXV, No. 1 (1960), 3–28.

Soupault, Philippe. *Last Nights of Paris,* trans. William Carlos Williams. New York: Macaulay, 1929.

Spencer, Benjamin T. "Doctor Williams' American Grain," *Tennessee Studies in Literature,* VIII (1963), 1–16.

———. *"Many Loves and Other Plays,"* *Modern Drama,* VI, No. 1 (May 1963), 97.

Stephens, Alan. "Dr. Williams and Tradition," *Poetry,* CI, No. 5 (February 1963), 360–362.

Sutton, Walter. "Dr. Williams' *Paterson* and the Quest for Form," *Criticism,* II (Summer 1960), 242–259.

———. "A Visit with William Carlos Williams," *Minnesota Review,* I (1961), 309–324.

Taupin, René. *L' Influence du Symbolisme Français sur La Poésie Américaine.* Paris: H. Champion, 1929.

Thirlwall, John C. "The Lost Poems of William Carlos Williams" or "The Past Recaptured," *New Directions 16* (1957), 3–45.

———. "Two Cities: Paris and Paterson," *Massachusetts Review,* III, No. 2 (Winter 1962), 284–291.

————. "William Carlos Williams as Correspondent," *Literary Review,* I, No. 1 (Autumn 1957), 13–28.

————. "William Carlos Williams' *Paterson,*" *New Directions 17* (1961), 252–310.

Thompson, Frank. "The Symbolic Structure of *Paterson,*" *Western Review,* XIX (1955), 285–293.

Tomlinson, Charles. "Dr. Williams' Practice," *Encounter,* XXIX (November 1967), 66–70.

Turnbull, Gael. "A Visit to WCW: September, 1958," *Massachusetts Review,* III, No. 2 (Winter 1962), 297–300.

Tyler, Parker. "The Poet of *Paterson* Book One," *Briarcliff Quarterly,* III (October 1946), 168–175. (Special Williams issue.)

Untermeyer, Louis. "Experiment and Tradition," *Yale Review,* XXVIII (Spring 1939), 612.

Van Duyn, Mona. "To 'Make Light of It' as Fictional Technique," *Perspective,* VI (Autumn–Winter 1953), 230–238.

Van Nostrand, A. D. *Everyman His Own Poet: Romantic Gospels in American Literature.* New York: McGraw-Hill, 1968.

Waggoner, Hyatt. *American Poets from the Puritans to the Present.* Boston: Houghton Mifflin, 1968.

Wagner, Linda Welshimer. "A Bunch of Marigolds," *Kenyon Review,* XXIX, No. 113 (January 1967), 86–102.

————. "A Decade of Discovery," *Twentieth Century Literature,* X, No. 4 (January 1965), 166–169.

————. "Dr. Williams' Prescription," *Laurel Review,* VII, No. 2 (Fall 1967), 23–28.

————. "*Pictures from Brueghel* and William Carlos Williams," *American Weave,* XXVII, No. 2 (Winter 1963), 37–39.

————. *The Poems of William Carlos Williams: A Critical Study.* Middletown: Wesleyan University Press, 1964.

————. "Pulitzer and Williams," *South Atlantic Bulletin,* XXVIII, No. 2 (March 1963), 3–4.

————. "William Carlos Williams: Giant," *College English,* XXV No. 6 (March 1964), 425–430.

————. "William Carlos Williams: Post-Physician of Rutherford," *Journal of the American Medical Association,* CCIV, No. 1 (April 1, 1968), 15–20.

————. "William Carlos Williams: Self Portrait," *Grande Ronde Review,* No. 2 (Spring 1964), n.p.

————. "William Carlos Williams: Traditional American Poet," *Renascence,* XVI, No. 3 (Spring 1964), 115–125.

————. "Williams' 'The Use of Force': An Expansion," *Studies in Short Fiction* (Summer 1967), 351–353.

Wallace, Emily Mitchell. *A Bibliography of William Carlos Williams.* Middletown: Wesleyan University Press. 1968.

————. "William Carlos Williams' Bibliography," *Literary Review,* IX, No. 4 (Summer 1966), 501–512.

Weatherhead, A. K. *The Edge of the Image.* Seattle: University of Washington Press, 1967.

————. "William Carlos Williams: Poetic Invention and the World Beyond," *English Literary History,* XXXII (March 1965), 126–138.

————. "William Carlos Williams: Prose, Form, and Measure," *English Literary History,* XXXIII (March 1966), 118–131.

Weimer, David R. *The City as Metaphor.* New York: Random House, 1966.

West, Nathaneal. "Some Notes on Violence," *Contact* No. 3 (October 1932), 132–133.

Whitaker, Thomas. *William Carlos Williams.* New York: Twayne U.S. Authors Series, 1968.

Whittaker, Ted. "Presumptions," *Open Letter,* No. 3 (April 1966), 18–24.

Wilbur, Richard. "On My Own Work," in Howard Nemerov, ed., *Poets on Poetry.* New York: Basic Books, 1966.

Willingham, John R. "Partisan of the Arts," *Nation,* CLXXX (January 22, 1955), 78.

Wilson, Edmund. *The Triple Thinkers.* New York: Harcourt, Brace, 1948.

Winters, Yvor. *In Defense of Reason.* New York: Swallow Press and William Morrow, 1947.

Worth, Katharine. "The Poets in the American Theatre," *American Theatre,* Stratford-Upon-Avon Studies 10. New York: St Martin's Press, 1967.

Zabriskie, George. "The Geography of *Paterson,*" *Perspective,* VI, No. 4 (Autumn 1953), 201–216.

Zukofsky, Louis. " 'The Best Human Value,' " *Nation,* CLXXXVI (May 31, 1958), 500–502.

————. "An Old Note on William Carlos Williams," *Massachusetts Review,* III, No. 2 (Winter 1962), 301–302.

Index